How to Relate Science and Religion

How to Relate Science and Religion

A MULTIDIMENSIONAL MODEL

Mikael Stenmark

WILLIAM B. EERDMANS PUBLISHING COMPANY
GRAND RAPIDS, MICHIGAN / CAMBRIDGE, U.K.

Wm. B. Eerdmans Publishing Co.
255 Jefferson Ave. S.E., Grand Rapids, Michigan 49503 /
P.O. Box 163, Cambridge CB3 9PU U.K.

Printed in the United States of America

09 08 07 06 05 04   7 6 5 4 3 2 1

Library of Congress Cataloging-in-Publication Data

Stenmark, Mikael.
How to relate science and religion: a multidimensional model / Mikael Stenmark.
p.   cm.
Includes bibliographical references (p.   ) and index.
ISBN 0-8028-2823-X (pbk.: alk. paper)
1. Religion and science.   I. Title.

BL240.3.S744   2004
201′.65 — dc22

2004053271

www.eerdmans.com

For Anna Romell Stenmark

Contents

Acknowledgments

M ore people than I can name have contributed to shaping this book through their helpful comments on earlier drafts and their questions in response to lectures on these topics. For critical readings of the manuscript or parts of it, I am indebted especially to Thomas Ekstrand, Philip Hefner, Eberhard Herrmann, Kenneth Nordgren, Anne Runehov, and F. LeRon Shults. I gratefully acknowledge financial support from the John Templeton Foundation and from Axel och Margaret Ax:son Johnsons Stiftelse, which made this whole project possible. Some of the material in this book appeared (in more or less modified form) in previous publications of mine. I have utilized material from the following sources: "Should Religion Shape Science?" *Faith and Philosophy* (forthcoming); "Contemporary Darwinism and Religion," in *Darwinian Heresies,* ed. Abigail Lustig, Robert Richards, and Michael Ruse (Cambridge: Cambridge University Press, 2004); "Science and a Personal Conception of God: A Critical Reply to Gordon D. Kaufman," *Journal of the American Academy of Religion* 71 (2003); "Evolution, Purpose and God," *Ars Disputandi: The Online Journal for Philosophy of Religion* (2001); "Theological Pragmatism: A Critical Evaluation," *The Heythrop Journal* 41 (2000); "The End of the Theism-Atheism Debate? A Critical Response to Vincent Brümmer," *Religious Studies* 34 (1998); "An Unfinished Debate: What Are the Aims of Science and Religion?" *Zygon: Journal of Religion and Science* 32 (1997).

Introduction

People throughout the ages have tried to understand the universe and their own place within it. They have developed a big picture, a worldview. Religions have traditionally played a very important role in shaping individuals' worldviews, but ever since the scientific revolution science has also played a crucial role. But how should we understand the relationship between these two powerful cultural forces? *How should we relate science and religion?* This is the key question of this book.

Within the academy today we can find two very interesting, but quite opposite, ways of responding to this profound question, which is of great importance for our lives. We have, on the one hand, those who believe that there are no real limits to the competence of science, no limits to what can be achieved in the name of science. Richard Dawkins, for instance, writes that since we have modern biology, we have "no longer . . . to resort to superstition when faced with the deep problems: Is there a meaning to life? What are we for? What is man?" (Dawkins 1989: 1). According to Dawkins science is capable of dealing with all these questions and constitutes in addition the only alternative to superstition. Edward O. Wilson is confident that science not only can fully explain religion but can even replace religion. The evolutionary epic provides us with a new mythology, and it can constitute the key element in our new religion, what Wilson sometimes calls "scientific materialism" and at other times "scientific naturalism" (Wilson 1978: 192). Peter Atkins is no less ambitious. He does not hesitate to talk about the "limitless power of science" or about science as "omnicompetent" (Atkins 1995: 122f.).

We have, on the other hand, a group of people with the very opposite view. They believe instead that science ought to be influenced or shaped in a significant way by religion. These thinkers share the idea that the boundaries of *religion* — and not the boundaries of science — can and should be expanded in such a way that religion influences science. For instance, Alvin Plantinga thinks that it is excessively naive to think that contemporary science is religiously and theologically neutral. Instead it often expresses a commitment to materialism or naturalism. His advice, therefore, is that "a Christian academic and scientific community ought to pursue science in its own way, starting from and taking for granted what they know as Christians" (Plantinga 1996b: 377). Christians ought to develop what he sometimes calls a "theistic science" and at other times an "Augustinian science." Some Muslims talk instead about a "sacred science" or an "Islamic science." Mehdi Golshani writes that some people deny that "the idea of Islamic Science" makes any sense. "They argue that science is an objective and universal enterprise, and it does not depend on any creed or ideology." But Golshani maintains that "this is a naïve interpretation of scientific activity" and that "'Islamic Science,' or for that matter, 'religious science,' has relevance at [both] the theoretical level and the practical level" (Golshani 2000: 1).

I shall call people like Atkins, Dawkins, and Wilson "scientific expansionists."[1] What characterizes scientific expansionists is that they have great confidence both in science and about what can be achieved in the name of science. What they all have in common is that they maintain that the boundaries of science can and should be expanded in such a way that

---

1. The term "scientific expansionists" is taken from Loren R. Graham's study, *Between Science and Values* (1981). He writes that "expansionists cite evidence within the body of scientific theories and findings which can supposedly be used, either directly or indirectly, to support conclusions about sociopolitical [e.g., moral, political, aesthetic, religious] values. The result of these efforts is to expand the boundaries of science in such a way that they include, at least by implication, value questions" (p. 6). Graham defines values as "what people think to be good" (p. 4). In my view, however, he unnecessarily limits scientific expansionism to value questions. Scientific expansionists could argue that the boundaries of science should be extended so that it includes values or value questions; but it must also be possible for them to claim that, for instance, all beliefs that can be known or even rationally maintained must and can be included within the boundaries of science. Science sets on such an account the limits for what we possibly can know about reality; the only kind of knowledge that we can have is scientific knowledge. So there is one crucial difference between how I shall use the term and the way Graham uses it.

something that has not been understood as science can now become a part of science. How exactly the boundaries of science could and should be expanded and what more precisely it is that is to be included in science are, as we will see, issues on which they disagree. In some versions, scientific expansionism (or "scientism," as this view has also been called)[2] even attempts to offer a substitute for traditional religions, and thus science itself becomes a religion or worldview.

People like Plantinga and Golshani shall in contrast be called "religious expansionists." Religious expansionists agree in general terms that the boundaries of religion could and should be expanded in such a way that religion in some way becomes an important element of the scientific enterprise; religion becomes relevant for areas that were not previously considered part of its domain. How exactly the boundaries of religion should be expanded into the scientific domain is, as we will see, an issue on which they disagree.

To some people the idea of a religiously shaped science seems utterly old-fashioned ("That is the way things used to be back in the Middle Ages, but today it is merely something that religious fundamentalists or very conservative people would still believe"), whereas the idea of scientific expansionism seems more promising and progressive. I do not believe that this is an appropriate attitude to adopt; rather, I think that religious expansionism must be taken as seriously as scientific expansionism. Why? Because more and more frequently we hear complaints from people both within and outside the academy that science is being used to support certain ideological agendas. Science is not ideologically neutral. R. C. Lewontin maintains in *The Doctrine of DNA* — with the significant subtitle, *Biology as Ideology* — that behind a lot of writing and research done by Neo-Darwinists and sociobiologists we can find ideological commitments that legitimate inequalities within and between societies (Lewontin 1993). Feminists claim with increasing frequency that "the modern western conception of science, which identifies knowledge with power and views it as a weapon for dominating nature, reflects the imperialism, racism, and misogyny of the societies that created it" (Jagger 1989: 156). In a recent article in *Newsweek* (April 21, 1997), we can even read about "the Science Wars,"

---

2. See Stenmark (2001b) for a detailed discussion of scientism. I have decided not to use this term in this work because here I want to contrast two types of positions that can best be labeled "scientific expansionism" and "religious/ideological expansionism."

about the critics of science saying that the practice of science is subject to the political, cultural, and social influences of the times, and that science therefore is a social construct.[3]

Many of these science critics thus agree with Plantinga when he writes that "it is a myth that science is a completely objective, dispassionate attempt to figure out the truth about ourselves and our world, entirely independent of religion, worldviews, political ideologies, and moral convictions" (Plantinga 1991: 16). But that is not all. Some of them also share his conviction that science cannot be and therefore should not be ideologically or religiously neutral. Lewontin and his colleagues Steven Rose and Leon J. Kamin, for instance, write that they "share a commitment to the prospect of the creation of a more socially just — a socialist — society. And we recognize that a critical science is an integral part of the struggle to create that society, just as we also believe that the social function of much of today's science is to hinder the creation of that society by acting to preserve the interests of the dominant class, gender, and race" (Rose et al. 1990: ix-x). They believe in the possibility of a left-wing science. Moreover, Sandra Harding maintains that we should not merely criticize conventional science for being an androcentric science but replace it with a "feminist science," that is, a knowledge-seeking that is directed by existing feminist theories and agendas. Feminist science is "politicized research" which is "directed by feminist rather than androcentric goals" (Harding 1986: 24; cf. 1991: 310).

These thinkers want to *politicize* or *ideologize* the sciences on the basis of class or gender. They are not religious expansionists, but they are instead what I shall call *ideological expansionists*. Hence, we have a quite different group of people than Christians and Muslims who believe that our worldviews or ideologies should play an important role in the conduct of scientific inquiry and practice. Again, how and to what extent the boundaries of ideology should be expanded into the scientific domain is an issue on which ideological expansionists disagree.

I shall maintain that an interesting parallel can be drawn between, on the one hand, the kind of left-wing science and feminist science that scholars like Harding, Longino, and Lewontin advocate and, on the other hand, the kind of theistic science that scholars like Plantinga and Golshani de-

---

3. The books that caused this debate were Gross and Levitt (1994) and Ross, ed. (1996).

fend. For instance, Helen Longino's idea that "in order to practice science as a feminist . . . one must deliberately adopt a framework expressive of that political commitment" is almost identical to Plantinga's advice to Christians that "a Christian academic and scientific community ought to pursue science in its own way, starting from and taking for granted what they know as Christians" (Longino 1990: 197; Plantinga 1996a: 178). This similarity is worth noting because feminists like Longino usually belong to the "progressive" side of the political scale, whereas Christians like Plantinga tend to be situated on the "conservative" side. There is a similarity in argument and strategy to be found between two groups of people who typically are understood to be in opposition to each other. Thus I think that we can see religious expansionists sharing a concern with a wider movement of intellectuals today, questioning the very possibility of a religiously or an ideologically neutral science.

In contrast to both scientific expansionists and religious or ideological expansionists, we can, of course, find scientists, philosophers, and theologians defending the idea that science and religion or ideology ought to be restricted to their own separate areas of inquiry. These people are *scientific* and *religious restrictionists*. (I shall most of the time simply call them "restrictionists.") Stephen Jay Gould has very recently defended a version of this view in *Rocks of Ages: Science and Religion in the Fullness of Life* (1999). He argues for a principle of respectful noninterference between science and religion, and treats them as two autonomous "magisteria" (Gould 1999: 5).

We can thus identify three main groups within the academy today which hold different views on how science, on the one hand, and religion, ideology, or values, on the other, ought to be related. One group maintains that they start with science and nothing but science and then want to expand its boundaries in such a way that religion, ideology, and values become a part of science. They believe in the *scientization of our worldview*. Another group believes rather in the *ideologization of science*. They start with an explicit commitment to a particular ideology or religion and then want to argue that it should shape in a significant way scientific practice. Although people within this group agree that science and ideology or religion could and should not be kept apart, they disagree about which particular ideology or religion is the right one to link science to. Moreover, they also adhere to these ideas to a further or a lesser extent. So there are stronger and weaker versions of ideological and religious expansionism. The

same, of course, is true of scientific expansionism. Restrictionists constitute the third group. They believe in the *separation of science and religion or
ideology*. The message is that we could and should uphold a clear distinction between the autonomous domains of science, on the one hand, and
ideology, religion, and values, on the other.

In this discussion contemporary biology is of special interest because
of its recent developments and its relevance for our understanding of human nature and culture, including morality and religion. We have scholars
like Daniel C. Dennett, who holds that Darwin's idea and its recent development is an idea "bearing an unmistakable likeness to universal acid: it
eats through just about every traditional concept, and leaves in its wake a
revolutionized world-view, with most of the old landmarks still recogniz-
able, but transformed in fundamental ways" (Dennett 1995: 63), and like
Richard Alexander, who believes that contemporary evolutionary biology
will force us to start all over again to describe and understand ourselves in
a way that is completely alien to our intuitions (Alexander 1987: 2). We
shall therefore focus in particular on biology in our attempt to understand
how to relate science and religion.

As the discussion of views held by scientific expansionists, religious
expansionists, and scientific or religious restrictionists proceeds, I shall introduce the conceptual tools that I think are necessary to understand how
to relate science and religion. For instance, the logical and static distinction between science and religion as (a) totally separate domains, (b) overlapping domains, or (c) a unity of domains will be linked to the ideas of
expansion and restriction to create a dynamic and evolving relationship
between science and religion. To avoid getting trapped into thinking of the
relationship between science and religion as one-dimensional, a multidimensional matrix will be proposed and different levels of possible engagement will be identified and evaluated.

The book is arranged as follows. In chapter 1 I introduce the topic by
focusing on the different views about how to relate science and religion
that we can find among some contemporary evolutionary biologists, and
also propose some of the conceptual tools which in my view we need if we
are to properly understand the relationship between science and religion.
These reflections are developed into a multilevel or multidimensional
model of science and religion. The thesis defended is that we need to take
into account at least four different levels or dimensions of science and religion in order to understand how to relate them.

The first of these levels or dimensions is developed in chapter 2. It is, simply, that both science and religion are social practices. Hence, we can talk about the *social dimension* of science and religion. Whatever else science and religion might be they are complex activities performed by human beings in cooperation within a particular historical and cultural setting. They are thus what I call "social practices," that is, complex and fairly coherent socially established cooperative human activities through which their practitioners (religious believers or scientists) try to achieve certain goals by means of particular strategies. The emphasis on religion and science as social practices is important for at least two reasons. First, and most obvious, religion and science can as social practices have areas of overlap. Second, I maintain that it is from this angle that we have to start our theorizing about science and religion. That is to say, all accounts of the other dimensions of science and religion, and how to relate them to each other, must take account of the actual practices of science and religion and therefore must be grounded in the sociological and historical study of these practices. This is so if we really want our views to be relevant for real science and real religion and their relationship.

A practice can be distinguished by identifying the goals that its practitioners more or less share and the means that they develop and use to achieve these goals. Only when we have a good grasp of the goals of science and religion are we in a position to determine whether the means their practitioners have developed to achieve these goals are successful and perhaps also in competition with each other. In chapter 3 we will take a closer look at the goals of science and religion. Hence, the second element of the multidimensional model consists of the *teleological dimension* of science and religion. What we are looking for is a cluster of goals that individuals or the community more or less consciously take to be the aims of religious or scientific practice. Here I introduce a distinction between epistemic and practical goals, individual and collective goals, and manifest and latent goals, and analyze in respect to these categories whether the goals of religion and science are identical, similar, or totally different.

The third dimension of the multilevel model is the epistemic one. Beliefs, theories, stories, and the like are acquired, discussed, rejected, or revised in the everyday practice of both science and religion. These processes involve reasoning of some sort. Do practitioners in both fields endorse the same kinds of reasoning and is the same kind of reasoning appropriate given the goals of scientific and religious practice? Hence, another fundamental set of issues concerns rationality, justification, knowledge, and truth, in short, the *epistemological dimension* of religion and science. This dimension is discussed in chapters 4 through 6.

In chapter 4 the question is raised whether it is possible and desirable to challenge the way beliefs are formed, rejected, and revised in religion by taking science as the paradigm example of rationality: should the epistemology of religion be informed by the epistemology of science? Could there or should there be an overlap between science and religion on the epistemic level? In response to these questions we first critically evaluate Gould's principle of NOMA, which is one recent statement of scientific/religious restrictionism, and second Vincent Brümmer's claim that a scientifically informed epistemology of religion is based on a conceptual confusion. I maintain that Gould's and Brümmer's arguments are not convincing and that everything we can learn in one area of life from another area which can improve our cognitive performance ought to be taken into consideration by rational people. We cannot, therefore, exclude the possibility that there could and should be an overlap between science and religion in respect to epistemology or methodology. But I also note that an attempt to impose epistemic norms of one practice (science) on another practice (religion) will prove convincing only if one has sufficiently understood what is going on in these practices.

In chapter 5 we examine a recent attempt by Wentzel van Huyssteen to locate epistemological overlaps (understood in terms of transversal rationality) between science and religion. His postfoundational model of rationality is meant to be a "middle way" between, on the one hand, foundationalism (or modernism) and, on the other, nonfoundationalism (or postmodernism, or, more exactly, the radical forms of it). I question, however, whether it is really rational for us — given our limited cognitive resources — to take the postfoundational model of rationality as the ideal for our cognitive behavior. Instead I try to show the benefits of presumptionism as our model of rationality and why we should not confuse scientific, theological, and religious rationality. Presumptionism should be our global belief policy, while at the same time we must not deny that as a local belief policy judgment-based, internal evidentialism (which in my terminology is what van Huyssteen's model of rationality amounts to) may be more appropriate, at least when it comes to scientists' and theologians' own research. This allows a cross-disciplinary justification that provides means to step beyond the limitations and boundaries of our own local disciplinary contexts as scientists, theologians, or philosophers.

Scholars disagree on a number of issues in the discussion about scientific rationality and religious rationality and about the possibility of an overlap between them. In chapter 6 an attempt is, therefore, made to make explicit the different levels where we encounter this kind of disagreement. I suggest that we could use different concepts of rationality (disagree about the nature of rationality), assume different epistemic norms or principles (disagree about the standards of rationality), have different ideas about the relevance or applicability of the epistemic norms or principles (disagree about the scope of rationality), or accept different kinds of evidence (disagree about the reasons of rationality). These disagreements are, in turn, often related to differences in assumptions about the teleology of science and religion. Moreover, I argue that other things rather than epistemic matters or goals are of relevance when understanding religious rationality. Religious practitioners are not to be understood to be purely epistemic agents, because religious practice has both epistemic and practical goals. In this chapter, however, the opposite danger is addressed, namely, the failure to take account of the fact that rationality in religion is about truth and other epistemically relevant aspects, and the tendency to focus merely on political and moral considerations. The epistemology of some contemporary theologians is therefore critically examined. The view they hold is called "theological pragmatism."

In chapter 7 we move on to the fourth level of the multidimensional model, which is perhaps the most obvious level of engagement between science and religion, and certainly the one at the center of contemporary science-religion dialogue. This fourth level concerns the *theoretical dimension* of religion and science. Do the theories of science and the beliefs and doctrines of religion have the same, similar, or totally different subject matters? Because the focus in the dialogue has been so heavily directed toward this fourth level of engagement between science and religion, I merely offer two illustrations about the possible unity, intersection, or separation of the theoretical content of science and religion. This is sufficient since the overall objective is to offer a model of how to relate science and religion, and for this reason I have given priority to the other levels of engagement because they are less well known and even neglected in many writings about science and religion. First, Gordon D. Kaufman's argument that the acceptance of modern science (especially the account of cosmic and biological evolution) is not compatible with a belief in a personal God who is the creator of the world is critically evaluated. Second, the relevance of evolutionary biology for a religious understanding of the meaning of life is examined. The outcome of the discussion is such that it makes possible a contact view with respect to the theoretical level of engagement between science and religion.

The science-religion dialogue has often been understood in terms of the relevance of science for religion. If there is any traffic between these practices, it is assumed to be a one-way traffic from science to religion. In chapter 8, however, we look at scholars who claim that religion or ideology is of great relevance for scientific theory construction and method development, and not merely for ethical issues of scientific conduct. According to religious or ideological expansionists, science could not and should not be thought of as religiously or ideologically neutral. They believe that, on the contrary, the boundaries of religion or ideology could and should be expanded in such a way that religion in some important way becomes a part of the scientific enterprise. In chapter 8 four versions of this form of expansionism are presented, namely, Augustinian science, Islamic science, left-wing science, and feminist science.

Religious/ideological expansionism, or the idea of a science shaped by religion or ideology, is critically evaluated in chapter 9. In what way is it appropriate that worldview values and beliefs such as those endorsed by feminists, Marxists, Christians, Muslims, or naturalists enter into the fabric of science? I try to show that the answer to this question depends in part on what exactly we mean by "science." In the first part of the chapter I therefore distinguish between different aspects of science, between actual and good science, and between the problem-stating phase (science$_1$), the development phase (science$_2$), the justification phase (science$_3$), and the application phase (science$_4$) of science. The key issue concerns the justification phase of science. I argue that even if we can accept a worldview-partisan science$_1$, science$_2$, and science$_4$, we should be much more reluctant to accept a worldview-partisan science$_3$. Science should instead strive to be religiously or ideologically neutral in the sense that it ought not to presuppose the truth of any particular worldview, religion, or ideology such as Christianity, Islam, feminism, Marxism, or naturalism in the justification phase. This holds true even if religious and ideological expansionists are right that violations of this ideal in the actual life of scientific inquiry happen more frequently than we have previously thought. Thus, the position taken here involves a rejection also of a traditional understanding of the idea of a religiously or an ideologically neutral science.

In the last chapter, the multidimensional model of science and religion is fully explicated and compared with the standard fourfold typology (developed by Ian Barbour) of this relationship within the science-religion dialogue, and an answer is given to the key question of the study, how to relate science and religion.

Chapter 1

Contemporary Darwinism and Religion

The relationship between Darwin's theory of evolution and religion has been, to say the least, a controversial topic ever since the publication of *The Origin of Species* in 1859. Interestingly enough, evolutionary biologists have had and continue to have quite different views about this relationship. On the one hand, we have Darwinians who hold that religion and the sciences (including biology) are logically distinct and fully separate domains with different subject matters, methods, and aims. On the other, we have those who think that science in general and especially biology severely undermines traditional religion, and that science, to some extent, even can replace religion. In this chapter I shall present these views, identify where and why they diverge, and also propose some of the conceptual tools I think we need in order to understand properly the relationship between science and religion.

Scientific Restrictionism

In *Rocks of Ages: Science and Religion in the Fullness of Life* (1999), Stephen Jay Gould has delivered one of the most recent statements about how we ought to understand the relationship between contemporary science and religion. He thinks that the idea that there has been and still is a war going on between science and religion is wrong. It fails both as a historical account of how science and religion have been related and as a normative account of how science and religion ought to be related. He maintains instead that each inquiry frames its own questions and criteria of assessment. Gould writes that

> the net, or magisterium, of science covers the empirical realm: what is the universe made of (fact) and why does it work this way (theory). The magisterium of religion extends over questions of ultimate meaning and moral value. These two magisteria do not overlap, nor do they encompass all inquiry. . . . (Gould 1999: 6)

Science and religion ask different kinds of questions, and to that extent they have different aims and subject matters.

Science and religion also have methodologies or epistemologies. Both scientists and religious people have to regulate what they believe in some way. They use some kind of standards of assessment. Let us call these standards "epistemic norms." Gould maintains that science and religion have different epistemic norms, and that we have to acknowledge and accept this difference without imposing one magisterium's norms on the other magisterium.[1]

Gould contrasts the different ways in which the disciple Thomas's request for evidence is evaluated in the Christian practice and in which a similar request would be evaluated in scientific practice. When the other disciples told Thomas that they had met the resurrected Jesus, Thomas responded by saying, "Unless I see the nail marks in his hands and put my finger where the nails were, and put my hand into his side, I will not believe" (John 20:25). A week later Jesus reappeared and this time Thomas was also present. Jesus let Thomas put his finger where the nails had been and put his hand into his side, and then Thomas believed and said to Jesus, "My Lord and my God." Jesus responded by saying, "Because you have seen me, you have believed: blessed are those who have not seen and yet have believed" (John 20:29). Gould accepts this as a proper epistemic norm of religion but also writes that he "cannot think of a statement more foreign to the norms of science. . . . A skeptical attitude toward appeals based only on authority, combined with a demand for direct evi-

---

1. Gould defines a magisterium thus: "A magisterium . . . is a domain where one form of teaching holds the appropriate tools for meaningful discourse and resolution" (Gould 1999: 5).

dence . . . represents the first commandment of proper scientific procedure" (Gould 1999: 16).

Despite this difference, Gould maintains that both science and religion are important and necessary if we want to reach a full understanding of human life in all its complexity. They "hold equal worth and necessary status for any complete human life" (pp. 58-59). Gould, moreover, suggests that we should accept what he calls "the principle of NOMA" (or Non-Overlapping Magisteria) (p. 5). According to the principle of NOMA, the relationship between science and religion ought to be one of respectful noninterference. The principle could, roughly, be explicated as follows:

> Both science and religion are valid human inquiries and ought to be respected but treated as logically distinct and fully separate areas of inquiry with their own questions and epistemologies (or methodologies).

This principle puts certain restrictions on what kinds of claims religious believers or scientists can make *as* religious believers or scientists. That is to say, there can be both a misuse of science and a misuse of religion. Religion is misused when one uses it as a *control belief* in scientific inquiry, in other words, as a way of restricting the kind of factual conclusions scientists are allowed to draw from the data they have access to. This is done, for instance, when religious believers reject the theory of evolution because it does not fit with their understanding of what the Bible teaches and therefore they want to impose on science a different research program ("creationism") that better fits these religious convictions (pp. 125f.).

But Gould also thinks, perhaps a bit more surprisingly, that religion is misused or more precisely that NOMA is violated when religious believers adhere to a certain conception of God. This is so because he maintains that the first commandment of NOMA is, "Thou shalt not mix the magisteria by claiming that God directly ordains important events in the history of nature by special interference knowable only through revelation and not accessible to science" (p. 84). Thus, religious believers cannot properly claim that God's action sometimes results in the occurrence of a miracle. Moreover, "people whose concept of God demands a loving deity, personally concerned with the lives of all his creatures" also violate NOMA, although in "a more subtle" way (p. 93). This means, I think, that religious people should not understand God's personal concern for them and others in such a way that they believe that God has prearranged natural history so that it will have a certain outcome, for instance, the origin of the human species or, more specifically still, the birth or death of particular individuals (pp. 201-2).

So NOMA implies at least three restrictions on religion: (a) a restriction against using religion as a control belief in scientific inquiries, (b) a restriction against the acceptance of miracles, and (c) a restriction against the acceptance of a belief that things in the world are prearranged in a certain way (without violating any natural laws) so that they show God's particular concern for somebody or something.

Gould maintains that science can be misused as well, and that scientists can in their profession violate the principle of NOMA. NOMA "forbid[s] scientific entry into fields where many arrogant scientists love to walk, and yearn to control" (p. 93). Gould thinks, in fact, that many contemporary biologists have "imperialistic aims" (p. 85). They are scientific expansionists because they attempt to expand the boundaries of evolutionary biology in such a way that it covers other areas of inquiry, for instance, ethics and religion. One example that Gould comes back to several times is the attempt by some Darwinians to provide answers to our moral questions. This is a misuse of evolutionary biology: "Any argument that facts or theories of biological evolution can enjoin or validate any moral behavior represents a severe misuse of Darwin's great insight, and a cardinal violation of NOMA" (p. 163). Another example is related to claims about determinism in biology:

> One of the saddest chapters in the entire history of science records the extensive misuse of data to support the supposed moral and social consequences of biological determinism, the claim that inequalities based on race, sex, or class cannot be altered because they reflect the innate and inferior genetic endowments of the disadvantaged. (p. 166)

Such attempts violate NOMA because the biologists involved are "misidentifying their own social preferences as facts of nature in their technical writings" (p. 166). Gould believes that the same is often true in respect to religion. He confesses that he is "discouraged when some of [his] colleagues tout their private atheism . . . as a panacea for human progress against an absurd caricature of 'religion,' erected as a straw man for rhetorical purposes" (p. 209).

4

So it seems — even if Gould omits to state it — as if the second commandment of NOMA is this: "Thou shalt not mix the magisteria by claiming that science directly ordains solutions to moral and existential concerns by special interference knowable only through scientific experiments and discoveries that are not accessible to religion."

Gould thinks instead that Darwin should serve as the model for biologists (as well as for scientists in general):

> Darwin did not use evolution to promote atheism, or to maintain that no concept of God could ever be squared with the structure of nature. Rather, he argued that nature's factuality, as read within the magisterium of science, could not resolve, or even specify, the existence or character of God, the ultimate meaning of life, the proper foundations of morality, or any other question within the different magisterium of religion. (p. 192)

Thus the principle of NOMA is violated when one tries to expand one's own magisterium into the other's magisterium (p. 211). Accordingly, a biologist is misusing science when he or she in the name of science uses evolution to promote atheism, theism, or any other solution to our existential concerns, or uses evolution to specify the proper foundation or content of morality or to totally reject a moral discourse altogether.

Scientific Expansionism

The idea that evolutionary theory has great implications for human society and our self-understanding has, however, always been a part of the Darwinian tradition. Contemporary biology is no exception. Thus, Richard D. Alexander talks about the recent development within evolutionary biology as the "greatest intellectual advance of the twentieth century," which should have a profound impact on our self-view and our understanding of morality (Alexander 1987: 2). In fact, he believes that we have to "start all over again to describe and understand ourselves," and we have to do it "in terms alien to our intuitions" (p. 2). Richard Dawkins writes that since we have evolutionary theory, "We no longer have to resort to superstition when faced with the deep problems: Is there a meaning to life? What are we for? What is man?" (Dawkins 1989: 1). Moreover, he agrees with zoologist George Gaylord Simpson that "all attempts to answer that question ["What is man?"] before 1859 are worthless and that we will be better off if we ignore them completely" (p. 1). Daniel C. Dennett, a philosopher of science, writes that "Darwin's dangerous idea [evolution by natural selection] is reductionism incarnate, promising to unite and explain almost everything in one magnificent vision" (Dennett 1995: 81).

What is it that evolutionary biology can teach us that goes beyond the empirical questions Gould thinks it should be occupied with? There are several things. Evolutionary theory is taken to be able to show that morality is ultimately about selfishness or maximizing fitness. Michael Ruse and Edward O. Wilson tell us that evolutionary biologists have discovered that "in an important sense . . . ethics is an illusion fobbed off on us by our genes to get us to cooperate" and that therefore there is no objectivity to morality (Ruse and Wilson 1993: 310). We are deceived by our genes into thinking that there is a disinterested objective and binding morality, which we all should obey (Ruse and Wilson 1986: 179). Dawkins agrees and tells us that evolutionary theory supports the idea that life is selfish all the way down and thus we can even talk about selfish genes. He describes our genes as "successful Chicago gangsters" that are ruthlessly selfish. Moreover, since we are "survival machines" which are "blindly programmed to preserve [these selfish] genes," no matter how much "we wish to believe otherwise, universal love and the welfare of the species as a whole are concepts that simply do not make evolutionary sense" (Dawkins 1989: v and 2). No wonder Alexander thinks that these claims, if true, would radically change our self-view.

Moreover, Dawkins proclaims that Darwinism makes it possible to be an "intellectually fulfilled atheist," and that because evolutionary theory undermines, if not refutes, traditional religious beliefs by showing that the universe lacks design or purpose, biologists ought to be atheists (Dawkins 1986: 5-6). Although Wilson thinks that religion constitutes the greatest challenge to biology, he maintains that we can "explain traditional religion . . . as a wholly material phenomenon" by using evolutionary theory (Wilson 1978: 192).

But Darwinism, Wilson tells us, can be used not merely to explain religion as a strategy solely adapted to secure genetic fitness; it can even replace traditional religion. The evolutionary epic provides us with a new mythology and can constitute the key element in our new religion, what Wilson sometimes calls "scientific materialism" and at other times "scientific naturalism" (p. 192). But Wilson does not think that it is possible now to predict the form religious life and rituals will take as "scientific materialism appropriates the mythopoeic energies to its own ends" (p. 206). He also admits that it is here where at least the present spiritual weakness of scientific materialism lies. It lacks the "primal source of power" that religion for genetic reasons is hooked up with, partly because the "evolutionary epic denies immortality to the individual and divine privilege to the society" (pp. 192-93). Wilson, nevertheless, believes that a way exists to divert the power of religion into the service of scientific naturalism, even if it must be left to the future to tell us how exactly this will be done.

It is thus not merely the case, Wilson believes, that Gould fails to realize the full potential of Darwinism; he also fails to understand what religion is or at least what kind of religion it is that ought to be taken seriously. Dawkins tells us that he pays

> religions the compliment of regarding them as scientific theories. . . . I see God as a competing explanation for facts about the universe and life. This is certainly how God has been seen by most theologians of past centuries and by most ordinary religious people today. . . . Either admit that God is a scientific hypothesis and let him submit to the same judgement as any other scientific hypothesis. Or admit that his status is no higher than that of fairies and river sprites. (Dawkins 1995b: 46-47)

Dawkins goes beyond mere "compliments." Instead he seems to think that religion or belief in God is a kind of scientific or quasi-scientific theory because religion contains truth claims:

> The claim of the existence of God is a purely scientific one. Either it is true or it is not. A universe with God would be completely different from one without. . . . If you're deeply steeped in evolution, you see that it is a way to get complex designs out of nothing. You don't need God. (Dawkins 1992: 3)

Moreover, Dawkins thinks that scientists can use scientific methodology to criticize religious attitudes and epistemic norms. He tells us that faith

> means blind trust, in the absence of evidence, even in the teeth of evidence. The story of Doubting Thomas is told, not so that we shall ad-

7

mire Thomas, but so that we can admire the other apostles in comparison. Thomas demanded evidence. . . . The other apostles, whose faith
was so strong that they did not need evidence, are held up to us as worthy of imitation. . . . Blind faith can justify anything. (Dawkins 1989:
198)

Presumably this means that if religious believers were really rational —
and on this point they can learn a lot from scientists — they would admire
Thomas and not the other disciples and consequently change their
epistemic norms in such a way that they would resemble scientific norms.

Wilson also maintains that he considers scientific epistemology to be
preferable to religious epistemology. He writes that "the reasons why I
consider the scientific ethos superior to religion [are]: its repeated triumphs in explaining and controlling the physical world; its self-correcting
nature open to all competent to devise and conduct the tests; its readiness
to examine all subjects sacred and profane . . ." (Wilson 1978: 201).

According to these biologists, Gould has got most things wrong
about the proper relationship between science and religion. It is, *pace*
Gould, the case that

(a) evolutionary theory can explain religion as a purely material phe-
    nomenon;
(b) evolutionary theory can demonstrate that morality is ultimately
    about selfishness or maximizing fitness;
(c) evolutionary theory can help us resolve our existential questions,
    and in doing this it supports naturalism (or atheism);
(d) religions are scientific or quasi-scientific theories; and
(e) scientific epistemic norms are superior and therefore ought to re-
    place religious epistemic norms.

In other words, science and religion occupy the same turf. Two strategies,
more exactly, are used (either separately or jointly) to show that there is a
union of domains. Either it is argued that traditional religion offers rival
explanations about the same (empirical) phenomenon and thus science
and religion are already on the same turf, or it is maintained that the
boundaries of contemporary science (especially of evolutionary biology)
can be expanded in such a way that science covers or will eventually cover
not only empirical questions but also moral and existential questions.

Thus science can move its position forward so that it ends up on the same turf that religion traditionally occupied.

Related to this point, it is important to notice that even if all evolutionary biologists discussed in this section are scientific expansionists in contrast to Gould, they do not agree about the exact way in which the boundaries of evolutionary theory ought to be extended. Whereas, for instance, Ruse and Wilson think that evolutionary theory can be extended to offer solutions to our moral questions, this is something Alexander and Dawkins seem to deny (Alexander 1987: xvi and Dawkins 1989: 2). Moreover, whereas Dawkins and Wilson think that evolutionary theory can be extended to offer solutions to our existential questions and to refute traditional religion, this is something Ruse explicitly denies (Ruse 1998: 294).

Three Science-Religion Views

What should one think about these radically different claims about the boundaries of contemporary science, especially of evolutionary biology, and its relationship to religion? We have at least three options:

1. There is no overlap between science and religion.
2. There is a union of the domains of science and religion.
3. There is overlap (or intersection) between science and religion.

Gould defends the first view, and Dawkins and Wilson seem to presuppose the second view in their writings, but it is, of course, also possible to maintain a middle position, namely, point 3. Call the first the "independence view," the second the "monist view," and the third the "contact view." More exactly, Dawkins and Wilson adhere to one particular version of the monist view, namely, the conflict version. They believe that science and religion offer different answers to the same kinds of problems. (But it is of course also possible to hold that they could offer the same answers to the same kinds of problems. Call this the harmony version of the monist view.)[2] Notice how-

2. It is easy to forget this perspective today, but this view was probably the dominant one among the scientists themselves during the seventeenth and eighteenth centuries and far into the nineteenth century. The historian of science Charles C. Gillispie writes that if there had been a war going on between religion and science, at least the scientist did not know about it until the latter half of the nineteenth century (Gillispie 1951: 3f.).

ever, that if one defends the contact view one can also understand the area of intersection in terms of either conflict or harmony. Hence, merely the fact that someone claims that science and religion are in conflict on a particular issue — say, the origin of life — does not entail that that person accepts the monist view. This person could very well at the same time maintain that typically, although not in this particular case, science and religion have different agendas or areas of expertise.

Which view is the most reasonable? To be able to determine which of these three science-religion views is the most reasonable one, we have to know in more detail what kind of activities science and religion are. What I want to stress, for reasons that will soon become clear, is that whatever else they might be, science and religion are complex activities performed by human beings in cooperation within a particular historical and cultural setting. In short, they are *social practices*. As social practices, they are performed by certain groups of people. These groups of people (call them the "practitioners") are organized in a particular way. The practices can be defined by identifying the goals that the practitioners have more or less in common and the means that they develop and use to achieve these goals. Further, these practices have a history and they therefore constitute traditions. Thus one possible level of intersection is social. We could perhaps find overlaps when it comes to the participants in these practices and how these practices are socially structured, the functions different groups of practitioners have, how knowledge or something else essential for the practice is transmitted from one generation to the next, and so on.

In what way is this relevant to our discussion? Gould would hardly deny that there is a social intersection in the sense that people can participate in both religious and scientific practice. He would not presumably claim that these two magisteria do not overlap in this sense. This is relevant because Gould points to the actual *social* intersection as a reason for thinking that there is no *methodological* and *theoretical* intersection or, more exactly, that there is no warfare between science and religion whether in terms of epistemology (or method) or in terms of areas of inquiry. He asks rhetorically, "if science and religion have been destined to fight for the same disputed territory" how could it then be possible that "science, at the dawn of the modern age, [has been] honorably practiced by professional clergymen (who, by conventional [warfare] views, should have undermined rather than promulgated such an enterprise)" (Gould 1999: 70)? Again, "If NOMA did not work, and religion really did demand the suppression of important factual data at key points of contradiction with theological dogma, then how could the ranks of science include so many ordained and devoted clergymen at the highest level of respect and accomplishment . . ." (p. 83)?

The argument seems to be as follows:

1. If the warfare view (or, more exactly, the warfare version of the monist view) is true, one would expect that people who are deeply religious would not be in the forefront in developing science.
2. But deeply religious people — including Galileo, Newton, Faraday, and Eddington — have been in the forefront in developing science.
3. Therefore, we ought to reject the warfare view and accept an independence view based on the principle of NOMA.

This argument, I think, undermines the plausibility of any view claiming that there has always been warfare between science and religion. But it is not quite as strong as Gould seems to believe. For one thing, a defender of the warfare view could argue that the recent development in, for instance, evolutionary biology is such that there is *now* a genuine conflict between science and religion. Thus, William Provine thinks it is true that "very few truly religious evolutionary biologists remain. Most are atheists, and many have been driven there by their understanding of the evolutionary process and other science" (Provine 1988: 28). In fact, he believes that contemporary science "directly implies" that there is no cosmic purpose, no God, no objective ethical principles, no immortality, and no free will (pp. 27-28).

In other words, *science (and, of course, religion as well) is a practice that changes over time, and, therefore, whether or not there is a conflict between science and religion depends on, among other things, the specific content of the scientific theories (and, of course, also the specific content of the religious beliefs) accepted at a given time.* Consequently, Gould's argument is not sufficient to establish the conclusion that the proper relationship between science and religion ought to be guided by the principle of NOMA. There is no shortcut possible on this issue. If Gould wants to convince us that NOMA also applies to the relationship between contemporary evolutionary biology and religion, then he needs to respond to the claims of his expansionistic colleagues. This is so because it is quite possible that the recent developments in evolutionary biology can justify an expansion of the scientific domain to what is now considered a part of the religious domain.

Therefore, although Gould is right that the social overlap between science and religion undermines any idea that we will always find scientists and religious believers in simple opposition, the ways religion and science are related can certainly vary during the course of history since both are dynamic and evolving social practices. Any plausible account of how to relate science and religion must be able to take that into consideration.

Now we are in a better position to see why the dynamic concepts of expansion and restriction are important complements to the logical and static concepts of separation, union, and intersection when we try to understand the relationship between science and religion. These concepts are important because they make a relational model possible that takes into account the fact that science and religion are social and dynamic practices and thus not static entities. Therefore it is not possible to determine *a priori* where the borderline goes between science and religion since that could change as these practices develop and transform over time.

The relationship between science and religion is also, however, a *multilevel* or *multidimensional* relationship. For this reason we need to consider the aspects where science and religion might be related. The idea is simply that there are many aspects to these complex enterprises. I suggest that there are at least four levels or dimensions of these practices that we need to take into account if we want to understand how to relate science and religion.

The first simple but important aspect, as I have stressed, is that both science and religion are social practices. Therefore we need to know how they are socially structured. For instance, who is allowed to participate and on what grounds? What functions do different groups of practitioners perform in science and in religion, and how is knowledge or anything else essential for these practices transmitted from one generation to its successor? I shall treat these issues as belonging to the *social dimension* of science and religion.

The second aspect concerns the *teleology* of religion and science. Practitioners of religion and science have some aims in mind when they do what they do; they are trying to achieve certain ends. Some fundamental issues concern the goals of the practices and the weight these different goals should be given. Are the goals of religion and science identical, similar, or totally different?

The third is the *epistemological dimension*. Beliefs, theories, methods, and concepts are acquired, discussed, rejected, or revised in the day-to-day activities of both science and religion. These processes involve reasoning of some sort. Do practitioners in both fields endorse the same kinds of reasoning? More fundamentally, can both science and religion be characterized as cognitive activities? And do they both have explanatory missions? Hence, another fundamental set of issues concerns rationality, justification, knowledge, and truth, and this is the epistemological dimension of religion and science.

The last dimension concerns the subject matter of science and religion. Religion and science are about something. They have what Gould calls certain "areas of inquiry." What are the beliefs, theories, and stories of religion and science about? Do theories of science and religious beliefs or doctrines have the same, similar, or totally different subject matters? Perhaps science is about factual matters, whereas religion is merely about ultimate meaning and values. Or are there factual matters other than purely empirical ones and are these or some of these addressed by religion but not by science? Here we have the *theoretical dimension* of religion and science.

The basic idea, then, is that *somebody who wants to successfully understand how to relate science and religion needs to take into account at least the social structure of science and religion, the aims of these practices, the kind of epistemology they exhibit, and their theoretical content (their theories, beliefs, or stories).*

Furthermore, these dimensions of science and religion can be studied either historically or from a contemporary perspective, and can focus on one particular science and one particular religion (or even more narrowly one tradition within one religion) or focus more generally on, for instance, the natural sciences and the world religions. They could thus be more universal or more contextual in scope. In the science-religion dialogue we have those who maintain that one cannot sensibly talk about science and religion in some abstract, universal, ahistorical, or gender/color-unrelated way. Instead one must always be specific about, for instance, the religion (or even the religious tradition within a particular religion), the science (or part of science), the historical period, the cultural setting, and so forth, one is dealing with. For instance, John Brooke and Geoffrey Cantor argue that neither religion nor science is reducible to some timeless essence; both must be understood in their historical particularities. Science and religion are inextricable from the times in which they arise (Brooke and Cantor 2000).

The historical studies are typically descriptive in character: they tell us how science and religion in a particular historical environment were related. The contemporary studies could be either descriptive or normative: they could tell us either how science and religion (or a particular kind of science or religion) are related or how they should be related to each other.

These distinctions give us the following matrix:

	Social dimension	Teleological dimension	Epistemological dimension	Theoretical dimension
I. Contemporary studies				
1. universal				
a. descriptive				
b. normative				
2. contextual				
a. descriptive				
b. normative				
II. Historical studies				
1. universal				
2. contextual				

Moreover, we should not forget that any practice that fulfills the same or similar functions as religion is of interest. Hence, secularized versions of environmentalism, existentialism, feminism, Marxism, and naturalism also need to be taken into consideration. These views have been called a number of things, for instance, "worldviews," "ideologies," and "views of life." Although our focus is on science and religion we will also pay attention to the wider question of how science and worldviews should be related (assuming that religion and ideology are subsets of this broader category).[3]

Let us start our inquiry by focusing first on the social and then on the teleological dimension of science and religion, before discussing the

3. See pp. 172, 194-96 in this volume for a discussion of the concepts of worldview and ideology.

epistemological and theoretical ones. As we shall see, the answer one gives with respect to one of these dimensions often has consequences for one's conception of the other dimensions as well. If we structure our discussion about the relationship between science and religion in this way, it will give us some of the resources we need to be able to evaluate the claims of restrictionists, scientific expansionists, and religious/ideological expansionists.

Chapter 2

The Social Dimension
of Science and Religion

S cience may be regarded as merely a set of theories and religion as only a collection of beliefs. Clearly science and religion include these aspects, but science should not be identified with its theories or religion with its beliefs. Moreover, we do not grasp enough of the character and function of scientific theories and religious beliefs if we abstract them from the processes in which they are generated, that is, from their social and historical context; scientific theories are one product of scientific practice and religious beliefs are one output of religious practice. I shall maintain in this chapter that we must take these social and historical aspects into account if we want to understand how to relate science and religion. To be able to identify the social dimension of science and religion we need to ask questions such as these: Who participate in these practices? Who is allowed to participate? What functions do different groups of practitioners perform? How is knowledge or anything else essential for the practice transmitted from one generation to the next?

Whatever else science and religion might be they are complex activities performed by human beings in cooperation within a particular historical and cultural setting. They are what I shall call "social practices"; this means, roughly, that they are *complex and fairly coherent socially established cooperative human activities through which their practitioners (religious believers or scientists) try to obtain certain goals by means of particular strategies.*[1] A prac-

---

1. See MacIntyre (1987: 187f.) for an illuminating discussion of the concept of practice, and see Tilley (1995: 30f.) for its application in religion.

tice can thus be distinguished by identifying the *goals* that its practitioners have more or less in common and the *means* that they develop and use to achieve these goals. (In chapter 3 we will, therefore, take a closer look at the goals of science and religion, and in chapter 4 move on to a discussion about the means of science and religion.) Science and religion conceived in this way consist of all the activities that scientists and religious people participate in while pursuing the goals of their particular practice; and since these two practices have existed for a long time, they have a history and constitute traditions.

The emphasis on religion and science as social practices is important for at least two reasons. First, and most obviously, religion and science can as social practices have areas of overlap. They can be socially structured in similar but also in totally different ways. Of course, the traditional picture has been that there is a huge difference in how science and religion are organized. The scientific community is taken to be the very paradigm of rationality, where claims are systematically criticized and nothing is believed on authority, where the members of the community dispassionately and disinterestedly apply the scientific method, and every use of it takes them closer to the goals of science (truth, avoidance of falsehood, knowledge, understanding, or whatever else the goal of science more exactly is taken to be). Religion, on the other hand, is instead taken to be a paradigm example of irrationality, where claims are not criticized and where things are believed on authority, and where emotions run high and subjectivity prevails. We shall see, however, that there are good reasons to nuance this picture a great deal.

Second, I shall maintain, as I have already pointed out, that it is from this angle that we have to start our theorizing about science and religion. That is to say, all accounts of the teleology, epistemology, and theoretical content of science and religion, and of how to relate these dimensions to each other, must be grounded in the actual practices of science and religion and therefore grounded in the sociological and historical study of these practices. This is so if we really want our views to be relevant for *real* science and *real* religion and their relationship. Otherwise we risk developing an account of their relation that is religiously and scientifically irrelevant because it is not in substantial contact with the actual practice of religion and science. If we, for instance, want to compare the epistemic norms employed in science with the ones used in religion, we have to take into account how practitioners of science and religion really form and regulate their beliefs. Philosophers in particular have had a tendency to overlook this, but scientists also tend to have an idealized and unrealistic image of the scientific enterprise.

Maintaining such a practice-oriented approach does not mean that there is no place for normative accounts of religion and science.[2] This is, after all, the main concern of this book. Both descriptive and normative accounts are appropriate, but we have to be clear about when we are doing what. Most of all, we must distinguish between (a) what we would prefer science or religion to be, and (b) how science and religion are actually understood by the majority of its practitioners. We ought to characterize science and religion so that we do not disqualify large numbers of practitioners whose self-understanding is different from the one we ourselves exemplify or prefer. Everyone of course has a right to his or her own particular view of religion and science, but these practices are shared collective enterprises. Therefore, the best approach is one that acknowledges that the real practice of religion and science puts constraints on (but does not determine) how religion and science and their relationship could be understood or conceptualized. Case studies of actual religious and scientific practice constitute evidence for or against proposed conceptions of religion and science and how they are related. In this chapter I shall, therefore, consider some similarities and differences between religion and science seen as social practices. I shall highlight only some of the aspects that such a comparison between science and religion might contain, thereby providing a necessary background for the analysis of the claims of scientific and religious expansionists that we shall consider later on and for the overarching agenda of how to relate science and religion. It is anyway beyond my competence as a philosopher to give a more detailed account; for such an account we have to rely on the work of sociologists and historians.[3] But my sketch of science and religion as social practices can, I hope, at least take us in the right direction.

2. I developed the idea of a practice-oriented approach for the first time in Stenmark (1995); see especially pp. 9f. and 115f.

3. See Stahl et al. (2002) for a recent book that offers a social perspective on the relationship between science and religion.

The Learning Process and the Place of Authority

The first thing to acknowledge is that social practices like religion and science are something the practitioners *learn* to do. They require a certain degree of knowledge and skills, things the practitioners are not born with. These practitioners are instead introduced or socialized into an ongoing practice that has a history and tradition, as well as a particular social structure, including a division of labor.

Religious practitioners either grow up in a religious community or at a later stage in life become a part of a religious community. The longtime members of the community train the newly converted in religious practice. These newcomers learn how to participate in worship, how to read and interpret sacred texts, how to encounter the divine reality, and so on. Hence we have at least two significant groups of religious people: the old and the new believers. In science too we can distinguish between old and new scientists, although one cannot grow up in a scientific community as one can in a religious community. With regard to this point we find a crucial difference between the two practices. The practitioners of science enter the scientific community at a later stage in life and the longtime members of the community train them in doing science properly. They learn the content of the currently accepted theories of the discipline, how to use instruments and collect information, how to interpret the phenomena of the natural and social world. Hence, looking at the world with the "eye of faith" or with the "eye of science" is something one has to learn. It is part of a social training process.

If this is correct then authority plays an important role not merely in religion but also in science. But here we seem to come into conflict with a popular view of science. Bertrand Russell, for instance, claims that the scientist's "beliefs are tentative, not dogmatic; they are based on evidence, not on authority or intuition" (Russell 1984: 514). Stephen Jay Gould agrees and writes that "a skeptical attitude toward appeals based on authority, combined with a demand for direct evidence . . . represents the first commandment of proper scientific procedure" (Gould 1999: 16). But contrary to what Gould and Russell maintain, assignments of authority are important also in science. Science could not be done unless scientists were prepared to take some matters on trust. In science just as in any other human context, we believe on authority. Philip Kitcher writes, "each of us begins, in childhood, by absorbing the lore of our culture, and we do so, initially, without questions. Later, apprentice scientists may submit themselves voluntarily to training by people whom the community regards as authoritative on certain matters. Still later, individual scientists identify certain people within the community as authoritative in issues that are not agreed on throughout the community" (Kitcher 1993: 84 n. 36). It is thus a misconception that scientists critically assess all the theories, methods, and instruments they use in their research and accept theories or hypotheses only to the degree that evidence warrants them.[4]

Scientists rely on authority for good reasons. This is so because scientists are not Cartesian egos or lone ideal observers. Rather, scientists (like the rest of us) are finite beings with limited cognitive resources who find themselves in a particular social environment with a particular task at hand. As a consequence, every application of their cognitive resources has a certain cost. Scientists, therefore, have neither the time nor the resources to check every scientific theory and method in their field or even all those which form the basis of their own research. If they were to try to do such a thing they would never get anywhere in their research. So without trust in others, individual scientists would neither be able to pursue their projects as rapidly nor be capable of developing projects that are impossible for a single individual to accomplish. Scientists do not even have the cognitive resources for rechecking the scientific information that is already a part of their own memories. They are not able to trace the justification of these beliefs.[5] This applies to all scholars. Many of us believe certain things to be true or false, plausible or implausible, in our particular fields. But on reflection we realize that we cannot retrace the original source of these beliefs by using our memory or notes we have made on papers or files in our computers or elsewhere.

Authority is, of course, also of importance in the religious context, and by paying attention to the social dimension of religious practice we can also see why it is justified. For instance, as they grow up, children in a Christian community are told that there is a God and that God created heavens and earth, and they receive this information, initially, without questions. Later in life they (and newly converted people) submit them-

---

4. For a criticism of this image of science see Kuhn (1970), Newton-Smith (1981), and Kitcher (1993).

5. For a discussion of the difficulty or impossibility of doing this see Cherniak (1986), Harman (1986), and Stenmark (1995).

selves to training by individuals whom they or the community regard as authoritative on religious issues, in order to become more "mature" believers. When there are disagreements in the community about certain issues, individual believers typically recognize certain people as authoritative. In these situations and just as in science, religious practitioners accept some of the claims made by other practitioners, investigate the ideas of some people and ignore the proposals of others. It seems, however, to be more common in religion than in science for people to hold on to authorities in too dogmatic a way; in other words, no matter what may happen, some of these authorities are still fully accepted and can never really be modified or rejected. (The reasons why this is so and how to respond to it are discussed in chapter 5.) Nevertheless, trust in authorities is necessary and therefore rational in complex social practices such as religion and science, where division of labor is required.

The reliance on authority in religion and science does not imply that the commitments involved in these practices are never altered or replaced; on the contrary, they constantly undergo change. This is not merely true of science but also of religion because, as Holmes Rolston points out,

> The history of religion is strewn with abandoned beliefs, largely overcome by more commanding creeds or made implausible by new ranges of experience. To the contemporary religious mind, primitive fetishes and taboos, superstitions and sacrifices seem quite as quaint as (and perhaps a form of) primitive science. Only a handful of the myriad religious hypotheses of the human race have survived the sifting in experience that makes them classic (that is, verified in experience), and for that handful this durability increases their categorical element. Most earlier religions are extinct; a few are relict. (Rolston 1987: 7)

Whether one can talk about "the contemporary religious mind" in this way is perhaps questionable, but it still remains true that religious practitioners' commitments are confirmed, modified, or rejected through (a) conversation with *other practitioners,* and (b) encounter with what is experienced as the *sacred* (or the divine reality). Their commitments are also conformed, modified, or rejected through (c) conversation with *outsiders,* in other words people who are not practitioners of the religion (or of the particular branch of the religion in question), or more broadly speaking by interaction with the surrounding society. In a similar fashion the scientists' commitments are confirmed, modified, or rejected through (a) conversation with other scientists, through what is taken to be (b) an encounter with the natural and the social world, and through (c) conversation with nonspecialists, people who are not scientists or at least do not belong to the scientific discipline in question, or more generally by interaction with the surrounding society. Although outsiders play an important role when it comes to what religious people and scientists believe or do, the "significant others" in both science and religion are typically other practitioners.

Nevertheless, in science the process of critical evaluation is done in a different and more systematic way than in religion. As we shall see in chapter 3, this is related to the fact that typically the epistemic goals of science and religion are significantly different. In short, I suggest that in science the epistemic goal is to increase the general body of knowledge about the natural and social world, whereas in religion it is to increase the knowledge of each of the believers to such an extent that they can live a religious life successfully. To contribute to the epistemic goal of religion is first of all to increase, up to a certain level, the religious knowledge (say, at least to the level necessary for salvation/liberation) of as many people as possible (although Judaism is one exception to this rule). It is not, as in science, to move the frontiers of knowledge of the social and natural world forward as much as possible.

To achieve this epistemic goal scientists work on different problems. They specialize, and there is thus a division of labor. Moreover, scientists try to provide individuals of different research groups with access to the data they discover and to the theories they develop. An integrated part of this process is not only cooperation but also competition among scientists, with scientists allowing and encouraging the critical scrutiny of other people's work, and thus being aware that their own work probably will receive the same treatment and therefore trying to make certain that it will stand up to such an evaluation.

In religion, on the other hand, the process of critical evaluation — if we take the understanding of the epistemic goal of religion that I have suggested for granted — is done in quite a different and less systematic way than in science. The key question is whether the means developed by the previous generations of practitioners of, for instance, a religion such as Christianity to allow contact with the divine reality (or God), to enable its practitioners to live a Christian life successfully, and to help other people become Christians are still appropriate or whether instead these means need to be improved or even radically changed in some way.

So whereas the mission of science is not to have all of us give up our old occupations and become scientists, the mission of many religions is something like that; it is to make all nonreligious practitioners into religious practitioners and to give people the religious knowledge they need to live such lives successfully. The social organization and the process and aim of critical evaluation will look different if, to put it bluntly, you are principally concerned with the question, "How can we improve our relationship to God and make the path to salvation/liberation understandable and compelling to people who are not yet practitioners?" rather than with the question, "How can we improve our understanding of and control over events in the natural and social world?"

Individual and Collective Practices

In religion we can distinguish between *common faith* (what all practitioners believe) and *individual faith* (what a particular practitioner believes). When it comes to questions of common faith (what should be believed, what rituals should be used, what stories should be normative, and so on), there is almost always a group of members that are viewed as authoritative. It may consist of priests, theologians, or church leaders, if we take Christianity again as our example. In science we also have to be aware of the differences between the commitments of individual scientists and the body of commitments that is shared by the scientific community (either within a particular discipline or within science as a whole). Also in the scientific case there is normally a group of people who are considered by the other scientists to be authoritative on what should be the generally scientifically accepted view (or views) on a particular issue.

Let us call the commitments of individual scientists and religious believers the *individual practice* and the ones that are shared within their communities the *collective practice* (cf. Kitcher 1993: 74f.). Precisely what the individual and collective practices of religion and science consist of and what the most important components in them are, is a matter of dispute. But, roughly, these practices contain language, questions, aims, methods, beliefs, models, and theories; and in the scientific case they contain also instruments and samples, and in the religious case, rituals and stories or myths.

23

Scientists' individual practice consists typically of the collective practice, but also of commitments that go beyond those that are shared with other scientists. They might, for instance, accept a particular hypothesis as the most likely explanation of a particular phenomenon, whereas a different hypothesis is the one accepted by most scientists in their field. This is often also the case in religion, but the collective practice is not as clearly defined as in science (at least not as it is in the natural sciences) and there is almost always a debate going on about what it should consist of (this, however, is also often the case in the social sciences and the humanities).

The collective practice changes in both religion and science in response to modifications in the individual practices. For instance, the changes in Paul's, Augustine's, Aquinas's, and Luther's individual practices caused modifications in the collective practice of Christianity. In science the paradigm examples of this influence of individual practice on collective practice are the discoveries of Galileo, Newton, Darwin, and Einstein. Changes in practice occur then both at the individual and the collective level in religion and science, and these levels further mutually affect each other.

The Plurality of Practices

Even though I frequently speak of "religious practice" and "scientific practice" because it is convenient to do so, we must not be misled into thinking that there is a single generic social practice of religion or science. Neither the sciences nor the religions could be grouped together as rather homogeneous collections of practices. Being a scholar working in physics is radically different in many ways from being one who is working in psychology or history. In a similar fashion, being a Christian is very different in many ways from being a Buddhist or an adherent of a so-called indigenous religion. It is therefore sometimes better to focus on how to relate a particular religion, like Christianity, to a particular science, like biology (or, at least, to a particular group of sciences such as the natural sciences).

But I also suggest that it matters what activity within a religious practice we compare science with. This is because even though both religion and science are social activities performed by human beings, science is something more; it is a set of *disciplines*. A special training and a much higher degree of cognitive competence than that needed for taking part in religion is required to be able to take part in an enterprise like biology, physics, or psychology. In fact, some religious practitioners including many Christians claim that to be a part of their religious practice requires no special cognitive competence at all. To become a Christian is taken to be an act of faith alone. So science is a highly theoretical or intellectual enterprise for the cognitively well trained, whereas religion is an activity in which anyone can, if she likes, participate. *In science, therefore, we have nothing similar to ordinary religious believers.* For this reason, as we shall see, it is sometimes better to compare religious practice with the practice of everyday life than with scientific practice.[6]

Some religious participants — namely, the theologians — could perhaps be considered equals in this respect to the members of the scientific practice. The theologians' task is to reflect on the life and commitments of the community, and to be considered a professional theologian requires a special training and a much higher degree of cognitive competence than is required for taking part in religion in general. Theology is the discipline within which the theologians work. Hence *religion is an intellectual enterprise like science only in the form of theology.* In this sense there is a crucial disanalogy between science and religion. This means that we have to be careful when we discuss (a) the relationship between science and religion and (b) the relationship between science and theology. Religion and theology are not interchangeable concepts.

But there is also a disanalogy between scientists and theologians in general. The task of the scientist is normally not to reflect on the life and commitments of the scientific community; it is rather to reflect on the natural world. Only historians, philosophers, and sociologists *of* science consider this to be a part of their work. Scientists in general spend very little time on that kind of reflection. Many theologians, on the other hand, take this to be their key occupation, although of course a significant group of them would think that their mission is also to study the interaction between the divine and the world. The members of the scientific community who most closely resemble the first group of theologians are thus the historians, philosophers, and sociologists of science.

What further complicates the picture is that theological reflection need not necessarily take place within the religious community. Sometimes theology is a subset of religious practice; at other times it is a study done independently of such a practice. It is independent at least in the sense that it

6. See pp. 89-103 in this volume.

is not a necessary requirement for working as a theologian that one must be a religious believer (or a religious believer of a particular kind, say a Christian). We must therefore make a distinction between confessional and nonconfessional theology. If theology is not an activity going on within the religious community, but merely has religious communities as its research subject, this further shows that it could be quite misleading on occasion to use theology as a substitute for religion when comparing religion with science. If we compare theology in this sense with science we might even end up comparing two academic disciplines,[7] which is something quite different from comparing science with religion, a non-academic practice. So it is important that we do not overlook the differences between religion and theology and that we are clear when we are comparing, on the one hand, science and theology and, on the other hand, science and religion.

Unfortunately this is a frequent mistake in the science-religion literature. Let me give a few illustrations: Ian Barbour says that a pluralistic dialogue "is also compatible with a closer *Integration* between science and religion." In the next sentence, however, he describes religion and science as "two disciplines," and then goes on to talk about the "theories of science" and the "beliefs of theology" (Barbour 1997: 161). But could not integration between science and theology be something different from integration between science and religion? Holmes Rolston says that he is going to give "a description characteristic of science and theology" by focusing on "good science and good religion" (Rolston 1987: 1). But good religion and good theology are presumably not quite the same thing. Last, Michael Peterson, William Hasker, Bruce Reichenbach, and David Basinger talk about possible conflict "between science and religion" when the proper objects, aims, and methods of "theology" are put on a par with the ones in science (Peterson et al. 1991: 198). But can we immediately assume that the objects, aims, and methods of religion and those of theology are the same? The answer to this last question is "no" for the reasons I have given above. I shall further develop them in the next chapter and in chapter 5.

WHAT THIS QUICK TOUR through the social landscapes of science and religion tells us, among other things, is that we should not expect that the phe-

---

7. Peacocke, for instance, seems even to think that theology is a science. It is the science that studies the most complex system of all — the interaction of God and the whole of creation; see Peacocke (1993); cf. Murphy and Ellis (1996).

nomena to which the notions of religion and science refer are either exact or fixed. Therefore, the ways in which religion and science are related will vary during the course of history since both are dynamic and evolving social practices. This means, at least, (1) that any rich conception of these practices must be contextually grounded. But it also implies (2) that when we try to determine how to relate science and religion, we should not only focus on the relations between beliefs and theories (the *theoretical relations*) and the relations between different methods or techniques (the *epistemological relations*); we should also take into account the relations between different groups of people (the *social relations*). As Ronald L. Numbers points out, the debates on how science and religion are related should focus not only on "what should be considered 'science' and 'religion' [but also on] who should be allowed to define them . . ." (Numbers 1985: 80). Therefore, a conflict, for instance, between religion and science can be social rather than theoretical in nature. It can be a conflict between different social groups and not between different sets of beliefs.

If the focus is merely on the epistemological and theoretical dimensions of science and religion, one important *overlap* and thus interaction between religion and science might be overlooked, namely, that individuals could be practitioners of both enterprises at the same time. They could be both religious believers and scientists. Recall also Gould's remark that "if science and religion have been destined to fight for the same disputed territory" how is it possible that "science, at the dawn of the modern age, [has been] honorably practiced by professional clergymen (who, by conventional [warfare] views, should have undermined rather than promulgated such an enterprise)" (Gould 1999: 70)? We could, therefore, easily distort a complex relationship if we confine the interaction between science and religion to merely the theoretical and methodological levels.

To take our discussion of how to relate science and religion further we must consider the goals of scientific or religious practice. What is the *teleological* relation between science and religion? It is only when we have an idea about the teleology of science and religion that we are in a position to determine whether the means (or the methodologies) they have developed to achieve these goals are successful and perhaps also in competition with each other.

Chapter 3

The Goals of Science and Religion

If we understand science and religion as social practices it becomes important to consider what the goals of these practices are taken to be by their practitioners. We need to investigate the *teleological* structure of science and religion, and thus add one more dimension — besides the social dimension — to our multidimensional model. What we are looking for is a cluster of goals that individuals or the community more or less consciously take to be the goal of religious or scientific practice. This will be the task of this chapter, and once we have done this we shall, I maintain, be in a better position to understand how to relate science and religion and to assess the claims of scientific expansionists and restrictionists and also those of religious expansionists.

Epistemic and Practical Goals

Let us first ask why people participate in practices such as religion and science. What do they hope to obtain from them? Recall our situation. Human beings are contingent beings; we depend on other things for our existence and flourishing. We value practices that, very broadly speaking, do certain jobs for us, such as the ones that keep us alive and healthy. Therefore, activities like religion and science do not exist in a vacuum. Instead, they are practiced and valued by finite beings with limited resources who, because of their constitution and environment, have certain needs. For instance, things happen to us that we do not anticipate and that sometimes threaten our lives and well-being. We also need things that are not always easy to obtain, such as nutritious food, medicine, houses, bridges, and vehicles. In dealing with these things *science* has proved to be of great value. It enables us to control nature, and when we cannot control it, at least to predict it, or to adjust our behavior to an uncooperative world. We could thus say that science, among other things, aims to make the world *technologically* and *predictively intelligible,* and we value science because it is useful and because it helps us control, predict, and alter the world.

We do not have to satisfy merely material needs to be alive and well, however. We also have to give attention to spiritual and existential needs. Our well-being thus also depends upon our ability to deal with our experiences of suffering, death, guilt, or meaninglessness. In dealing with these phenomena, *religion* has proved to be of great value. It enables us to make sense out of these existential experiences, to diagnose them, and find a way through the barriers to our well-being. We might say that religion aims to make the world *existentially intelligible.*

Many people seem to think that this is the major difference in goals between religion and science. For instance, Peacocke writes that the "religious and scientific enterprises" have in common "their search for *intelligibility,* for what makes the most coherent sense of the experimental data with which they are each respectively concerned. What proves to be intelligible is applied, in science, to prediction and control and, in theology [sic!],[1] to provide moral purpose and personal meaning and to enable human beings to steer their path from birth to death" (Peacocke 1981: xii). Further, Rolston says this: "Science and religion share the conviction that the world is intelligible, susceptible to be logically understood, but they delineate this under different paradigms. In the cleanest cases we can say that science operates with the presumption that there are *causes* to things, religion with the presumption that there are *meanings* to things. Meanings and causes have in common a concept of order, but the type of order differs" (Rolston 1987: 22).

There is an overlap between religion and science in that both practices search for intelligibility, although they search for different kinds of intelligibility. Religion and science are useful to us, but they are useful for doing different things or solving different problems.

---

1. See again the discussion about the difference between religion and theology on pp. 24-26 in this volume.

Religion is often said to aim at the *transformation of personal life* (and perhaps by implication also the transformation of society). According to John Hick, the goal of religion (or more exactly, of postaxial religions) is "the sudden or gradual change of the individual from an absorbing self-concern to a new centering in the supposed unity-of-reality-and-value that is thought of as God, Brahman, the Dharma, Sunyata or the Tao" (Hick 1989: 36). The concept of "salvation/liberation" is taken by Hick to refer to this transformation of the human situation from self-centeredness to Reality-centeredness. The function of religion is to provide a context for the transformation of human existence from a state of alienation from God or Ultimate Reality to a state in harmony with that reality. The practitioners of religions differ in their accounts of what the appropriate *means* are for bringing about this change, but they all agree that this is a primary aim of religion. We could say that religion on this account has a *soteriological goal*. In Christianity this typically means that salvation lies in a personal relationship with God.[2]

Science, on the other hand, is generally understood to lack this kind of concern. It is not taken to have the aim of giving us salvation, of delivering us from self-centeredness, or of overcoming our alienation from God or Ultimate Reality. But, as we have seen, some scientists think that we now are in a position to add also this goal or something akin to it to the scientific agenda, namely, the goal of answering our existential questions. Dawkins, for instance, writes, "so where does life come from? What is it? Why are we here? What are we for? What is the meaning of life? There's a conventional wisdom which says that science has nothing to say about such questions. Well all I can say is that if science has nothing to say, it's certain that no other discipline can say anything at all. But in fact science has a great deal to say about such questions."[3] Thus some scientific expansionists are ready to expand the boundaries of science so that it covers the domain or at least parts of the domain of traditional religion. In this ambition, they reflect the basic idea of scientific expansionism (or scientism), namely, the idea that any question that can be answered at all can best be answered by science (narrowly conceived).

2. Other goals that have been proposed for religion are the expression of an agapeistic way of life, freeing people from sin and guilt, effecting a personal encounter with God, worshiping God, and liberating the oppressed.

3. Dawkins quoted in Poole (1994: 57).

All of these aims, however, could be interpreted as different kinds of pragmatic or practical aims. It might be *useful* for us to achieve these aims. For instance, a transformation of human existence from self-centeredness to Reality-centeredness could help us cope with the world better. Some people like J. Wesley Robbins (inspired by Richard Rorty) think that the only value or aim that both science and religion actually have is usefulness, in the sense that they help us to cope with the world. Robbins does not deny that religion and science are useful in different ways, but maintains that usefulness, and nothing else, is the aim of these activities: "The only intellectual value that representations have is that of their usefulness to us in some respect or another. Scientific ideas are no different from any others, religious or otherwise, in that respect. Their connection to reality is a function of their embeddedness within the practices in and by which we cope with the world" (Robbins 1988: 234; see also Robbins 1993).

But of course many others think that either science or religion, or both, have aims other than usefulness. Wentzel van Huyssteen, for instance, says, "Religious beliefs are normally held to be true, not merely useful" (van Huyssteen 1988: 247; cf. 1999: 111). Religious practice provides people not only with useful symbols, stories, and rituals that guide their actions and are meaningful for them but also with doctrines, claims, and beliefs that can be true (or false). A religious practice like Christianity is meant to tell us something true about who God is, what God's intentions are, and what God has done. Less controversially, one can maintain that science aims to say something true or approximately true about the natural and social world. Philip Kitcher, for instance, claims that "the cognitive goal of science is to attain significant truth" (Kitcher 1993: 157).

So on these accounts both religion and science aim at *truth*. They aim to say something true about reality in general or some part of it. Or more exactly, I think we should say that religion and science aim at truth and the avoidance of falsehood. These practices strive toward both goals, because if truth was all their practitioners were after, a good strategy to adopt would be simply to try to believe as many things (or propositions) as possible and thereby automatically increase the number of true beliefs. By doing this, however, the practitioners would very likely also increase the number of false beliefs, which is hardly their intention. The aim must be to try to increase the number of true beliefs *without* increasing the number of false beliefs. We could say that on this account religion and science both

31

aim to make reality *epistemically intelligible,* that is, they aim at truth and the avoidance of falsehood.

We have thus encountered a fundamental disagreement about the nature of religious and scientific practice. In relation to this disagreement, we can also make an important distinction. We can distinguish between two groups of goals: *epistemic goals* and *practical goals.* Broadly speaking, the epistemic goals are those that aim at truth and the avoidance of falsehood, and the practical goals are those that aim at something else. For instance, when a religious believer takes religious practice to reveal truths about God and about salvation/liberation, these goals should be characterized as epistemic ones because they aim at truth and the avoidance of falsehood. A believer might instead, however, be aiming at happiness, peace of mind, a meaningful life, or relief from feelings of guilt or alienation. Such values do not, or at least not in any straightforward way, increase the number of true beliefs and decrease the number of false beliefs and should therefore be classified as practical goals.

It is, of course, also feasible for a religious practitioner to combine epistemic and practical goals and to aim, for instance, at both truth and peace of mind or salvation. The same is also possible in a scientific context. A scientist might think that the goal of the scientific enterprise is both to establish accurate predictions and to gain empirical knowledge. We thus infer that religion and science could share a *complex goal,* since they could both have epistemic and practical ends.

A fundamental issue we face is thus to determine *what* the goals of science and religion exactly are. The question is essentially *whether both religion and science have epistemic and practical goals or if only one of them has both sets of goals.* Perhaps science aims both at true beliefs about the world and at helping us control and alter parts of it, whereas religion aims merely to express and provide means for a self-sacrificing way of life; perhaps religion's only concern is values and moral conduct. Here it seems that we can choose between and argue for one of three possibilities:

(a) The goals of either religion or science or both are only (or at least essentially) practical ones;

(b) the goals of either religion or science or both are only (or at least essentially) epistemic ones;

(c) the goals of either religion or science or both are practical and epistemic ones.

I suggest that both (a) and (b) are, at least in their stronger versions, phenomenologically speaking, clearly false. That is, if we take what in general practitioners of science and religion do and say seriously or at face value, these statements are not true. (As it is understood here, a phenomenological account is based on how things appear to be, whether they really are that way or not.) As I have already pointed out, science is assumed to have practical goals such as the prediction and control of nature. Someone might, however, distinguish sharply between *science* and *technology* and claim that what I just said applies only to the latter. Such a distinction cannot, I think, be maintained consistently (see p. 227). But suppose it could. We can still see that scientists typically do not take science as having a purely epistemic goal if we consider that a central norm in the evaluation of a scientific theory is *simplicity*. The norm of simplicity says, roughly, that all else being equal, the scientist should believe the simplest theory that explains all the relevant data. It would be very difficult to justify the use of this norm if the correct values for science are merely to increase true beliefs about the world and to eliminate false ones. How can we justify saying that the simpler of two theories, all else being equal, is more likely to be true? It seems impossible. Of course, if we allow science also to have practical goals, it is not so hard to find a justification. A simpler theory is easier for the scientist to *use* than a complex theory; it is easier to test and control. Consequently, it is theoretical and practical convenience, not epistemic values, that makes the scientist prefer the simpler theory.[4]

Nor do most scientists seem to think that science is aiming only at practical goals, since science is also understood to give us information about the world (i.e., a body of true or approximately true propositions). For instance, scientists typically believe that there really are such things as planets, oxygen, molecules, and genes in the world, and this knowledge is something that science has discovered for us. Furthermore, these things exist whether we are here or not and whether these things are useful for us or not, in contrast to social facts such as money or football games (see Searle 1995).

This observation also shows that the distinction between epistemic and practical goals is not a sharp one. We should instead view the distinction as a continuum with one epistemic pole and one practical pole. If this is correct, simplicity is not a straightforward epistemic goal, but it is obvi-

---

4. For a discussion of simplicity, see Hempel (1966: 40-45) and Foley (1988) and (1991).

ously closer to the epistemic end of the continuum than, for instance, the goals of staying out of trouble with the government or just feeling good.

Practical goals clearly *shape* the epistemic goals in science, however. Scientists seem not — if we take a closer look — to seek just any kind of truths about the world. They do not try merely to increase our stock of true beliefs and eliminate false ones. Scientists seek the kind of truths that are useful for them (or for society) given the questions and problems that they (or, for instance, governments or industry) consider significant and therefore try to solve. They are not trying to acquire true but trivial beliefs about the world concerning, for example, the precise number of trees, stones, or leaves in the world.[5] Scientists thus try to find significant or important truths, truths that are, broadly speaking, useful for them (or society).

At least with regard to a religion like Christianity (a) and (b) are, at least in their stronger versions, phenomenologically speaking, false. We can see this if we try to understand what an ordinary Christian practitioner affirms that an ordinary atheist denies. First of all, the atheist might deny that the Christian faith is an adequate means to overcome experiences of guilt and meaninglessness and to create a lasting happiness or any other practical goal of Christianity. (The very opposite might even be true, as Karl Marx thought.) Sometimes this (the practical and existential adequacy of Christianity) is what the atheist and the Christian believer disagree about, but at other times it is not. Sometimes the atheist might think that Christianity is quite helpful in overcoming these problems. But atheists deny the existence of the Christian God; that is, they deny there is a being of the sort Christians believe in (or any other divine being, for that matter). Ordinary Christian practitioners recognize this as a genuine disagreement; Christians believe that it is true that a God of this sort exists and that an atheist denies this. Thus the Christian practitioner confirms, and the atheist presupposes, that Christianity also has an epistemic goal.

In religion as in science, however, the practical goals typically shape or inform the epistemic goals. This is true, at least, in the sense that Christian practitioners do not merely affirm the truth of such beliefs as that there is a God, that God is love, or that God created the world. Instead their aim is to have an appropriate relation to God so that they can imple-

---

5. Truth is in fact quite easy to find. One just needs to add disjuncts to the truth one already has. For a discussion of this possibility and other ways of arriving at trivial truths, see Goldman (1986) and Cherniak (1986).

ment the divine dimensions of reality in their lives. Christians believe that God's revelation (however defined), although it is incomplete, gives knowledge that is adequate for believers' needs. For Christians it is sufficient to know what is necessary so they can live the life they must in relation to God. Vincent Brümmer thus says, "The questions which [Christian] believers ask about God's factual nature are never asked out of mere curiosity in the way in which they might out of curiosity ask questions about the factual nature of the world around them" (Brümmer 1992: 59). "Never" is probably a too strong word here; "not typically" would, I think, be more correct. Nevertheless, believers aim at *significant* or *important truths,* truths that are useful for them in their relation to God.

This demonstrates that it is not belief *that* God exists that is the focus of Christian believers' concern, but belief *in* God — that is, trusting God, accepting God's purpose, committing one's life to God, and living in God's presence. This does not, however — and this might be overlooked — change that the belief that God exists is a necessary condition for Christian practice. It shows only that it is not a sufficient condition. Belief in God is much more than accepting the proposition that God exists, but it is at least that. The practical goals of living a Christian life determine to a very high degree the epistemic goals of Christian practice. The belief that God exists is no significant truth *within* the Christian practice. It is simply presupposed. The significant truths are rather about the relation between God and believers and about the fruits that relationship should have in the lives of believers. From an external perspective, things may be different, especially when the question arises as to which (religious or nonreligious) worldview one should be committed to. In such a context belief that a personal God exists becomes a significant, and sometimes controversial, belief.

Hence, one version of option (c) above, that the aims of religion and science are both practical and epistemic, has the best support from the actual practices of religion (at least of Christianity) and of science. This is the way things are whether we like it or not. This is, of course, how it looks provided we adopt a phenomenological point of view, that is, if we take what scientific and religious practitioners in general say and do at face value. It is clearly possible that both scientific and religious practitioners in general are wrong and that they have even deeply misunderstood what their practices aim at. There are also groups of them whose self-understanding is different from the more generally accepted one I have tried to outline. Neither science nor religion consists of strictly unified practices. My account thus offers at most a *prima facie* justification of one version of option (c). But this implies that the burden of proof falls on those who disagree with the phenomenological account, especially those who propose radically different interpretations of these practices. After all, we have, as I pointed out earlier, to distinguish between what one personally would prefer science or religion to be, and how we ought to characterize science and religion as they are understood by most of their practitioners.

Thus far we have established at least that religion (at least Christianity) and science seem to have both epistemic and practical goals, although exactly what these are and which of them should be considered predominant are still questions that need to be considered. Once we accept option (c) above, we must consider *whether religion and science have the same or different kinds of epistemic and practical goals.* We must determine what particular types of practical and epistemic goals science and religion try to promote. We can choose between one of four possibilities:

   (d) The epistemic and the practical goals of science and religion are of
        the same kind;
   (e) the epistemic and the practical goals of science and religion are of
        different kinds;
   (f) the epistemic goals of science and religion are of the same kind but
        the practical ones are not;
   (g) the practical goals of science and religion are of the same kind but
        the epistemic ones are not.

We have seen these possibilities exemplified by many of the thinkers we have already discussed. For example, Dawkins seems to assume that the epistemic goals of science and religion are the same. Recall that Dawkins writes that he pays

> religions the compliment of regarding them as scientific theories. . . . I
> see God as a competing explanation for facts about the universe and
> life. This is certainly how God has been seen by most theologians of
> past centuries and by most ordinary religious people today. . . . Either
> admit that God is a scientific hypothesis and let him submit to the
> same judgement as any other scientific hypothesis. Or admit that his
> status is no higher than that of fairies and river sprites. (Dawkins
> 1995b: 46-47)

If one treats belief in God and other religious beliefs as scientific theories then it follows that one presupposes that both science and religion have the very same epistemic goals, even if, as in Dawkins's case, the exact content of these goals is not stated.

Another possible view is that the epistemic emphasis in science is essentially on eliminating false beliefs (as Karl Popper thought), whereas in religion it is to attain a few essential truths. In Christianity it might be to know that God is love and that Jesus is God incarnated. Such a view stands as an example of either option (e) or (g).

More common is the claim that it is the practical goals of the two practices that are different, that is, a version of either (e) or (f). One could, as we have seen, maintain that science aims at prediction and religion at the discovery of patterns of meaning. Stephen Wykstra expresses such a view when he writes that,

> Sometimes, when our lives cry out for redemptive change, what is important is not precise predictions, but the disclosure of unanticipated new meanings where old ones have been shattered. Demanding that religious discourse here provide precise predictions would be obtuse. Sometimes we find our lives in pits where what we most need to be delivered from is our way of taking things in our own hands. (Wykstra 1990: 137)

Wykstra does not, however, claim that religion and science lack an epistemic goal: "For religion and science do not merely provide useful linguistic constructions; they make claims about reality which either should or should not be *believed*" (Wykstra 1990: 122).[6] Religion and science should be understood as making claims about reality, claims that are either true or false. But he does not go on to consider whether religion and science have the same or different epistemic goals. This might, however, be an important question, because for one thing, truth in religion seems to be something at least in some respects different from truth in science. Louis Dupré claims that "If one thing distinguishes traditional religious conceptions of truth from modern philosophical ones, it is the absence of, or secondary role of, epistemological concerns. Despite their substantial differences, all religious traditions agree in stressing the ontological and moral

---

6. Recall also what Peacocke and Rolston said in the quotations on p. 29.

qualities of truth over the purely cognitive ones. Truth refers to *being*, rather than to knowledge" (Dupré 1989: 260).

One way of interpreting this difference is to maintain that truth in religion is a richer notion than truth in science (or philosophy) because it includes more than the epistemic dimension (see Stenmark 1995: 266-67). Religious truth is not reducible to correct beliefs because truth is also something to be done, to be lived. Therefore, epistemic truth can be a necessary condition for religious truth, but it is clearly not a sufficient condition. Such an interpretation, however, also supports the view that religion can typically be characterized as having a complex goal. The aim of religious practice is on such an account not only to make reality epistemically intelligible but also, and perhaps primarily, to guide people's actual way of life so they can achieve genuine well-being, which religious practitioners think can be obtained only if we let our lives be transformed by the Divine Reality or if we enter into a right relation to it. Its aim is also to make reality existentially intelligible. So it seems that only a worldview that can also successfully guide religious practitioners in their lives can be really true, satisfying both the epistemic and practical aims of religion.

But, as I have pointed out, contrary to Wykstra and the view that the practical goals of science and religion are different (in short, that science helps us satisfy our material needs, whereas religion helps us satisfy our existential needs), scientific expansionists such as Dawkins and Wilson hold that the boundaries of science could be expanded in such a way that science eventually if not at present could answer our existential questions and thus fulfill our existential needs. This is essentially to presuppose not merely option (c) concerning the first issue, but also option (d) concerning the second issue.

We have seen that among practitioners of science and religion we can find different assumptions about what the aims of these practices are. These goals are sometimes understood to be mutually exclusive and sometimes to be complementary. But even if we understand the aims as complementary and we agree that both science and religion have epistemic and practical goals, the emphases may still differ. One kind of goal (or goals) could be considered more important or more essential to the practice than other kinds. People may disagree not only about *what* the aims of religion or science are, but on what *weight* they should be given.

One issue arises when we recognize that the practitioners of science and religion might give very different weights to the different aims not only within the practical set of goals they maintain but also within the epistemic set of goals. In Christianity we might see this if, for example, we contrasted feminists and liberation theologians with more traditional theologians. The most essential practical goal of feminists and liberation theologians is usually liberation from oppression (the oppressed being primarily either women or the poor). Salvation is consequently interpreted in sociopolitical terms. This does not necessarily mean that these theologians have to deny the more traditional idea of salvation as establishing a personal relationship with God, but it does mean that the practical emphasis is strongly on the social, and not the personal, aspect of it. Hence we find among religious practitioners that the weight they give different practical goals can vary significantly.

Scientists too might emphasize their practical goals differently; for example, they might disagree about whether the scope or the simplicity of a theory is more important, everything else being equal. Here I instead focus on the different ways scientists might conceive the epistemic goals. In a previous section I maintained that the epistemic goal of science should not really be just truth but rather truth and the avoidance of falsehood. One might easily think that this is just another philosophical distinction of no importance in actual scientific practice, but it does have certain practical consequences.[7] Assume that some scientists think that seeking true beliefs is more important than eliminating false ones. They would when ascertaining that a hypothesis is true or false believe that it is true not only in situations where the evidence for it is stronger than that against it but also in cases where the evidence pro and con is equally balanced. This, however, would not be true about scientists who thought that avoiding errors was more important than discovering truths. More generally, the relative emphasis we place on these two epistemic values has consequences for the appropriate level of epistemic risk-taking in science. On one side of the spectrum we have radical "Popperians" like P. K. Feyerabend, who seems to fear that we might reject some truths that we should after all have accepted. On the other side we have people who are concerned that we might accept something that is false and that we therefore should have rejected. Between avoiding all risks and taking all risks, scientists must make their epistemic choices.[8]

---

7. For a classic discussion of this, see section 7 in William James's essay *The Will to Believe* (1897).

8. For a more detailed analysis of risk-taking in epistemology see Rescher (1988: 54-60).

Feminist and liberation theologies also illustrate a related issue, the issue of what weight the set of practical (in this case religious) goals should be given in comparison with the epistemic set. Clearly the emphasis of feminist and liberation theologians is strongly on practical goals. A feminist like Mary Daly, for example, thinks that one should reject Whitehead's process theism or for that matter classic theism if it does not actively encourage "human struggle against oppression in its concrete manifestations" (Daly 1973: 20).[9] So a necessary condition for accepting a religious belief would be, it seems, that it must somehow promote social liberation (especially of women). This of course puts feminists like Daly in sharp contrast to those religious practitioners who that think that truth questions matter greatly in religion and are distinct from political considerations.[10] C. Stephen Evans exemplifies this view when he writes,

9. This is so even though in process theism God is portrayed as not being omnipotent and transcendent, which seems to be in line with feminist thought.

10. The problem with Daly's account is that the motives of religious believers do not determine the truth or rationality of these people's religious beliefs. God might be omnipotent even if men (or rich people) have used this idea to oppress women (or poor people). Logically speaking, we need some additional premises if we want to reach the conclusion that we should not believe in an omnipotent God on the basis of the empirical claim that men (or white and rich people) have used the idea of an omnipotent God to oppress women (or people of color and poor people). Call this the "oppression argument against belief in an omnipotent God."

From the premises that

(1) *God is using God's omnipotent power to oppress other beings,* and
(2) *(white and rich) men should act in a way similar to God's,*
male (white and rich) religious believers might validly infer (an argument is valid if its conclusion must be true if the premises are true) that
(3) *therefore, (white and rich) men should, to the extent they can, oppress women (people of color and poor people).*
Then feminist (liberation and nonwhite) theologians would be right, not about the fact that such a God does not exist, but that such a God is not worth believing in. That follows if we add the premise that
(4) *it is morally wrong to oppress other human beings.*

But male (white and rich) believers have of course not typically maintained (either consciously or unconsciously) a premise such as (1). Nor, more importantly, should they according to Christianity. So the truth of (1) seems very hard to prove or confirm. Hence, the oppression argument is not likely to be sound (an argument is sound if it is valid and its premises are true) even if it could be stated in a valid way.

Many writers center their attention on whether religion is or is not socially useful, an aid or an impediment to progress. Or they try to find
out whether religion is or is not psychologically beneficial, a contribu-
tor to neurosis or buttress of mental health. Such questions are important and interesting and the answers to some of them might bear on
the question of truth. However, we must remember that the primary
question about any religion is not whether it is useful but whether it is
true. That is the question we must keep uppermost in our minds. . . .
(Evans 1996: 16)

Some of these religious practitioners might even think that the epistemic
goals are by far the most important and thus hold a position very contrary
to feminist and liberation theology of the sort described above.

Scientists might also think that although science proper has both
epistemic and practical goals, they should in general aim at the development of practically useful theories, because, for example, science should
first of all serve society and the needs of people. (At least a lot of politicians
seem to think in this way.) Perhaps the emphasis should be on practical
goals because one thinks that epistemic goals are hard to satisfy; there are
not many things we really can know, especially about what is not directly
observable (and things that are not directly observable are, after all, science's main business). A scientist influenced by Peacocke's writing, who
thinks that "Critical realism recognizes that it is the aim of science to de-
pict reality as best it may . . . [but] this purpose may well be achieved by
scientists with but varying degrees of success," could (but need not) argue
in this way (Peacocke 1993: 12).

I have given a *prima facie* justification for the idea that both science
and religion have complex goals (that is, both practical and epistemic
goals). I shall therefore stick to this assumption in what follows, well
aware — as I have just pointed out — that different accounts could be
given. Neither science nor religion constitutes a unified practice, and this
is particularly true about religion. Things are a bit more complicated
when it comes to the issue of whether religion and science have the same
or different kinds of epistemic and practical goals. For the moment I just
want to highlight the different possibilities we have and point out that
scholars who address the issue of how to relate science and religion often
presuppose a particular answer to this question. Some of these views
about whether science and religion have different kinds of epistemic and

practical goals and about how to weigh them will be critically scrutinized in chapters to follow.

Personal and Collective Goals

It is important never to lose sight of the fact that religion and science are not merely sets of statements, beliefs, theories, or linguistic discourses; as I emphasized in the previous chapter, they are necessarily also social practices performed by human beings within particular historical and geographic settings. Religion and science have communities of practitioners that do certain things with certain goals in mind, within certain social situations, and within a common tradition or history. Hence, what I have been saying so far can be interpreted on two levels: the *individual* level and the *social* level.

It can be understood either in terms of what individual practitioners take their own religious or scientific activity to be aiming at (part of what I previously called the "individual practice") or in terms of what the practitioners taken together understand as the goals of religion or science (a part of what I previously called the "collective practice") (see p. 23). Consequently, we must add to the philosophical distinction (between epistemic and practical goals) a sociological distinction, namely, a distinction between *personal* goals and *collective* goals. By "personal goals" I simply mean the goals of individual scientists or religious believers themselves in science or religion. The term "collective goals," on the other hand, refers to those goals that a scientific or religious community maintains, that is, the goals that are shared by the members of the community.[11]

A realistic understanding of the situation and motives of individual scientists will recognize that scientists always have their own epistemic and practical goals as well as the ones maintained by the scientific community. A biologist is probably not just attempting to expand the scientific community's understanding of evolution when trying to discover, say, some mechanism in the evolutionary processes (a *collective epistemic goal*). If that was all a biologist cared about, it would not matter who actually discovered it. But, of course, biologists want to make the discovery them-

---

11. I am indebted to Philip Kitcher (1993) for much of what I say in this section. He, however, focuses only on science.

selves, either as the result of their own effort or through the work of a team to which they belong. Perhaps the biologist wants, in addition to knowledge, to be recognized as the first to know (a *personal practical goal*). Such a practical goal is, of course, not part of the goals maintained by the community. The collective goal is that such discoveries be made, that our understanding of nature increases. Who makes them is irrelevant from the perspective of the scientific community.

In the actual practice of science, epistemic and practical goals as well as personal and collective goals are then probably woven together in a rather symbiotic fashion. A remark by Kitcher aptly captures how these four types of goals specify what scientists (more or less consciously) could be aiming at with their research: "a scientist may have the goal of contributing to the long-term community project of understanding some aspect of nature [a collective epistemic goal], the goal of advancing her own knowledge in a particular area [a personal epistemic goal], the goal of promoting a more egalitarian society [a collective practical goal], and the goal of attaining a position of eminence within her specialty [a personal practical goal]" (Kitcher 1993: 73). The goal of promoting a more egalitarian society is surely a collective goal. Another perhaps less controversial collective practical goal is the goal of controlling and predicting forces or processes in nature. (We will come back to this issue in our discussion of feminist science in chapter 9.)

In a similar fashion a religious practitioner may have the aim of contributing to the religious community's long-term goal of understanding the Divine Reality, to the extent that is considered possible for beings in our predicament (a *collective epistemic goal*). (Different religions, or denominations within a religion, may be more or less optimistic about the achievement of this goal.) Note that even though this formulation parallels that of science, it is, I think, a more controversial characterization in the religious case. I suggest that this is because the emphasis in religion is so much on *being* religious, on *living* a life in the presence of God. The epistemic goals of religion are typically not purely epistemic but rather are complex in character. Therefore, we should perhaps say that a collective epistemic goal of Christianity, for instance, is to promote as much knowledge of God as is necessary for people to live a religious life successfully (knowing that God is love and that God wants to redeem us, and so on). A religious practitioner can then try to contribute to that collective goal. Further, religious practitioners may have the goal of advancing their own knowledge in a particular area of religious thought — a Christian about Jesus Christ, a Buddhist about karma, and so on (a *personal epistemic goal*).

Notice again a crucial difference between the epistemic collective goals of religion and those of science. In science the aim is to increase the *general body of knowledge* about the social and natural world, whereas in religion it is to increase the *knowledge of each of its practitioners* to such an extent that they can live a religious life successfully. To contribute to the collective epistemic goal of religion is first of all to increase, up to a certain level, the religious knowledge (say, at least to the level necessary for salvation/liberation) of as many *people* as possible (although, again, Judaism is one exception to this rule). It is not, as in science, to move the frontiers of *knowledge* of nature forward as much as possible. This difference would help us understand why religious journals look so different from those of science. Here again we find a reason why we ought not to place religion on an equal footing with theology. The aim of academic theology — to increase our general body of knowledge or justified belief about religious matters — is rather similar to the aim of science.

Let us now turn to the practical goals of religion. Here also we can distinguish between personal and collective goals. A religious practitioner may want to contribute to the long-term goal of the religious community of bringing salvation/liberation to all people (a *collective practical goal*), and to become a more loving, understanding, and caring person (a *personal practical goal*). People may, of course, also have personal goals that are incompatible with the collective goals of the religious community. A person might, for instance, participate in religious practice merely because he wants to marry a woman within the community or because it gives him social status.

There is clearly a whole complex of issues facing us here: In what way should the differences between the individual and collective goals of scientific and religious practitioners be taken into account when trying to understand the relationship between science and religion? To what extent are unity and diversity with respect to goals possible and desirable in religion and science? Are there any differences between how individual and collective goals actually interact (or should interact) and are maintained in religion and science? How are the individual and collective goals of religion and science related to one another? I shall not pursue these issues any further in this context, but merely point out that if we attempt to understand the teleological structure of science and religion we need to add to the distinction between epistemic and practical goals also one between individual and collective goals. In both cases I suggest that we understand the distinctions as marking the end poles on a continuum, rather than as stating a dichotomy.

Recognizing that religion and science are essentially social practices always performed by people living in certain cultural and historical situations should alert us to the fact that religion and science change over time. But what changes in these practices? Do they change only in terms of who practices them, how the relationship between the practitioners in the practice is organized, and what is believed? Or *do religion and science also change on a more fundamental level, in terms of what the aims of these enterprises are?* One could, of course, say that here we simply face a choice between two options: either the goals change or they do not. I do not, however, think this really captures the discussion, especially in the philosophy of science, about the stability of the goals. Instead I propose that our choice here is between three options:

(h) the goals of either religion or science or both do not change;
(i) some of the goals of either religion or science or both change and others stay fairly stable;
(j) most goals of either religion or science or both change drastically.

There are not many now in the philosophy of science who claim that the aims of science do not change at all. There seems to be a growing consensus that the goals of science do change, at least to some extent. These philosophers have come to that conclusion after many detailed historical studies of the development of science. Larry Laudan, one of the most influential philosophers of science today, concludes that these studies show that there is no single set of goals that holds for all sciences and for all times. One of his paradigm examples of a teleological shift in science is the debate among scientists in the late 1700s and early 1800s concerning whether scientists should restrict their theories to observable entities and processes (Laudan 1984: 55-62). Up until that time, scientists had, officially at least, claimed to be "inductivists," aiming to understand the observable world by purely inductive methods; all hypotheses should be avoided. But during this period scientists developed a number of theories in electricity, embryology, and chemistry that seemed to depend essentially on postulating unobservable entities. These theories received widespread criticism because they were in conflict with the accepted aims of science. To make a long story short, however, the "hypotheticalists" won the debate and the aims of science changed drastically. It was from then on generally accepted that science should also value and aim for theories with depth, and what we today call the hypothetico-deductive method was recognized as a scientific method.[12]

Philip Kitcher, on the other hand, argues that the conclusion of these historical studies should rather be that "the goals of science do not change over time — although scientists may offer different ideas about subgoals in the light of their beliefs about the world" (Kitcher 1993: 157). He thinks, for instance, that the goal of biology (that it should, among other things, explain the diversity of living things and trace the patterns in that diversity) is stable. Kitcher's interpretation of cases like the one given by Laudan is that it is only our formulations of derivative goals (i.e., the goals we actually hope to achieve at a given time) that change; the more fundamental goals of science do not change. He writes, "On a closer view, I claim, changes in formulations of the aims of science can be understood as expressions of the enduring goal of discovering as much significant truth as human beings can in light of changing beliefs about what is significant, what nature is like, and what the nature of our relation to nature is" (Kitcher 1993: 160). Hence, Kitcher should not be understood as claiming that the goals of science do not change at all (option [h] above), but as maintaining a version of option (i), namely, that some of the goals of science stay fairly stable whereas others change.

To some extent the answer to this question depends on how *broadly* we interpret the aims of religion and science. The more broadly we understand the aims, the more reasonable the "stability option" seems; and the more narrowly we conceive them, the more justified the "reversibility option" seems to be. The same is true for religion. If we accept that one of the goals of religion is to deal with existential concerns or questions, it seems that this goal does not change over time. By "existential questions" I mean,

---

12. Laudan thinks that many historical examples of changes in the goals of science could be given. He writes, for instance, that "The history of science is rife with controversies between, for instance, realists and instrumentalists, reductionists and antireductionists, advocates and critics of simplicity, proponents of teleology and advocates of purely efficient causality. At bottom, all these debates have turned on divergent views about the attributes our theories should possess (and thus about the aims of scientific theorizing)" (Laudan 1984: 42).

roughly, questions of who we are, why we are here, where we came from, and where we are going.[13] In fact, something would probably not be a religion if it did not address those kinds of questions. On the other hand, some things appear clearly to change in religion. Today there is, for instance, a growing awareness that an ecological disaster threatens the earth. More and more religious practitioners therefore seem to be concerned that their religions should deal with environmental issues. So although a religion like Christianity in its early forms was not understood by its followers to have as one of its essential goals the overcoming of ecological crises, today that appears to have changed. The goals of Christianity have undergone a transformation.

The answers to the question of whether the goals of religion and science change over time are thus relevant when we try to understand how they are related. If the goals drastically change, then the relations between religion and science will also change; hence, the ways religion and science are related can vary significantly in different time periods. If, on the other hand, the goals do not change at all or only insignificantly, then such grounding is not necessary. We can talk about the teleological relations between religion and science without paying much attention to historical circumstances.

Scholars engaged in the science-religion dialogue do not typically state their views on this issue. By looking more closely at what they say we can ascertain whether they presuppose a more or less static conception or a more or less evolving conception of the goals of religion and science (and indeed of science and religion as a whole). The distinction between individual and collective goals will turn out to be of relevance for our discussion about the epistemologies of science and religion.

Manifest and Latent Goals

The focus on the issue of whether the goals of religion and science change also shows that we need to add one further dimension to the picture of the goals of science and religion that I have been trying to develop so far. It is a distinction similar to the one between *manifest* and *latent ideology* often used in studies of ideologies. Roughly, the manifest ideology is what, for

13. See Stenmark (1995, chapter 9) for a fuller account of existential questions.

instance, a political party explicitly states in its official documents as its views and policies, and the latent ideology of the party is what we can discover if we read between the lines.

In religion we can sometimes find official documents that state the aims of that religion. We can further ask the official spokespeople, or just ordinary practitioners, what they consider the goals of their religious activity to be. This is one way of proceeding if we want to find out the actual goals of a religion. Another way is to study what practitioners actually do, focusing on their actions and choices. Let us call the goals discovered by using the first strategy *manifest goals* and the ones discovered by using the second strategy *latent goals*. Sometimes there is no tension between these goals. We can approach religious practitioners and say that it looks as if this is something they do not claim to be aiming at with their activity, but it is something we can infer from their actions and choices, and religious practitioners might recognize it as something that is actually a part of their goals. At other times, however, practitioners may not accept what we say they are actually trying to do with their religious engagement. This is perhaps especially the case when what we claim are latent goals are in tension or even conflict with the manifest goals.

As we saw in the last section, conflicts of this kind also emerge in science. Laudan pointed out that one of the manifest collective goals of an entire community of scientists was discovered to be in conflict with the goals that actually seemed to guide the research done within the scientific community. In addition, individual scientists may realize that in their actual work they proceed in a way that is contrary to the aims they explicitly acknowledge.

For instance, a group of scientists (or maybe a whole scientific community) may at a certain time maintain that they have the Popperian goal of (1) always laying down in advance what would lead them to reject a theory and (2) actively trying to falsify it (a *collective manifest epistemic goal*). But by analyzing scientific journals, we discover that we cannot find any papers that either explicitly or implicitly state what would falsify the proposed theories, and by studying how scientists actually behave in face of arising anomalies we discover that, contrary to what these scientists say, scientists never seem to reject a theory they believe has something going for it even when many anomalies have been found. In fact, in practice scientists seem never to reject a theory no matter how many anomalies there are unless they have a better theory to put in its place. We thus have reason to believe that scientists have a *collective latent epistemic goal* that is different from, and even in conflict with, the manifest one.[14]

In a similar fashion many Christians claim that they are God's stewards on earth, by which they presumably imply a respect and responsibility for the things that God created (a *collective manifest practical goal*). But by studying how these believers actually act and make choices concerning nature we come to realize that they have no such goal in practice, or that it has a very low priority in comparison with their other goals. A last example: Christianity officially seems to aim for the mutual respect and love of all human beings (a *collective manifest practical goal*): "We are all one in Christ." But after empirical studies we may come to understand that Christianity also has the implicit goal of maintaining a patriarchal relationship between men and women in religion and society. Christianity has then a collective latent practical goal of patriarchalism. These manifest and latent religious goals seem at least to be in tension with each other, perhaps even in conflict.

The distinction between manifest and latent goals in religion and science creates some specific problems for those of us who try to understand how to relate science and religion. For example, on what kind of goals should we base our comparison of religion and science, the manifest or the latent ones? And to what set of goals should we give priority when there seems to be a tension or conflict between manifest and latent goals in the actual practice of religion or science?

The centrality of both of these questions can be demonstrated if we focus on the account of religion developed by philosophers and theologians influenced by the writings of Ludwig Wittgenstein. D. Z. Phillips, for instance, thinks that religion is vastly different from science, especially in that religions do not involve any factual beliefs or claims, whereas science does (Phillips 1976 and 1988). Any understanding of how science and religion are related that assumes that religion has some factual content is therefore based on a deep misunderstanding of the nature of religious practice. Phillips does not, however, take this to be a normative claim. Instead he says that we would all be able to see this if we paid close enough attention to the way religious believers speak about and deal with religious matters. A number of people have said that Phillips is simply wrong. A great number

---

14. These are some of the reasons why a majority of contemporary philosophers of science have rejected Popper's account of theory choice in science.

(maybe even the vast majority) of Christians believe, as a matter of fact, that God exists, that God is morally perfect and almighty, that there will be a Judgment Day, and so on. Phillips, however, is probably not denying this (that would surely be stupid) but would still claim that his account is not normative. Why? I suggest that we should interpret him as saying that although the manifest goals of religion often seem to include a factual element, the latent goals of religion do not. And it is, in fact, these goals that Phillips takes as having more *weight* when he develops an account of the proper aims of religion. We should therefore not be misled by the surface grammar of religious language (as some or many religious people and even scholars seem to be). Suppose Phillips is right; then it matters greatly whether we put our emphasis on the set of manifest goals or the set of latent goals. Even if he is wrong, which I think is the case, his claims at least show that it is important for us to try to be explicit about which set of goals forms the basis of our theories about the relationship of religion and science, especially in cases where there seems to be a tension between the two sets. Probably a lot of confusion and misunderstanding could then be avoided.

I HAVE SUGGESTED that scholars who write about the relationship between religion and science should address certain teleological questions, and their views typically have such presuppositions at least implicitly. The reason why they sometimes come to such different conclusions and seem to be talking past each other is often that they are, in fact, committed to different accounts of the goals of religion and science, which are not clearly stated.

Our inquiry has led to the development of a three-dimensional picture of the teleological structure of religion and science: The first dimension consists of the distinction between *epistemic* and *practical goals,* the second of the distinction between *individual* and *collective goals,* and the last of the distinction between *manifest* and *latent goals.* These dimensions could be addressed from either a historical or contemporary perspective. We could either focus on a particular historical situation or discuss how to understand the goals of science and religion as these practices are practiced today. These studies could also be more universal or contextual in scope, focusing on one particular religion such as Christianity (or more narrowly, the Protestant tradition, the Lutheran tradition, or Luther's own religious beliefs) and one particular scientific discipline such as biology (or more narrowly, evolutionary biology, sociobiology, or Edward O. Wilson's own theories).

Hence, to be able to know how to relate science and religion we must pay attention to the fact that they are practices (and not merely sets of beliefs or theories), which entails that not merely the social structure but also the goals of science and religion must be investigated.

Do the differences in the teleology of scientific and religious practice have any consequences for the *epistemological* issues we face? Would they explain, for instance, the contrast Gould highlighted and I described in chapter 1, between how the request of the disciple Thomas for evidence is evaluated in the Christian practice and how a similar request is evaluated in the scientific practice? Wykstra explains why there are reasons to suspect that differences in teleology have consequences for the epistemological issues when he writes,

> if we approach the claims of a theistic complex like Christianity — claims having to do with Creation, Covenant, Sin, Judgment, Grace, Incarnation, and the like — as if they must embody the values of scientific theorizing, we will not assess them by appropriate criteria; indeed, we will probably not even understand them. Their point is not to help us predict, control, and contrive the world. (Wykstra 1990: 138)

The choice of aims for religion and science determines the appropriate criteria or norms for assessing what is going on in these activities. If Wykstra is right, the answers to the teleological questions have serious implications for the epistemological issues. Hence, disagreement about the goals of religion and science may lead to disagreement about how to achieve these goals, that is, to disagreement about the methodology or epistemology of science and religion. It is time for us to turn to these issues now.

Chapter 4

The Epistemologies
of Science and Religion

B eliefs, theories, and the like are acquired, revised, or rejected in the actual life of both science and religion. These processes involve reasoning of some sort. Do practitioners in both fields endorse the same kinds of reasoning or, if not, should they endorse the same kinds of reasoning? In particular, is it legitimate for scientists to critically challenge the way beliefs are formed, rejected, and revised in religion by taking science as the paradigm example of rationality? If one does that, would it mean that one assumes that science and religion have the same epistemic and practical goals? Issues of this kind belong to the epistemology of religion or science, and these issues will be the main concern of this chapter and the two which follow.

The epistemology of religion and the epistemology of science can be defined in a similar way. I suggest that we define them, roughly, as *the attempts to understand and explain how belief (in science, typically, theory) formation and regulation is conducted within religion or science and to assess whether these belief formations and regulations are acceptable and successful ways of carrying out one's cognitive affairs in these realms of human life, and, if they are not acceptable, to propose alternative ways of conducting religious or scientific belief formation and regulation.* This could be done, for instance, in the case of religion by articulating the norms or standards implicit in the process by which people form, revise, and reject religious beliefs and by critically comparing them with norms used in other human practices such as the sciences, everyday life, or politics.

Defined in this way, the epistemologies of religion and science have both a descriptive and a normative task. The descriptive task is to investigate how practitioners (of different social status, color, and sex, and at both an individual and a collective level in different societies, in different cultures, and during different historical periods) form, reject, revise, and replace their religious or scientific beliefs. In short, the aim is to explicate the epistemological norms of actual religious and scientific practice. The normative task is to evaluate critically these norms and the cognitive behavior of people in religious or scientific matters, and, if necessary, to suggest ways of improving them. In essence, the mission is to assess the rationality, justification, and general epistemic status of religion and science.

We will not be able to take into account all or even most of the issues that properly belong to the study of the epistemologies of science and religion. Instead the idea is to focus our attention on the question whether science and religion should be related in such a way that the apparently successful methodology of the sciences should be implemented also in religious practice: Is it possible and desirable to challenge the way beliefs are formed, rejected, and revised in religion by taking science as the paradigm example of rationality? Should the epistemology of religion be informed by the epistemology of science? Could there or should there be an overlap between science and religion at the epistemic level? Various epistemological aspects of science and religion will be explored in relationship to these key questions. This is an important set of issues, especially if Arthur Peacocke is right in asserting that

> there has been, in the West, at least, a collapse in the credibility of all religious beliefs, notably Christian ones, as they are perceived as failing to meet the normal criteria of reasonableness, so strongly present in the practice of science, namely: fit with the data, internal coherence, comprehensiveness, fruitfulness and general cogency. . . . Thus all religions, and especially Christianity in the West, face new challenges posed by the successful methodology of the sciences and by the worldview it has generated. (Peacocke 2001: 12)

This chapter is structured in such a way that we shall first critically evaluate Gould's principle of NOMA, which is one recent statement of scientific/religious restrictionism and thus of the independence view. In the second part we shall critically examine Vincent Brümmer's claim that the notion of a scientifically informed epistemology of religion is based on a conceptual confusion.

Scientific Evidentialism and Doubting Thomas

Gould denies, as we saw in chapter 1, that it is legitimate for scientists to critically challenge the way beliefs are formed, rejected, and revised in religion by taking science as the paradigm of rationality. He does this by maintaining that the epistemic norms of one magisterium should not be imposed on the other magisterium; the relationship ought to be one of respectful noninterference (Gould 1999: 5). He acknowledges that the norms of religion are foreign to the norms of science, but refuses to pass any judgment on those norms. Other scientists, on the other hand, such as Dawkins and Wilson, feel no such obligation and quite straightforwardly maintain the superiority of the epistemic norms of science on all matters.

But Dawkins, Gould, and Wilson seem to agree that rational scientists endorse what philosophers call *evidentialism* as their model of rationality. Evidentialism is, roughly, the view that it is rational to accept a theory or belief only if, and to the extent that, there are good reasons (or evidence) to think that it is true.[1] Gould believes evidentialism to be mandatory in science, but he thinks it is at best permissible within religion (that is, in Christianity) because the ideal is the one embodied not in Thomas's but in the other disciples' response to the resurrected Christ. The message the biblical narrative delivers, according to both Gould and Dawkins, is that the proper way to acquire a belief within religious practice is to accept it on the basis of trust and authority, and not on the basis of evidence. Dawkins is very critical of such an epistemic norm because this kind of faith, this "blind trust" that he thinks the other apostles express (their faith was so strong that they did not need evidence), is not worthy of imitation since it can justify anything (Dawkins 1989: 198).

Suppose for a moment that Dawkins is right in that religious faith (and not merely Christian faith) is a matter of blind trust. Why would it not be appropriate for him to suggest that a different epistemic norm, one that has proved to be successful within science, would be a better norm to

---

1. See Stenmark (1995) for a discussion of two different versions of evidentialism, formal evidentialism and social evidentialism.

adopt also within religion? If we in this way can improve our cognitive performance, by taking what we have learned in one area and applying it in another area of life, it is hard to understand why anyone would object. Whether such an attempt to impose the epistemic norms or methods of one practice on another practice will prove to be convincing, however, depends on *whether one has sufficiently understood what is going on in this other practice.* The reason why we sometimes respond very negatively to a proposed "improvement" of a particular practice concerns exactly this; we anticipate a lack of awareness and sophistication in understanding what the context and the goals of the practice in question are.

This applies to academic disciplines as well. Wilson, for instance, argues that the explanatory categories and methods of evolutionary biology ought to be extended to the social and human sciences as well. He writes, "It may not be too much to say that sociology and the other social sciences, as well as the humanities, are the last branches of biology waiting to be included in the Modern Synthesis" (Wilson 1978: 4).[2] If this is done properly then, presumably, the cognitive performance of the scholars working in these fields can be improved. It is unclear to what extent Wilson wants to replace, for instance, the traditional methods of sociology with biological methods. But suppose it would mean that sociologists could keep their statistical and mathematical methods but would replace their hermeneutic methods with biological methods. Under such conditions it is fully understandable that many sociologists would object to the attempt to impose biological methods on sociology, by maintaining that Wilson fails to do justice to the subject matter of sociology. Some of the data that sociologists try to understand consists of meaningful phenomena such as texts. These texts could be legal documents, letters, political manifestos, and so on. Thus, it is reasonable to believe that some of the phenomena studied by sociologists are not detectable by biological means; they escape biological methods. Therefore, hermeneutic methods, at least, cannot be replaced by biological methods.

The same kinds of considerations are, of course, relevant in the case of religion. Have then Dawkins and Gould properly understood the epistemic norms of religion? These could be different in different religions so here we shall merely focus on Christianity. Let us consider in more de-

2. This theme is further developed by Wilson in *Consilience: The Unity of Knowledge* (1998).

tail the biblical narrative that Gould and Dawkins believe illustrates a central religious epistemic norm, namely, the story about doubting Thomas. Dawkins takes the difference to be that Thomas (as scientists do) demanded evidence, whereas the other disciples had a faith that was so strong that they did not need evidence; therefore, their faith expresses a blind trust (Dawkins 1989: 198). Gould takes the difference to be that Thomas (as scientists do) demanded evidence and had a skeptical attitude toward appeals based only on authority, although he (like the other disciples) should have known that Jesus was resurrected and alive through faith (Gould 1999: 16). Thus, the epistemic norm of religion in question is, roughly, taken to be that *a religious belief ought to be accepted only (in Dawkins's case) or preferably (in Gould's case) on the basis of trust and authority, and not on the basis of evidence.* This is thus a norm that conflicts with evidentialism.

But is it really reasonable to believe that the conclusion we should draw from this biblical narrative is (to follow Dawkins) that the other disciples had a faith that was so strong that they did not need evidence and (to follow Gould) that their faith in Christ was based only on authority? I do not think so, because if we return to the text, we can actually read about how the other disciples arrived at their faith in the resurrected Christ. We can read that when they were gathered in a room, "Jesus came and stood among them and said, 'Peace be with you!' After he said this, he showed them his hands and side. The disciples were overjoyed when they saw the Lord" (John 20:19-20). But if this is true then they did not violate the evidentialist norm. They held their belief on the basis of evidence and not merely on the basis of authority.

What is then problematic from a religious point of view with Thomas's doubt, if it is not that he attempted to base his faith on evidence whereas the other disciples had no such intention? Two things would seem to be involved.

First, Thomas questioned the testimony of his close friends, the other disciples. They had been together for a long time and had gone through much hardship together. But when the other disciples told Thomas that they had met the resurrected Jesus, he did not believe them but asked for more evidence. In this way Thomas's behavior indicated that he did not really trust them in a situation where their friendship was put to a crucial test.

Second, his skepticism was too severe; in other words, his demand for evidence was beyond what one should require to be convinced of something. This theme is well captured in Mark Tansey's painting "Doubting Thomas," which Gould also brings to our attention (Gould 1999: 14f.). In this 1986 work Tansey depicted a man who would not accept continental drift in general, or even the reality of earthquakes in particular. An earthquake has fractured both a road and the adjoining cliff, but the man still doubts. So he instructs his wife to straddle the fault line with their car, while he gets out and thrusts his hand into the crack in the road. Then, and only then, he believes.

It is difficult to determine how skeptical one should be in life. The price of skepticism is the risk of failing to hold a substantial number of true beliefs, whereas the price for credulity is the risk of ending up with too many false beliefs. But contrary to what both Dawkins and Gould believe, I think that neither the biblical version nor Tansey's version of the doubting Thomas would be a very good role model even for evolutionary biologists. Many of the theories accepted in evolutionary biology are such that the evidence they are based on, to put it crudely, is not such that one can feel it directly with one's hands, and the conclusions (i.e., the theories) always go beyond the actual evidence. Nor would they typically, I believe, be worthy of imitation in everyday life situations. The reason for this is that we have finite cognitive resources and limited time at our disposal, but still we need to believe and do a number of things every day to function properly.[3] We would, therefore, not have time to do most of these things if the norms of rationality were set at the level of the ancient or modern version of doubting Thomas. Moreover, there are people in Western society who do not believe that the Holocaust happened or that Caesar was a Roman emperor. Why they do not believe these things might be hard to know, but it could be that they do not think there is sufficient evidence to support these beliefs. If that is the case we would not consider such people rational, not because of their credulity but because of their extreme skepticism.

We have seen that there are good reasons for questioning that the conclusion we should draw from the biblical narrative is (as Dawkins argued) that the other disciples had a faith that was so strong that they did not need evidence and (as Gould claimed) that their faith in Christ was

---

3. I return to this theme in chapter 5, where a discussion is undertaken about how the human constitution and predicament affect the formulation of an appropriate model of rationality.

based only on authority. Nevertheless, I think — and to return to the first theme about what makes Thomas's doubt problematic from a religious point of view — that Dawkins and Gould have captured one feature of religious belief regulation that makes it different from scientific theory regulation. (At the same time, as we saw in chapter 2, authority and trust play a much more important role in science than they seem to realize.) There are, however, reasons to believe that Dawkins's negative assessment of this feature of religious belief regulation is somewhat premature. The difference is this: *the critical questioning of the beliefs of other people (exemplified by Thomas) is typically regarded as an epistemic virtue within science, whereas that is normally not the case in religion.* Gould maintains, as we have seen, that the first commandment of science is a skeptical attitude toward appeals based only on authority and a demand for evidence, and Dawkins thinks that Thomas's demand for evidence is what is worthy of imitation and is also what characterizes the scientific attitude. In religion, on the other hand, people frequently believe things on the basis of authority, discourage critical questioning, and talk instead about trust.

Should we then adopt the skeptical scientific norm in religion and perhaps also in every other practice we participate in? Not necessarily. In fact it might even turn out to be quite imprudent. To see this, compare two scenarios. In the first scenario imagine that one of Dawkins's colleagues in zoology tells him that she has developed this great new theory about the genes that cause certain animals, say chimpanzees, to behave in a particular way. This theory runs contrary to most things zoologists previously have thought. Dawkins says, "Great, very interesting indeed. But what evidence do you have that supports your extraordinary claim?" Dawkins perhaps adds, "I am so sorry but I can't believe what you say until you supply me with this information." In the second situation imagine that Dawkins's wife comes home and tells him that she fell from the third floor of a building but miraculously, apart from a few bruises, she was not hurt. Dawkins, being consistent in his epistemology, says, "Great, very interesting indeed. But what evidence do you have that supports this extraordinary claim?" Dawkins perhaps adds, "I am so sorry but I can't believe what you say until you supply me with this information." In fact, imagine that this is also the way Dawkins responds to everything that his friends tell him. My point is that in the scientific scenario Dawkins's response is just standard procedure, but by proceeding in the way he does in the second scenario Dawkins probably would run the risk of losing both his wife and his friends.

I am not going to go into all the details of why we assume, for good reasons, I think, that different epistemic norms apply in these cases, but it is sufficient to say that the scenarios illustrate the danger of taking norms from one (no matter how successful) practice and thinking that the application of them would automatically improve another practice. One could also claim on good grounds that the context of religion resembles more the context of these everyday life situations than it does the context of science. To believe in God is not, at least in the major theistic faiths, just a matter of mentally assenting to a set of propositions, but of relating to and trusting God — just as we relate to and trust our spouses and friends. Maintaining this does not mean, however, that one could not argue that religious believers sometimes are too dogmatic and uncritical in their religious belief regulation. I, for one, think this is true, and therefore would maintain that the epistemic norms of many religious believers could be improved. We shall return to this theme in chapter 5.

Even if Dawkins fails to capture the epistemic norms embedded in the biblical narrative and its rationale, it is still, I think, a mistake to adopt Gould's position of respectful noninterference between science and religion when it comes to issues of epistemology. To do so is to assume that relating science and religion is best done in accordance to the independence view, which means that there could not and should not be any overlap between science and religion. The reason it would be a mistake to adopt this position is that everything we can learn in one area of life from another area which can improve our cognitive performance ought to be taken into consideration by rational people. We can, therefore, not exclude the possibility that there could and should be an area of contact between science and religion with respect to epistemology or methodology.

But *being cautious* seems to be a good virtue to cultivate in this context. Certainly, there is nothing in the scientific training that Dawkins and Wilson have received that makes them particularly qualified to understand what religion is all about, to understand, for instance, what kind of epistemic norms are and ought to be used in religious practice, given the goals of religion. If scientists fail to take this into account, their proposed improvements may turn out merely to reflect the imperialistic aims which Gould, as we have seen, is afraid drive some of his colleagues (Gould 1999: 85). Moreover, even if there could and should be an epistemic overlap between science and religion, biologists like Wilson or Dawkins have no special authority *as* scientists to suggest epistemic improvements, other than those that concern their own scientific practice. Epistemological evaluations of human practices other than the scientific one are no part of their assignment as evolutionary biologists. A kind of misuse of science would then be to pretend that the comparison of religious and scientific "ethos" (to use Wilson's term) is something that can be made in the name of science (Wilson 1978: 201).

But is being cautious perhaps not enough? Perhaps there is a reason of a more principal nature for accepting Gould's principle of NOMA? In the next section we shall take a closer look at one proposed reason of this sort.

Science and Religion as Different Language-Games

Some philosophers and theologians inspired by the writings of Ludwig Wittgenstein have argued that religious language has a particular use which we must leave as it is rather than forcing it into confrontation or conformity with the language of science. I have in *Rationality in Science, Religion, and Everyday Life* (1995) responded to some of these ideas. Here I shall merely focus on one recent and interesting attempt by Vincent Brümmer to defend this idea of a strict separation between science and religion. His context is primarily contemporary philosophy of religion, but his ideas apply just as well to the science-religion dialogue.

What is it that Brümmer is so critical of? It is the attempt to treat religious belief as a kind of scientific or quasi-scientific hypothesis (as Dawkins does) and maintain that there are or must be neutral rational grounds for adopting belief in the existence of God and that the truth of this belief must be demonstrated or shown to be more probable than not, to be rationally acceptable (Brümmer 1993: 88, 95, and 100). It is the idea of using scientific methods or criteria to assess what is going on in religious practice, which presupposes that belief in God is to be understood as a conjecture or hypothesis. His key examples of philosophers involved in this kind of *scientifically informed epistemology of religion* are Anthony Kenny and Richard Swinburne, and the debate they participate in is (somewhat misguidedly) referred to as the "theism-atheism debate."[4]

Notice that Brümmer's criticism, if justified, would apply also to par-

4. See Kenny (1969) and Swinburne (1977 and 1979).

ticipants in the science-religion dialogue who, like Philip Clayton, Steven Knapp, and Arthur Peacocke, think that inference to the best explanation (we infer what would, if true, provide the best of the competing explanations of the data we generate) used in science is also appropriate within the epistemology of religion. Peacocke quotes and agrees with Clayton and Knapp that

> this [Clayton's and Knapp's] theory of rationality is best understood in terms of the "inference to the best explanation" model adapted from the philosophy of science. On this view, many Christian beliefs are potential explanations: they tell why certain data that need to be explained are the way they are; they account for certain facts about human existence. When I believe them, I believe they do a better job of explaining the data than the other explanatory hypotheses of which I am aware. (Clayton and Knapp 1996: 134; Peacocke 2001: 29)

The reason why Brümmer maintains that scientifically informed epistemology of religion ought to be rejected is that in this kind of enterprise the belief that God exists is not used in a way that is appropriate with the way it is used in the religious language-game, and that those engaged in it therefore misconstrue and even make that belief as well as other religious beliefs meaningless.

To evaluate this argument we have to know what a language-game is and the characteristics of the religious language-game within which the belief that God exists is expressed. Brümmer does not himself say very much about the concept, though he writes that "language-games are primarily forms of actions involving the use of language" and continues talking about "the religious language-game" (Brümmer 1993: 90).

The basic idea seems to be, however, that we come to understand how an expression is used by focusing on what the users of a language do with it. Hence a language-game is more or less a unified practice of using language. Thus we can say that the religious language-game is constituted by, roughly, what religious people do with linguistic expressions in their religious practice or in the religious form of life in which they participate.[5]

---

5. Notice that Brümmer is limiting the concept to a high level of abstraction. We could use it also in a more concrete way, talking about the language-game of shopping, counting, praying, holding speeches, and so forth. Hence, we can talk about language-games

(This means that a language-game is always embedded in a form of life.) Brümmer seems also to allow that we can talk about language-games within the religious language-game (Brümmer 1993: 100). Hence, the Christian language-game is what Christian practitioners do with words, phrases, or sentences in their religious practice. In a similar fashion we can talk about the scientific language-game and about the language-games within science, such as the language-game of biology and the language-game of sociology.

Given this explication, what are the characteristics of the religious language-game and what role does the claim that God exists play in it? We should first notice that there are religious language-games where this particular claim plays no role at all, for example, in some forms of Buddhism. Hence, what Brümmer really is talking about is what we could call "the theistic language-game." Let us therefore instead use this term whenever he is writing about the religious language-game. What then, according to Brümmer, are the characteristics of the theistic language-game, and what role does the claim that God exists play in it? He writes,

> the claim that God exists is to be understood as a constitutive presupposition of the form of life in terms of which the theist makes sense of life and experience, and of the language-game in which this is expressed. Within the language-game, this presupposition cannot be doubted or denied since denying it would entail taking leave of the form of life as such. Divorced from the language-game and its form of life, the claim becomes superfluous and loses all significance. (Brümmer 1994: 428)

Therefore,

> Doubting or denying the existence of God or looking on it as a conjecture of which the relative likelihood or unlikelihood could somehow be established, would be quite absurd within the language-game of religious belief. Clearly Swinburne's conclusion that "on our total evi-

---

within language-games in many layers. For instance, the language-game of counting could be a part of the language-game of describing objects, which could be a part of the language-game of physics, which could be a part of the physical world language-game, and so on. For this reason I myself normally try to avoid using the language-game lingo because it creates unnecessary ambiguities.

dence theism is more probable than not" should strike the believer as decidedly odd. (Brümmer 1993: 94-95)

These statements indicate that there are "logical limits" to the theistic language-game. According to Brümmer, these limits help us distinguish one language-game from another, and they have to do with the internal inferences which can or cannot be correctly drawn from the beliefs within the language-game. The logical limits of the theistic language-game are, among others, that within it the claim that God exists cannot be denied or even doubted and cannot be considered a hypothesis with a certain probability. This is so because for the believers God necessarily exists (that is, God's non-existence is wholly unthinkable in any circumstances). If one does not recognize these limits, it only shows that one has already left the theistic form of life, and in such a situation the claim that God exists becomes automatically superfluous and loses all significance. Hence, the claim that God exists functions as a "constitutive presupposition" for the whole theistic form of life. These logical limits, or at least some of them, are exceeded by Kenny and Swinburne and by implication by many participants in the science-religion dialogue since in these debates the claim that God exists is not only affirmed but also denied and often treated as a conjecture or hypothesis. As a result, scientifically informed epistemology of religion is an expression of conceptual confusion and should be abandoned.

Brümmer's argument seems to involve the following points:

1. In scientifically informed epistemology of religion the belief in the existence of God is denied, doubted, or looked upon as a hypothesis.
2. The belief in the existence of God cannot be denied, doubted, or looked upon as a hypothesis within the theistic language-game.
3. Therefore, scientifically informed epistemology of religion is based on conceptual confusion and should be rejected.

If Brümmer were right in his characterization of the theistic language-game, it would have severe consequences for the project for a scientifically informed epistemology of religion. But is (2) true? Is Brümmer not himself, in fact, misconstruing the nature of the theistic language-game? By writing as he does, Brümmer gives the impression that the theistic language-game is unified in a way that it is clearly not. This impression is evident when he writes,

[The theism-atheism debate] is only meaningful if it is construed as a debate about the coherence and adequacy of a form of life. Atheists reject the claim that theistic faith is coherent or adequate for coping with the demands of life and therefore feel no need for the presupposition that God exists which is constitutive for this faith. . . . Christian theists, however, hold that the Christian faith can be coherently conceptualized in a form which is adequate for making sense of the demands with which life confronts them. If for this reason they can authentically make this form of life their own, then it is for them absurd to deny its constitutive presupposition, namely that the God in whose sight they live and move and have their being exists in reality. (Brümmer 1994: 431-32; see also again the citations above)

Brümmer here assumes that the atheistic language-game is unified in the sense that the criticism of theism by atheists is understood to be of one kind. It is not that atheists reject the *truth* of the claim that God exists but that they all reject the coherence and adequacy of theism and therefore have no need for the claim that God exists. How does Brümmer know this?

The answer appears to be that he knows it because he has studied the way atheists *use* their atheistic expressions. But what about atheists like Bertrand Russell, J. L. Mackie, and Richard Dawkins? Do they not reject the truth of the claim that God exists? If we study what Russell, Mackie, and Dawkins do with their atheistic concepts must that not be our conclusion? Brümmer would probably not deny this, but claims that atheists like Russell, Mackie, and Dawkins have misunderstood the logical limits of the theistic language-game and therefore that what they are saying makes no sense. Russell, Mackie, and Dawkins would have understood this if they had paid more attention to the way theists use their religious expressions. So what Brümmer is saying is not really that "atheists reject . . ." but that atheists *should* understand their rejection of theism (whether they say that or not) as a criticism of its coherence and adequacy.

This same conjecture applies in the case of Swinburne. Brümmer writes that Swinburne's claim about the likelihood of theism "should strike the believer as decidedly odd" (Brümmer 1993: 95). It should even be "absurd" to him or her. But is not Swinburne himself a Christian believer, and is he therefore not "playing" the theistic language-game? Again Brümmer would probably not deny this but claim that Swinburne has misunderstood his own religious commitments.

The problem is, however, that *this is not the kind of answer Brümmer can give if he intends to stick to a language-game analysis of religious faith.* Brümmer's approach picks out a certain kind of believers' use of religious expressions as the *norm* that all others should conform to. But this does not follow merely from a language-game analysis because according to it, the theistic language-game is what people with a theistic faith (or perhaps better, what Christians, Muslims, and other theists) are doing with words, phrases, and sentences in their religious practices. It is thus primarily a *descriptive* notion. As a result, what Swinburne and other religious believers are doing with religious expressions is as valid as what some other group of them does. This means that Brümmer could go on talking about the theistic language-game in the way he does only if all theistic believers were doing (at least roughly) the same thing with linguistic expressions in their religious practice. This, of course, is not the case. This is also the way things are irrespective of whether we like it or not. After all, we have to distinguish between what we personally would prefer religion to be and the various ways in which religion is in fact understood by its practitioners.

Brümmer also admits that language-games *change.* Perhaps, then, this is one of the changes! Perhaps nowadays religious believers really have started to think that it could be true that God does not exist (not only as a purely logical possibility but as a live-option — as an existential possibility) or even that there is a certain likelihood (though a low one) that that is the case. What Brümmer does not acknowledge is the *pluralism* of theistic language-games within the theistic form of life. What a language-game analysis applied to religion shows is that there is not one but many grammars of faith. What Brümmer is picturing as *the* theistic language-game is in fact merely *a* sub-theistic or sub-Christian language-game.

Hence, when Swinburne writes that "on the total evidence theism is more probable than not," it will strike some believers as odd because, as Brümmer points out, they think that God necessarily exists. Others — while denying that God necessarily exists in this sense — will think it is odd because Swinburne's talk about probability sounds as though it is possible to measure or quantify the likelihood of God's existence (something they would never dream of believing), or because they think that the belief that God exists is a properly basic belief and is therefore not supported by other beliefs that can make it more or less probable (see Plantinga 1983). Still other believers, like Swinburne, believe that it is quite proper to talk about theism in this way (though they would never deny that belief in God is more than believing that it is probable that God exists). In essence, there are different ways of being religious.[6] There is no unified grammar of faith.

Let us consider one more passage where Brümmer does not acknowledge the pluralism of theistic language-games. He writes, "Religious beliefs are not open to doubt or refutation within the context of the form of life itself, any more than the constitutive presuppositions of science are open to scientific doubt or refutation" (Brümmer 1993: 95).[7] But some religious practitioners do not view the belief in the existence of God in a fashion analogous to how scientists view belief in the uniformity and comprehensibility of nature or the belief that material objects which scientists observe continue to exist at times when they do not observe them. Rather, these practitioners view the belief in the existence of God in a fashion analogous to how scientists treat the hard-core beliefs in theories such as the relativity theory and the theory of evolution, and they understand atheism (i.e., naturalism) in a fashion analogous to how competing theories to the relativity theory and the theory of evolution are viewed by scientists. Which, if any, group of religious practitioners is right cannot, therefore, be determined merely by a language-game analysis. It cannot be settled by simply focusing on what practitioners do with their religious expressions, because they do *different* things with them.

Looking back on Brümmer's argument against Kenny and Swinburne and its consequences for a scientifically informed epistemology of religion, the above remarks indicate that his premise (2) is false. It can be true only if it is formulated as follows:

6. Psychologists C. Daniel Batson and W. Larry Ventis give empirical support for thinking that some religious believers could be classified as being religious in the sense of having "religion as a quest." The quest orientation is in general characterized by complexity, doubt, and tentativeness and "involves honestly facing existential questions in all their complexity, while resisting clear-cut, pat answers. An individual who approaches religion in this way recognizes that he or she does not know, and probably never will know, the final truth about such matters. But still the questions are deemed important, and however tentative and subject to change, answers are sought" (Batson and Ventis 1982: 149-50). There is thus empirical evidence indicating that there really exist ordinary religious believers — and not only a number of religious philosophers — who *within* their religious language-games do not deny that God's existence can be doubted or denied.

7. It seems that Brümmer thinks that all religious beliefs are constitutive presuppositions of religion. He probably means to say that just as some scientific beliefs are constitutive presuppositions of science and others are theories assessable within science, so different groups of beliefs can also be understood within religion.

(2′) The belief in the existence of God cannot be denied, doubted, or looked upon as a hypothesis within *some* theistic language-games.

But, of course, (1) and (2′) do not entail (3).

Even if what Swinburne maintains strikes virtually all theistic practitioners as odd, however, this does not necessarily mean that this is not the attitude they *ought* to have. That is, even if what Swinburne says goes against one of the main features of all current theistic language-games, that does not automatically imply that he is wrong in treating the belief that God exists as he does. What is customary or normative among religious people is not necessarily right. Perhaps nearly all theistic language-games need to be revised in this way; this is probably what Dawkins had in mind when he proposed that Christians should have Thomas as their epistemic role model and not the other disciples (see pp. 7-8).

We can see this by comparing religion with science, returning to the example mentioned in the previous chapter. From the beginning of the scientific revolution until at least the late 1700s, virtually all scientists believed that proper science must be restricted to observable entities and processes only (see Laudan 1984: 55-62). They all claimed to be "inductivists," aiming to understand the observable world by purely inductive methods so that all hypotheses should be avoided. But during this period scientists developed a number of theories in electricity, embryology, and chemistry that seemed to depend essentially on postulating unobservable entities.[8] As I noted, these theories received widespread criticism because they were in conflict with the accepted view of science, but in the end the "hypotheticalists" won the debate and what was considered proper science changed drastically. It was from then on generally accepted that science should also value and develop theories about unobservable entities and processes. As a result what we today call the hypothetical-deductive method was recognized as a scientific method. Thus, even if the scientific method of all scientific language-games at that time was not construed as being hypothetical-deductive, this merely indicates that a profound revision of that method was needed.

By way of analogy, what is considered by most or even all religious believers to be true religion (or the correct attitude toward the belief that

---

8. For instance, Franklin's fluid theory of electricity, the Buffonian theory of organic molecules, the gravitational theory of Lesage, and the neurophysiological theory of Hartley.

God exists) may drastically change. Someone like Swinburne may actually turn out to be right in the long run.[9] Thus, the actual practice of religion can correctly be subject to criticism by somebody inside or outside the religious forms of life, just as science can be criticized by scientists as well as by people within other professions. As a result, we must conclude that Brümmer's argument is invalid. Hence, even if it is true that

> (2″) The belief in the existence of God cannot be denied, doubted, or looked upon as a hypothesis within *any* existing theistic language-game,

that premise cannot entail (3).

Even if this is so, however, I think that Brümmer is correct if we understand him as saying that if (2″) is true, it should make us very suspicious. I suggest that participants in the science-religion dialogue are, *most of the time*, in serious trouble if their way of treating the content of religion turns out to be at odds with all (or most) religious language-games.

To see the rationale behind this, consider again philosophers' attitude in general today toward science. Most philosophers of science consider that logical positivism and Popper's scientific rationalism do not give an adequate account of scientific practice and therefore fail in their critical intentions. Remember our earlier discussion of Karl Popper, for example. Popper thought that what is characteristic of good scientists is that they always lay down in advance what would lead them to reject a theory and always actively try to falsify the theory (see Popper 1963). But by analyzing scientific journals, philosophers of science discovered that they could not find any papers that explicitly or implicitly state what would falsify the proposed theories. By studying how scientists actually behave in the face of arising anomalies, these philosophers of science came to discover that — contrary to Popper's thesis — scientists never seem to reject a theory that they believe has something in its favor even in situations where many anomalies have been found. In fact, in practice, scientists seem never to reject a theory no matter how many anomalies there are unless they have a *better* theory to put in its place.[10] This by itself does not show that scien-

---

9. We thus return to the distinction between descriptive and normative epistemologies of religion. This illustrates why the concepts cannot be equated.

10. The most important contribution to this change to a "practice-oriented ap-

tists ought not to behave as Popper prescribes (it is possible that he is correct after all). It only demonstrates that actual scientists do not behave in such a way. In this situation, however, philosophers of science give priority to actual scientific practices, hence leaving the burden of proof to Popper.

I think that we should view scholarly theories of religion in a similar fashion if they do not fit the history of religions. In the science-religion dialogue a discrepancy between a theory and actual religious (or scientific) practices also constitutes *prima facie* evidence against that theory.[11] We thus again see the importance of descriptive epistemology of religion (and of science).

Brümmer has been kind enough to respond to my criticism (Brümmer 1999).[12] I shall here merely comment on some of the issues he raises. It seems that our views are closer to each other than I previously thought. For instance, he does — contrary to what I thought — actually think that in a discussion about the rationality of religious beliefs questions of truth are relevant and not merely questions about coherence and adequacy. Although Brümmer confesses that he is surprised at my interpretation of his view (p. 90), one may perhaps excuse me for thinking so when he writes things such as, "the debate about the truth or falsehood of the claim that God exists .. has no future" (Brümmer 1994: 426). It is important for our overall objective that we consider his objections.

He maintains that it is a mistake to describe him as indulging in what I call a language-game analysis of religious faith, which I claim is primarily a descriptive notion. Instead Brümmer denies altogether the relevance of descriptive epistemology of religion (and by implication of science) as a philosophical task, claiming that what he intended to do was to develop "innovative proposals." "As a philosopher should, I am only putting forward reasoned proposals for coherent and adequate ways of understanding our religious forms of thought" (Brümmer 1999: 96). It is therefore a "serious misunderstanding" of his position that I offer because he has "not been put-

---

proach" in philosophy of science was Thomas Kuhn's influential book *The Structure of Scientific Revolution* (1962). For a discussion of this approach, its alternatives (the "formal approach" and the "contextual approach"), and its relevance for the question of rationality in philosophy of religion, see Stenmark (1995, especially pp. 7-11 and chapters 3, 5, and 11).

11. This is not the place to develop a full argument for such a view. For this see Gutting (1982: 1-4) and Stenmark (1995: 167-73).

12. This criticism was originally published as a part of a larger article in *Religious Studies* (see Stenmark 1998).

ting forward any descriptions at all!" (p. 96). Hence, when he writes, for instance, that "the claim that God exists is to be understood as a constitutive presupposition of the form of life in terms of which the theist makes sense of life and experience, and of the language-game in which this is expressed," the "is to be" in the sentence ought to be understood as a "should," and "the theist" and "the language-game" do not necessarily refer to any actual theists or language-games (Brümmer 1994: 428). Or when Brümmer claims that "doubting or denying the existence of God or looking on it as a conjecture of a kind where its relative likelihood or unlikelihood could somehow be established, would be quite absurd within the language-game of religious belief," this may sound like a description of a real religious language-game, but it is to be read as a normative statement about how things ought to be (Brümmer 1993: 94-95). Or when Brümmer writes, "Religious beliefs are not open to doubt or refutation within the context of the form of life itself, any more than the constitutive presuppositions of science are open to scientific doubt or refutation," we should add after "the context of the form of life itself" the words "as we should conceive it," and so on (p. 95).

If this is how we should interpret Brümmer, then it will not do to criticize his view, as I have done, by pointing out that within some theistic language-games the existence of God could actually be looked upon as a hypothesis and could be doubted or even denied. Brümmer cannot be understood to maintain that scientifically informed epistemology of religion ought to be rejected since within this kind of enterprise the belief that God exists is not used in a way that accords with the way it is used in the religious language-game, simply because there is no such thing as *the* religious language-game. It follows that his basic claim is not that (a) all (or at least most) religious practitioners think that God necessarily exists, describing the actual theistic language-game, but that (b) they *should* think so; they *should* participate in a theistic language-game which has belief in God as a constitutive presupposition. He writes in his reply to my criticism,

> I logically cannot claim to live my life in fellowship with God without at the same time presupposing the existence of the God in whose fellowship I live, nor can I logically understand my experience of the world in terms of the agency of God without at the same time presupposing that there is a God in terms of whose agency my existence can be said to make sense. In this way Christians have traditionally claimed that for them the existence of God is not contingent but necessary.

Thus J. N. Findlay is correct in pointing out that for believers partaking in the theistic form of life and understanding, God's non-existence must be wholly unthinkable in any circumstances. (Brümmer 1999: 93)

There is thus a difference of principle between science and religion: "truth claims *in the context of religion* differ from truth claims in the context of science. The latter remain empirical hypotheses which are methodologically subjected to doubt and conjecture regarding their probability or relative likelihood," whereas in religion that is not so, or it is even impossible for it to be so (p. 93). It follows that a scientifically informed epistemology of religion is completely misguided.

The tricky part when it comes to understanding this line of argument is whether we should interpret Brümmer as he says we should, namely, as giving an innovative proposal about how to improve religious practice, or instead as stating what must necessarily be the case. Should we interpret his argument in the should-mode or in the must-mode way? I think the quotations above indicate that we have to interpret him in the latter way because that is the only way to distill an argument out of what he says. Hence his claim might actually be that (c) religious practitioners *must* (whether or not they realize this) think that God necessarily exists and therefore that God's existence cannot be denied, doubted, or looked upon as a hypothesis.

But notice if we do so that what Peter Berger thinks is his big sociological insight then turns out to be a major mistake. His big insight is that pluralism (the coexistence and social interaction of people with very different beliefs, values, and lifestyles) has in contemporary society undermined the taken-for-grantedness of beliefs and values. He writes that where socialization processes are uniform our

> view of reality is held with a high degree of taken-for-granted certainty. Pluralism ensures that socialization processes are *not* uniform and, consequently, that the view of reality is much less firmly held. Put differently, certainty is now much harder to come by. People may still hold the same beliefs and values that were held by their predecessors in more uniform situations, but they will hold them in a different manner: what before was given through the accident of birth now becomes a matter of *choice*. Pluralism brings on an era of many choices and, by the same token, an era of uncertainty. (Berger 1998: 782)

This Berger holds to be particularly true of religious beliefs and values. But then it seems that for many people today, God's non-existence is not, as Brümmer and Findlay believe, "wholly unthinkable in any circumstances." Instead they treat God's non-existence as a real possibility; they might even doubt God's existence, and perhaps also treat it as a hypothesis. But on Brümmer's analysis this must be taken to mean that they have rejected the theistic language-game since if you play that game "the claim that God exists is not only rational but also necessary" (Brümmer 1999: 93). They therefore play another game now. Berger's big mistake is that he has failed to see that these people are not religious, or at any rate no longer Christians.

Brümmer's argument seems thus to be:

(4) In scientifically informed epistemology of religion the belief in the existence of God is denied, doubted, or looked upon as a hypothesis.

(5) It is wholly unthinkable in any circumstances for a religious believer within the religious practice to deny, doubt, or look upon the existence of God as a hypothesis.

(6) Therefore, scientifically informed epistemology of religion is based on conceptual confusion and should be rejected.

So one could not inform the epistemology of religion scientifically because one then would turn religion into a nonreligious practice; one would violate the logical limits or the grammar of this kind of human activity. It is like saying that in soccer you should allow the players only to throw the ball and not to kick it with their feet. Brümmer's point is that by doing so, you change the game's constitutional presuppositions in such a way that you turn soccer into a different sport, perhaps into handball.

Why should we then think that (5) is true and that consequently Berger is talking about something other than religion or Christianity? Brümmer starts by maintaining, as we have seen, that "I logically cannot claim to live my life in fellowship with God without at the same time presupposing the existence of the God in whose fellowship I live, nor can I logically understand my experience of the world in terms of the agency of God without at the same time presupposing that there is a God in terms of whose agency my existence can be said to make sense." This is supposed to support the claim that "God's existence is not contingent but necessary" and that "God's non-existence must be wholly unthinkable [for religious believers] in any circumstances" (p. 93). But is this really so?

It seems obviously true that I logically cannot claim to live my life in fellowship with God without at the same time presupposing the existence of God. To deny that would be like claiming that I do biological research as a Darwinian without at the same time presupposing that natural selection takes place. You simply fail to be a Darwinian if you do not believe that. Or to take another example, you logically cannot claim that you have fallen in love and want to marry the woman you have been corresponding with for the last two years without at the same time presupposing the existence of this woman. But as these parallel cases show, this says nothing about whether the existence or non-existence of natural selection or of this woman is contingent or necessary, thinkable or unthinkable in any circumstances, or could or could not be understood to be a hypothesis. We, therefore, must conclude that also in this version Brümmer's argument is unsuccessful. A scientifically informed epistemology of religion is not necessarily based on conceptual confusion.

Is Belief in God a (Scientific) Hypothesis?

Having criticized Brümmer's argument, I shall nevertheless try to show that his ideas are not completely unfounded but for other reasons than those Brümmer gives and with different consequences for the science-religion dialogue. There is indeed something problematic about treating belief in God as a hypothesis, even if it does not entail that God's existence cannot be denied or doubted, or imply the end of the atheism-theism debate.

We have seen that scientific expansionists like Dawkins and Wilson think that science and religion compete, not merely because (a) science can be expanded to deal with our existential concerns, but because they believe that (b) traditional religions actually are scientific or quasi-scientific hypotheses or theories. They believe their colleague Gould to be wrong on both of these accounts. Recall that Dawkins writes,

> I pay religions the compliment of regarding them as scientific theories and . . . I see God as a competing explanation for facts about the universe and life. This is certainly how God has been seen by most theologians of past centuries and by most ordinary religious people today. . . . Either admit that God is a scientific hypothesis and let him submit to

the same judgement as any other scientific hypothesis. Or admit that his status is no higher than that of fairies and river sprites. (Dawkins 1995b: 46-47)

Either religious practitioners have to treat belief in God as a scientific hypothesis or they have to admit that it has merely a fairy-tale status, that it is merely a superstition. These are apparently the only options that Dawkins thinks possible. Even though Wilson does not explicitly state that he sees traditional religion as a scientific hypothesis, he at least sometimes writes as if this is his position. Wilson maintains, for instance, that

the reasons why I consider the scientific ethos superior to religion [are these]: its repeated triumphs in explaining and controlling the physical world; its self-correcting nature open to all competent to devise and conduct the tests; its readiness to examine all subjects sacred and profane; and now the possibility of explaining traditional religion by the mechanistic models of evolutionary biology. (Wilson 1978: 201)

We could say that Dawkins and Wilson raise a scientific challenge to religious belief. It consists of the following claim: *It is rational to believe in God only if (a) this belief fulfills the same or at least similar standards of rationality as scientific hypotheses do and (b) this belief can compete with scientific hypotheses.*[13] If belief in God (or theism) does not satisfy these conditions, it is an irrational belief to hold.

Others have of course argued against Dawkins and Wilson. Swinburne has, for instance, in *Is There a God?* (1996) argued directly against Dawkins. Swinburne accepts part (a) of the scientific challenge and maintains that there are close similarities between religious theories and large-scale scientific theories. But he rejects (b), that is, that theism competes with science. Instead, he believes, it competes with materialism or naturalism. His basic idea is that in the same way that science explains phenomena with hypotheses about atoms, genes, forces, and so on, other phenomena can be explained by the hypothesis "God exists" — phenomena such as the fact that there is a universe at all and that scientific laws operate within it. Therefore it is rational to believe in God and theism cannot be equated with belief in fairies.

13. In this study I make no distinction between a theory and a hypothesis.

We face here two different questions: (1) Is belief in God a hypothesis? (2) Is belief in God a scientific or quasi-scientific hypothesis? These are two separate issues because it is possible that something can be a hypothesis but nevertheless not be a scientific hypothesis. For instance, my belief that you are tired and perhaps did not sleep very much last night is a hypothesis I reach by looking at your face, but it is not a scientific hypothesis.

To be able to answer these questions, however, we have to narrow our focus. Belief in God comes in many radically different versions, so it is difficult to determine the answer to these two questions in respect to all that variety. Let us, therefore, merely focus on belief in God as it is traditionally understood by Jews, Christians, or Muslims (that is, on theism), which after all seems to be the main target of both Dawkins and Wilson.

We first need to know what a hypothesis is. I suggest that by a hypothesis we mean *an assumption made in order to explain a phenomenon or an event.* For instance, when I see footprints outside my kitchen window I explain this by assuming that a human being has passed by my window. Further thought and observation allows this hypothesis to be made more precise. The size of the footprints together with their depth seems to indicate that a large human being, probably a man, has passed by my window. All hypotheses have in common the feature of speaking about things which transcend the evidence. They tell us more than we can see for ourselves. My hypothesis tells me that a male person passed by outside my window, even though all I can see is footprints in the mud. Thus, what makes something a hypothesis is that it explains or helps us understand a phenomenon. Different hypotheses differ in their credibility, however. Some of them are merely "working" hypotheses, which are only tentatively accepted. They are believed to be true but need to be investigated further. They are, perhaps, only minimally tested. Other hypotheses are not only believed to be true but in addition one thinks that there is no need to investigate them further. These are hypotheses with a high degree of certitude. We take hypotheses of this latter kind for granted in life in general, in politics, and in science, and we feel no need to question them. For instance, evolutionary theory is a hypothesis (or rather a set of hypotheses) in this sense because it functions as a paradigm for much of the research done in contemporary biology.

Is belief in God a hypothesis? There are reasons to doubt this because for many religious practitioners God is taken to be an experienced reality and not a derived entity of some sort. Their faith is not a hypothesis invented to explain natural events in the world. It is, rather, an expression of an experience of something holy, something beyond the mundane, something which is of supreme value and, therefore, worthy of worship and prayer. In short, they have had an encounter with what they experience to be a divine reality. This is well captured by Keith Ward when he writes,

> Many people, perhaps most, occasionally experience a sense of something transcendent, something beyond decay and imperfection. . . . Perhaps religious faith begins, for many of us, in such small epiphanies, in "a sense and taste for the Infinite." It is from such glimpses of a spiritual reality underlying this phenomenal world that one may develop a desire to seek a deeper awareness of it, and, if possible, seek to mediate its reality in the world. If that happens, religious faith is born. Worship and prayer are, basically, ways of deepening this awareness and transforming the self to reflect and mediate the divine spirit. (Ward 1996a: 102-3)

The primary aim of a traditional religion such as Christianity is, on such an understanding, not to explain and predict observable events but to transform people's lives as a response to an encounter with a divine reality — a reality that religious practitioners claim helps them in their lives to deal with experiences of suffering and anxiety, and that gives their lives a meaning. It involves one's deepest personal commitments. Belief in God is, therefore, probably more closely related to belief in other persons than to belief in the existence of genes, electrons, planets, or any other scientific stuff. This explains why it could be deeply problematic to treat belief in God as a tentative hypothesis. To understand, for instance, one's relationship with the beloved, in love affairs, as a tentative hypothesis (as something one should test by actively searching for counter-evidence) would seem to destroy the very foundation necessary for a loving relationship — it undermines the trust and loyalty that must exist between two lovers. But this seems also true about belief in God because it is not just a matter of mentally assenting to a set of propositions, but of trusting God. It is, therefore, probably correct to say, as Ward does, that to treat belief in God as a tentative hypothesis would typically be "like saying that a good marriage is best achieved by always seeking evidence of infidelity" (Ward 1996a: 97).

What follows? For one thing, it follows that it is not surprising if many religious practitioners and theologians do not consider their religious faith to be a hypothesis. Consequently, to discuss the rationality of religious commitment as if people's belief in God *is* for them a hypothesis is to seriously misunderstand the nature of many people's religious faith. Moreover, to treat the issue as if these people's belief in God *ought to be* a hypothesis is unjustified. The reason why is perhaps best explained by going back to the everyday life situation I described earlier. Imagine that this morning I was in my kitchen and saw a man pass by outside my kitchen window. Assume now that a skeptic would claim that it is rational for me to believe this only if I treat my belief as a hypothesis. In other words, I must go out and check whether there are any traces left after the man and, in addition, for me to be rational in accepting this conviction I have to believe this on the basis of this evidence. Suppose, further, that neither the skeptic nor I am able to find any traces, any mark of footprints. The skeptic's conclusion is clear. He claims that it is irrational for me to hold this belief. Stammering, I maintain, however, "But, but, but I saw him!" I would claim that many religious believers are in an analogous situation in respect to their belief in God.[14] They have experienced God's presence in their lives; they have encountered at least glimpses of a divine reality. In a similar way to my believing that a man passed by my window, they believe that God exists and believe in God's presence in their lives. If this is correct, it is unreasonable to demand that these people should view their belief in God as a hypothesis of some kind. Their belief, just like mine, is *directly* experientially grounded. This is in contrast to the belief the skeptic would have adopted if there had been footprints outside my window. The skeptic's beliefs would then have been *indirectly* experientially grounded because he or she would have derived the existence of this man from certain facts or evidence (such as the presence of footprints, their depth, and so on). The same is true in all other cases when hypotheses are assumed or proposed.

Notice, however, that the things we believe which are directly experientially grounded can nevertheless be things we are uncertain about. I was quite certain because I clearly saw a man outside the kitchen window. But the situation could just as well have been that I merely saw the contours of a man in the window, but because my focus was elsewhere or because the sun shone through the window I am uncertain about what I really saw. The same thing can be true about religious belief. Some religious

---

14. See Alston (1991) for an attempt to justify this analogue.

practitioners have experienced merely glimpses of what they think is God in their lives and, therefore, they believe in God but still feel uncertain. Others have had more profound experiences of God's presence, experiences which are harder for them to doubt.

Thus, religious practitioners do not have to treat their belief in God as a hypothesis because for many of them this belief is directly experientially grounded. But would this mean that no religious practitioners whatsoever or any other person (say Dawkins, Peacocke, Swinburne, and Wilson) would be justified in seeing belief in God as a hypothesis? I do not think this follows. Consider an example from another context. My belief that my wife loves me is for me not a hypothesis. This does not mean, however, that it could not be a hypothesis for somebody else. Suppose, for example, two persons hear me say that my wife loves me. One of them believes me but the other does not. So they decide to treat my belief as a hypothesis and try to collect evidence for or against its truth which they both could accept. I can see nothing problematic about that. The same seems to be true about religion. Take a person who has never experienced God's presence firsthand. Suppose she attaches some importance to the believers' testimony, but what makes her believe in God is after all that she thinks that she can see God's footprints in the universe. The existence and beauty of the cosmos convince her that God exists and is worthy of worship. This person's belief in God is, thus, indirectly experientially grounded. Perhaps from a religious perspective there is a better way of obtaining a belief in God, but there is no reason to doubt that this is a genuine faith. This person can hardly be said to have misunderstood belief in God or the theistic language-game in some fundamental way. Or take skeptics who wonder about the rationality of religious faith. They know about the believers' testimony but that is not sufficient for them. Instead they wonder whether it would not be reasonable to assume that if the God whom believers are talking about really exists, really has created heaven and earth, then somehow this divine reality should have left some marks, some footprints in the world. The nonbeliever might even, like J. J. C. Smart, want to be a believer, if only there were sufficient evidence of this sort supporting belief in God (Smart 1996: 6).

Hence we should not confuse the questions, "*Must* or *should* religious practitioners see their belief in God as a hypothesis?" and "*Can* a religious practitioner (or somebody else) see belief in God as a hypothesis?" The answer to the first, as we have seen, is that religious practitioners need not treat their belief in God as a hypothesis because for many of them this conviction is directly experientially grounded. The answer to the second is that religious practitioners could understand their belief in God as a hypothesis if it is indirectly experientially grounded, and the same is true about skeptics or "seekers."

Where does this leave us? One thing we realize is that there is a crucial difference between religion and science on this point. Scientists, whether or not they believe a particular theory to be true, always treat it as a hypothesis in the sense that it is an assumption made to explain a phenomenon and it needs to be supported by other things which function as evidence, whereas religious practitioners and skeptics do not share such an agreement when debating whether or not it is true or rational to believe in God. In other words, scientists who disagree face a situation analogous to one in which two persons are looking at some marks in the ground that look like two footprints, and person A believes that a human being has been standing there, whereas person B does not think so. (They interpret the evidence in different ways.) The religious practitioner and the skeptic, on the other hand, face typically a situation analogous to one in which person A claims that she has seen a man passing by outside the window and person B doubts this to be the case (perhaps on the grounds that person A was drunk at the time or that no footprints can be found outside the window). This asymmetry between scientific and religious believing is something which, for instance, Peacocke fails to take into account in his (and others') attempt to develop an epistemology of religion based on the model of inference to the best explanation used in science.

Second, and of great importance for our inquiry, is that even if we cannot find any evidence of the presence of God in the physical world, this would not automatically undermine the credibility of religious faith, whereas the credibility of a proposed scientific theory would typically be undermined if no evidence could be found supporting it. The reason for this is that belief in God is not held on the basis of other beliefs that function as evidence; instead it is directly experientially grounded. Just like my belief that I have seen a man pass by outside my window is not automatically undermined by the lack of footprints in the grass, people's belief in God is not necessarily challenged if God has not left any physical footprints detectable by the sciences. But that is, of course, not to deny that if such divine footprints could be found, it would strengthen the case that God really exists, just as the credibility of my belief in this man passing by outside my window would be strengthened if footprints could be found in the grass. The discrepancy is that belief in God is typically a direct knowledge claim (it is more than this, of course), whereas beliefs in electrons, natural selection, mutations, and so on are indirect knowledge claims. (An indirect knowledge claim is, roughly, a claim about a state of affairs that people maintain they know by means of inference from other beliefs known to be true [see Stenmark 2001b: 26f.].) Again, an epistemology of religion based on the model of inference to the best explanation used in science fails to take this into account.

Third, the beliefs within a person's noetic structure (that is, the cluster of accepted beliefs and their epistemological relations to one another) can function in different ways in different contexts, and it would, therefore, not necessarily be improper for religious practitioners to sometimes treat their religious faith as a hypothesis (or set of hypotheses).[15] I would typically not treat my belief that my wife loves me as a hypothesis, but in a context where there are flowers on the table of my office and I cannot find any card telling me who put them there, one possible explanation might be that my wife left them there as a sign of her love and affection, and the reason why there is no card is that it fell off on the way to my room but my wife did not notice this. In this particular case my belief that my wife loves me functions as a hypothesis explaining a particular phenomenon, the flowers on my desk. I suggest that religious practitioners can in a similar way use their belief in God as a hypothesis explaining a certain range of phenomena, for instance, consciousness, or the order and the beauty of the world; and this has also been the case. The same holds true for participants in the science-religion dialogue.

Thus belief in God can at least sometimes function as a hypothesis for religious practitioners. But is it in these circumstances a *scientific* hypothesis? Dawkins maintains, as we have seen, that God is an explanation for facts about the universe and life, and therefore is a scientific theory. We have seen that this is misleading. It is misleading because belief in God is not a theory or hypothesis invented to explain particular facts about the physical and biological world as a scientific theory is; rather, it is taken by religious practitioners to be the outcome of an encounter with a divine reality, a reality which these practitioners claim helps them in their lives to

---

15. See Plantinga (1983: 48-50) for a more detailed discussion about what a noetic structure is.

deal with experiences of suffering and anxiety, and which gives their lives a meaning. Dawkins's claim also gives the impression that if religion cannot successfully compete with science then religion is superfluous and undermined by science. But this is to miss the point of a religion such as Christianity. The point of Christianity is to make possible a relationship with a divine Other, a relationship deepening through worship and prayer. Christianity does not seek to offer a competing explanation to scientific theories in accounting for facts about the universe and life.

IT FOLLOWS THAT my previous conclusion seems still to be valid: everything we can learn in one area of life from another area that can improve our cognitive performance ought to be taken into consideration by rational people. We can, therefore, not exclude the possibility that there could and should be an overlap between science and religion in respect to epistemology or methodology. Whether an attempt to impose the epistemic norms of one practice on another practice will prove to be convincing, however, depends on whether one has sufficiently understood what is going on in this other practice. Certainly, there is nothing in the training of natural scientists such as Dawkins, Gould, and Wilson that makes them particularly equipped to understand what religion is all about, to understand, for instance, what kind of epistemic norms are and ought to be used in religious practice, given the goals of religious practice. Therefore, caution about such methodological expansions, as I have already emphasized, seems to be a virtue worth cultivating in the religion-science dialogue. But let us nevertheless examine a recent and very interesting attempt by Wentzel van Huyssteen to identify epistemological overlaps (understood in terms of transversal rationality) between science and religion. This is an attempt that really tries to be sensitive to the different characters of scientific and religious practice.

Chapter 5

Rationality in Science, Theology, and Religion

In *The Shaping of Rationality,* Wentzel van Huyssteen addresses the question of whether "theology exhibits a rationality that is comparable to the rationality of science, overlaps with, or is informed by the rationality of science" (van Huyssteen 1999: 119). One of his key claims is that both science and religion have found their identities challenged by a new and pervasive postmodern culture. In this new postmodern world, the modernist ideas of objective truth, universal rationality, and the autonomous individual have been challenged. Van Huyssteen's objective is to take seriously this postmodern challenge to rationality while still upholding a credible form of interdisciplinary rationality, and at the same time to show why it is not the case that science finally has claimed rationality at the expense of religious faith and theological reflection. Rationality may have many faces but van Huyssteen still believes that it holds the important and only key to bridging the different domains of our lives responsibly, and that only if this is possible can theology's epistemic isolation be overcome and theology become a public voice within our secular and postmodern culture.

In developing his account of rationality van Huyssteen employs ideas that he finds in particular in the writings of Harold I. Brown, Nicholas Rescher, and Calvin O. Schrag (Brown 1988; Rescher 1988; Schrag 1992). But he also brings in some of the ideas I have developed in *Rationality in Science, Religion, and Everyday Life* (1995), while explicitly or implicitly rejecting others. I shall therefore in what follows respond to his proposals and criticism and in this way try to improve our understanding of the epistemologies of science and religion, with the overall goal in mind of understanding how to relate science and religion.

A Postfoundational Model of Rationality

In developing his "postfoundationalist" account of rationality, van Huyssteen believes that we must abandon the modernist (or classical) model of rationality. According to this model a belief is rational only if it is based on an evaluation of relevant evidence through the application of appropriate rules (van Huyssteen 1999: 120f.). The standards of rationality must be universal and necessary to function as the appropriate rules and the procedure we need for deciding when it is rational to accept a belief. The rules must be applicable in any domain or practice, or to any set of beliefs, and all rational persons must therefore arrive at the same conclusion in all areas of life. Universality is a necessary condition for rationality. Another condition is that a rationally acceptable conclusion must follow with necessity from the information given. Advocates of this model disagree about the exact content of these rules, but they all agree that rationality is essentially rule-governed. In the modernist model of rationality the emphasis is thus placed on the logical relations between evidence and the belief, while the role of the agent (the holder of the belief) is minimized (p. 146). Moreover, scientific rationality is given a privileged position (p. 29). Science is taken to be the paradigm of rationality in action. Therefore, any practice that does not exhibit a rationality that is comparable to the rationality of science is dubious, if not automatically considered as irrational.

Van Huyssteen takes modernism and thus the modernist model of rationality to be rooted in *foundationalism* since central to both of them is the quest for a secure foundation for our knowledge. Foundationalism is understood as the view that some of our beliefs are immediately justified because they are self-evident, self-justifying, or the like, whereas other beliefs are mediately justified, that is, they require evidential support from immediate beliefs by means of the appropriate rules (p. 62). Postmodernism, on the other hand, is characterized by a rejection of foundationalism and an adoption of *nonfoundationalism* or *contextualism,* which is a reaction against universalist notions of rationality which highlights the fact that every historical context, and every cultural or social group, has its own distinct rationality. The problem with this kind of nonfoundationalist or contextualist conception of rationality is, however, that it "easily leads to a relativism of rationalities, where every social or human activity could in principle function as a framework for human rationality" (p. 63).

Hence, the postfoundational model of rationality van Huyssteen sets out to defend and develop is meant to be a "middle way" between, on the one hand, foundationalism (or modernism) and, on the other, non-foundationalism (or postmodernism or, more exactly, the radical forms of it). The postfoundational model,

> *first,* fully acknowledge[s] contextuality and the embeddedness of both theology and the sciences in the different domains of human culture; *second,* affirm[s] the epistemically crucial role of interpreted experience and the way that tradition shapes the epistemic and nonepistemic values that inform our reflection about both God and the world; *third,* at the same time creatively point[s] beyond the confines of the local community, group, or culture, toward plausible forms of transcommunal and interdisciplinary conversation. (p. 9)

F. LeRon Shults characterizes an "ideal type" postfoundationalist of van Huyssteen's kind as someone who claims the following:

> (PF1): interpreted experience engenders and nourishes all beliefs, and a network of beliefs informs the interpretation of experience.
>
> (PF2): the objective unity of truth is a necessary condition for the intelligible search for knowledge, and the subjective multiplicity of knowledge indicates the fallibility of truth claims.
>
> (PF3): rational judgment is an activity of socially situated individuals, and the cultural community indeterminately mediates the criteria of rationality.
>
> (PF4): explanation aims for universal, transcontextual understanding, and understanding derives from particular contextualized explanations. (Shults 1999: 43)

What are then the key components of the postfoundational model of rationality? First of all, van Huyssteen goes along with Thomas Kuhn and in particular Harold I. Brown in maintaining that rationality is not rule-governed. Instead rationality is ultimately about making *informed* or *responsible judgments* (van Huyssteen 1999: 143). Judgment is the ability to evaluate a situation, assess evidence, and come to a reasonable decision without following rules. But only those who have adequate knowledge and training within a particular domain or practice can make informed judgments. Hence our ability to act as rational agents is limited by our expertise.

It follows that the locus of rationality cannot anymore be rational beliefs, but must be *rational persons* or *agents*. Thus, in contrast to the modernist model, where the emphasis is placed on the logical relations between the evidence and belief while the role of the agent is minimized, a postfoundational model of rationality takes rational agents to be the basic notion and rational beliefs as derivative (van Huyssteen 1999: 145; cf. Brown 1988: 184). This, van Huyssteen argues, opens up the possibility of taking our social and communal embeddedness seriously, which postmodern thinkers have strongly emphasized. Moreover, rationality requires other people: "For a belief based on judgment to be a rational one, it must be submitted to the relevant epistemic community, a community of those who share the relevant expertise" (van Huyssteen 1999: 146). Hence peer evaluation is taken to be a necessary condition for rationality.

What both the modernist and the postfoundational model of rationality have in common, however, is *evidentialism;* as we have seen, evidentialism is, roughly, the view that it is rational to accept a theory or belief only if there are good reasons (or evidence) to think that it is true. The difference is that the modernist model contains a rule-governed form of evidentialism, whereas the postfoundational model includes a judgment-based version of evidentialism (cf. Stenmark 1995, chaps. 3 and 6). Van Huyssteen's basic idea is that in evidentialism we have the unit that holds together all different human practices (including science and theology). The shared resource of rationality we all can have in common is the ability to exercise informed judgments:

> If rationality is not just a matter of having reasons for what one does, but of aligning one's beliefs, action, and evaluations with the best available reasons within specific contexts, then *all domains or levels of rationality are held together in the common or shared quest of including the best available reasons to attain the highest form of intelligibility.* This reveals a common or shared dimension of all human rationality and a way to integrate the performative presence of rationality in various

domains of our lives without again totalizing it into a modernist, rationalistic vision where different modes of knowledge are united in a seamless unity. (van Huyssteen 1999: 134, emphasis added)

Hence, even if van Huyssteen's focus is on theological rationality, his overall thesis is clear. It is that all forms of human rationality, in practices such as science, politics, religion, and so on, are (or should at least be) held together by judgment-based evidentialism. On this point there is an overlap between the epistemology of religion and the epistemology of science. Because it is (or at least should be) a matter of overlap and not unity, van Huyssteen wants us to talk about "transversal rationality" rather than universal rationality (pp. 135f.). The concept of transversal is taken from Schrag and it contains the idea of a line that intersects other lines and indicates the intersection of differing practices and modes of thought and action (Schrag 1992: 148f.). Transversality thus refers to the shared resources of rationality in our diverse assemblages of belief and practices, and locates the claims of reason in these overlaps. But what counts as good reasons in the two practices — that is, the type of data, evidence, or experiences appealed to — may vary considerably (van Huyssteen 1999: 187f.).

In sum, the core elements of a postfoundational model of rationality are these:

1. Persons and not beliefs are the locus of rationality, and therefore agents of rationality are always socially or contextually embedded.
2. Rationality is ultimately about making informed or responsible judgments and not about rule-following.
3. Persons are rational only if they have good reasons for their beliefs and can provide those reasons on request.
4. Peer evaluation is a necessary condition for rationality.
5. The shared resources of rationality are the ability and responsibility to exercise informed judgments in all areas of life (transversal rationality).

While I believe that van Huyssteen is on the right track when it comes to characterizing what rationality is about within *disciplines* like science and theology, his notion of rationality nevertheless fails as a plausible account of what human rationality in general and religious rationality in particular ought to be. The reason for this is that even if van Huyssteen tries to be sensitive to the character of religious practice, he still falls into the modernist trap of focusing too much on science. The postfoundational account of human rationality (just like, as we saw in the previous chapter, a model of rationality understood in terms of the inference to the best explanation) is too much modeled on science. As a consequence, van Huyssteen fails to take seriously something else he wants to take seriously, namely, everyday-life belief formation and regulation.

He writes, "Stenmark makes a persuasive case by arguing that, if not the 'best' we have, everyday believing . . . is in a sense a stronger paradigm case for rationality [than science] — not in the sense that it is the *best* we humans can do, but in the sense that it is the *most* we do" (van Huyssteen 1999: 155-56). As I point out, everyday beliefs are by far the largest domain of beliefs we human beings have, and everyone must be able to form, sustain, and evaluate them to be able to function appropriately in the kinds of situations one encounters every day in life. Everyday beliefs are about such things as other people, living, driving, and knowing what one's own name is, how to buy things, how to know when to trust someone, what love means, what good relations are, and so on. Because these beliefs normally account for the vast majority of the beliefs in our belief system, an adequate model of rationality must be able to make sense out of them and the processes that are used to arrive at and regulate them. It is in this way that everyday beliefs are a paradigm or control case of rationality. In fact, they are in a way more fundamental than scientific beliefs in our belief system, because we cannot avoid believing them and at the same time function appropriately as human beings (Stenmark 1995: 200f.). Hence, a postfoundational model of rationality must be able to make sense out of everyday belief formation and regulation to be an adequate model of human rationality. Is this the case?

By arguing that the locus of rationality ought to be people and neither beliefs nor propositions, van Huyssteen paves the way for a particular understanding of what rationality is, which is consonant with my suggestion that *rationality* consists of the intelligent use of our intelligence (or the proper exercise of our reason) in the situation in which we find ourselves (Stenmark 1995: 22; cf. van Huyssteen 1999: 114). Hence, we can say that *scientific rationality* consists of the intelligent use of our intelligence within the domain of science and *theological rationality* consists of the intelligent use of our intelligence within the domain of theology. If, as I have previously argued (and I shall soon return to this point as well), theology and religion are not identical, we can also say that *religious rationality* consists of the intelligent use of our intelligence within the domain of religion, and so on for any other practice we identify.

If we in this way locate rationality in a concrete kind of creature, human beings, we can easily see that what reasonably can be expected of humans when it comes to the intelligent use of their intelligence depends on their resources and situation. This means that a proper model of rationality must take into account the constitution and the actual predicament of the agent of rationality. This thesis, that a notion of rationality should be realistic, relies on the truth of what I have called the "axiom of reasonable demand." It states that one cannot reasonably demand of a person what that person cannot possibly do.[1] Human rationality is thus ultimately *a matter of seeking to do the best we can realistically manage to do in the circumstances in which we find ourselves, given our cognitive (and other relevant) resources.* Hence, the demands of rationality must be related to

(a) who we are,

(b) where we are, and

(c) what we are (or should) try to achieve (by, for instance, participating in practices such as science or religion).[2]

What does it then mean according to van Huyssteen to use our intelligence in an intelligent way? What does it more exactly mean to be rational? His answer is, as we have seen, that "being rational is . . . not just a matter of having some reasons for what one believes in and argues for, but having the *best or strongest reasons* available to support the comparative rationality of one's beliefs within a concrete sociohistorical context" (van Huyssteen 1999: 129, emphasis added). In short, we ought to be evidentialists with sensitivity for the concrete sociohistorical context in which the agents of rationality find themselves. Evidentialism is something not merely van Huyssteen but also Brown and Rescher take to be at the core of their models of rationality. Rescher writes, "All domains of rationality are . . . united by the common mission of finding 'the best reasons' . . . rationality calls for

---

1. This axiom needs to be qualified so it does not follow from it that people who, for instance, are insane or whose cognitive equipment malfunctions can be rational (see Stenmark 1995: 228f.).

2. See Stenmark (1995, chap. 8) for a detailed argumentation along these lines.

proceeding on the basis of good reasons for whatever we do" (Rescher 1988: 7 and 16). Brown maintains that "a belief that we arrive at on the basis of an adequate body of appropriate evidence is a rational belief" (Brown 1988: 185). On this point we find a crucial difference between the models of rationality that Brown, van Huyssteen, and Rescher advocate and the model of rationality I defend because the latter entails the rejection of evidentialism.

Problems with Postfoundational Rationality

What is the problem with judgment-based evidentialism and is there any good alternative? There are at least two difficulties. The first is that it entails taking skepticism as the norm for our cognitive life and the second is that it makes deliberation a necessary condition for rationality. In both of these ways, the postfoundational model of rationality does not take sufficiently into account that we are finite beings with limited cognitive resources (or intelligence) and time at our disposal.

So first, then, what does it really mean, according to evidentialists, for people to be rational in what they believe? It means that they must ask themselves what good reasons they have for every belief they have acquired through their socialization, and if they cannot come up with good reasons they ought to try to abandon these beliefs. Rational persons should, therefore, go over all beliefs and ideas they have about people in their neighborhood, about politics, economy, science, religion, cooking, traveling, their own memories, other people's testimony, and so forth and check whether they actually have good reasons for all of them. If not, they should dump them like hot potatoes. But this means that everything we believe is, so to speak, intellectually guilty until proven innocent. Rational people are therefore skeptical about everyone and everything until the opposite has been established.

I have in another context argued against evidentialism and maintained that it is not really rational *for us* — given who we are and our predicament — to be evidentialists (Stenmark 1995: chap. 8). Why? To make a long story short, the constant questioning of our beliefs, the constant search for evidence or the good reasons that evidentialism implies, is not an intelligent way for humans to govern their believing, simply because they have neither the time nor the cognitive resources needed. We are finite beings with limited cognitive resources. This entails that if *we* want to be rational beings, we cannot set aside time and resources to critically evaluate all our beliefs. Time, memory, and so on are too precious, and any waste of these resources must be avoided. Someone could, in fact, waste his or her entire lifetime searching for evidence for all kinds of beliefs. Therefore, evidentialism as a basic cognitive attitude or as a model of human rationality should be rejected.

Instead, it seems as if the most rational thing for us to do is to continue to believe what we already believe about God, life, and love until we find good reasons to believe something else. I call this model of rationality *presumptionism,* because it is based on the claim that our belief-forming processes and their deliverances (beliefs) should be presumed to be intellectually innocent until proven guilty. These processes and their deliverances do not first need to be justified (i.e., provided with good reasons) before it is rational for us to believe in them.[3] The initial attitude toward our beliefs should be one of trust, not distrust.

Presumptionism should not, however, be confused with the view that belief in God is properly basic (the view that is called "Reformed epistemology") because presumptionism is neutral in respect to the issue whether belief in God is a basic belief (that is, a belief that religious practitioners hold but not on the basis of other beliefs that they hold) or a nonbasic belief (that is, a belief that religious practitioners hold inferentially, on the evidential support of other beliefs that they hold).[4] It is not even committed to the distinction between basic and nonbasic beliefs. It is thus compatible with both foundationalism and coherentism.

The second problem with judgment-based evidentialism is that rationality understood in this way always involves *deliberation,* that is, careful exercises of thought about what to do and believe. It even seems, at least in van Huyssteen's case, to involve maximizing the role of deliberation in one's life. He writes that "to be rational we have to believe on the basis of some form of appropriate and carefully considered evidence" and that "rationality is not just a matter of having some reasons for what one does, but of aligning one's beliefs, action, and evaluations with the best

3. Similar ideas about rationality have been developed in Wolterstorff (1983), Andersson and Furberg (1986), Harman (1986), and most recently in van Inwagen (1996), Clayton and Knapp (1996), and Gellman (2000).

4. The most well-know defender of Reformed epistemology is perhaps Alvin Plantinga (see Sennett 1998).

available reasons within specific contexts" (pp. 132, 134). Rational people are those who are consciously aware (a) of the evidence for the beliefs they accept, (b) that what is taken to be evidence really is evidence for the beliefs, (c) that it is also good, even the best possible, evidence, and probably also (d) of the alternatives to one's beliefs.

Let us call this form of evidentialism "internal evidentialism" because it requires that people have been engaged in careful deliberation (making informed judgments) about what to believe and that they can provide those good reasons on request. The following statement from Max Black is a clear example of evidentialism of this kind:

> A man will be acting reasonably to the extent that he tries to form a clear view of the end to be achieved and its probable value to him, assembles the best information about available means, their probable efficacy and the price of failure, and in the light of all this chooses the course of action most strongly recommended by reason. (Black 1972: 44)

Brown thinks that internalist, judgment-based evidentialism is an appropriate model to use to evaluate and state what scientific rationality is all about. Scientists have (or ought) to carefully investigate the evidence for and against a theory before deciding consciously whether or not to accept it — though this is done without explicitly following certain rules. Van Huyssteen also believes that this is an appropriate model to use to explicate and evaluate theological rationality.

I think we should go along with them up to a certain point. Scientists are people who have been paid to think at least eight hours a day on certain problems and to develop certain theories to solve these problems. It seems reasonable to maintain that in doing this they ought to make an informal judgment, to try to base their reasoning on the best available evidence. Scientists ought to be engaged in careful deliberation about the evidence they have and its strength and possible alternatives to what they are inclined to believe, in order to be rational, that is, to use their intelligence in an intelligent way. This is a plausible model of scientific rationality.

This is also true about theologians working within the academy. They are also paid to think at least eight hours a day on certain problems and to develop certain theories to solve these problems. In Sweden philosophy of religion is located in the theological department of the universities, so I take the liberty to exemplify this view with my own work. One problem that I personally have been working on is the problem of how to understand religious rationality (and irrationality). It therefore seems quite reasonable to demand that I as a rational scholar should carefully investigate the evidence for and against a particular theory of rationality before I reject or propose it as an adequate theory to be used in understanding and evaluating religious beliefs and practices. Hence, van Huyssteen is probably right that this also is a plausible model of rationality for theology.

But let us now consider our everyday-life belief formation and regulation. Suppose, for instance, you are out driving in the countryside and see a bridge. Without thinking much about it, you drive across it and park at the nearest parking space to drink a cup of coffee. In that situation you suddenly start to think about Brown's, van Huyssteen's, and Rescher's views of rationality. It strikes you that you have in fact been irrational in what you have been doing. According to judgment-based, internal evidentialism, you should have carefully evaluated the evidence pro and con your beliefs and come to an informed judgment about whether it was safe for you to drive across that bridge. But you have done none of these things. You should even try to find out the best possible reasons for your belief. This could perhaps mean that the rational procedure would be, before crossing the bridge, to get out of one's car and examine closely the bridge and if one is not an expert in the field to contact those who are experts, because if one lacks the relevant expertise the rational thing to do according to this understanding of rationality is to seek expert advice.

When you come to think about it, you start wondering about your other beliefs: "What about the car I am driving? — have I carefully considered the reasons I have to believe it to be reliable?" You go deeper still and ask yourself, "What reasons do I have to rely on my own perception and memory?" In other words, you start to realize that if you follow this kind of model of rationality you would probably not be able to do as many things in life as you thought you could do because you do not have the cognitive resources needed or the time to assess the evidence in respect to the beliefs you have formed in life. This example, I suggest, clearly shows why people in general — philosophers, theologians, or scientists — cannot estimate the strength of various arguments for or against everything they do, not even all the important things. They do not and they ought not do this, simply because they do not have the time or cognitive resources needed.

My point, however, is that your conclusion should not be that you are behaving irrationally, but that this kind of model of human rationality ought not be accepted, because it violates the axiom of reasonable demand. In fact, we enter a paradoxical situation: realizing our limited cognitive resources and the limited time at our disposal as well as our needs and interests, we become aware that it is not rational for rational people to try to satisfy the demands of judgment-based evidentialism.

Let me push this point a little further. I read somewhere that we form around 50,000 thoughts a day about the things we experience, that is, beliefs about the weather, people we meet, and what we eat, beliefs about cars, bicycles, trees, houses, news, commercials, and so on. Suppose that this is true. Now, if we take the postfoundational rationality as a model for human rationality in general, this implies that on all these matters we ought to make informed judgments. We ought to be aware of the evidence we have for our 50,000 everyday thoughts or beliefs and form judgments about whether this is good evidence. In fact, we should strive to find the best available evidence for them. Furthermore, we must be ready to demonstrate to others the reasonableness of our thinking, choices, and actions. If we do so we are behaving rationally and we are using our intelligence in an intelligent way. But notice that if we do this the number of beliefs we have to process every day drastically increases; suddenly we have to handle, say, 150,000 beliefs, and perhaps we are starting to have second thoughts about some of these justifying beliefs, but then we suddenly may have to process 200,000 beliefs. The risk we run is of becoming epistemically paralyzed. We therefore have to use our limited time and cognitive resources more wisely.

Let me clarify my view on these issues. In *Rationality in Science, Religion, and Everyday Life* I gave another example similar to the one about the bridge. I wrote that sometimes when I drive I think about the people driving the cars I meet on the road. Often we pass each other at a speed of, say, 110 km/h, and there is, perhaps, 2 meters between the cars, sometimes less. Do I have good or sufficient reasons for trusting the drivers I meet to a degree that it is reasonable or rational for me to drive on the road? Certainly not. I do not know anything about them except that they are driving the cars I pass and perhaps what kind of car they are driving (Stenmark 1995: 211). In correspondence, Brown responded to this by maintaining that we in this case have more evidence than I suggest because during our lives we accumulate evidence for believing that people stay on the correct side of the road. So my belief is not without a basis in the evidence. I am not, however, denying this (and on this point I was not as clear as I would have liked to be in my previous writings). What I deny is that (a) in general people in this kind of situation have sufficient evidence to satisfy the evidentialist account (remember that judgment-based evidentialism is modeled on scientific investigation and evaluation of evidence), and that (b) to be rational people have to engage in careful deliberation about what evidence they have and its strength and other possible alternatives to what they are inclined to believe in cases such as this one.

What I pointed out in my reply was that in Brown's response, the gathering of evidence is assumed to be an unconscious and nondeliberating process. He writes, "I think that we regularly evaluate evidence without explicitly formulating data statements and applying formal rules — and that this ability is built into our biology." But this is a different form of evidentialism than the judgment-based, internal evidentialism he argues for in *Rationality* (1988).[5] This is a species of *external evidentialism* because it merely assumes that reasons can (and ought to) be operative in what we do and believe without being explicitly called to mind.

It is clearly so that external evidentialism is much more economical than internal evidentialism and that it does not waste as much of our limited cognitive resources. Brown, in fact, thinks that external evidentialism is built into our biology. He is probably right. This is compatible, however, with the basic idea behind presumptionism, namely, that we ought to trust our cognitive faculties and their deliverances unless experience provides us with substantial grounds for questioning those beliefs. The presumptionist says that we have a right to take all things that we find ourselves believing at face value unless we believe (or ought to believe) we have a special reason not to do so. Responsiveness to counter-evidence is thus central to this account of rationality. If people lose the capacity to respond appropriately to reasons against their favorite beliefs, they become irrational or dogmatic. So we ought to trust our biological belief-forming processes and what they automatically deliver. We do not have to start asking what evidence we have for everything we believe (that is, make informed judgments) and submit it to peer evaluation to be rationally entitled to believe

5. This is something that Brown admits. In one of the letters to me, he writes, "The view that I proposed in *Rationality* does, as you note, require explicit deliberation and I argue that the ability to exercise judgment kicks in only in the context of such deliberation. As a result, you are right in pointing out that my remarks about our biologically based, unconscious evidence assessing processes do seem to support the opposite of the point I wanted to make."

what we believe. Thus I suggest that presumptionism ought to be the rule in human life and judgment-based evidentialism the exception.

Let me try to avoid some confusion that might arise at this point. In trying to give reasons for the acceptance of presumptionism it may sound as if I am an evidentialist after all and not a presumptionist. In arguing *for* presumptionism I must be an evidentialist! Hence my position seems to be self-referentially incoherent. We can see that that is not the case, however, if we notice the difference between questions of *rationality* and questions of *justification.* The basic idea behind the distinction is that it is one thing for me to be rationally entitled to believe what I believe, quite another thing to be able to convince other people that they should believe the very same thing as I do. Roughly, rationality has to do with when a person (or a group of persons) is entitled to believe what he or she believes. Justification, on the other hand, has to do with when a person (or a group of persons) has provided sufficient grounds for a belief to render it generally acceptable. What I am trying to do is to convince the readers that they should accept the principle of presumption. Thus, I am writing in the context of justification about issues of rationality. In other words, nothing stops me from being an evidentialist in questions of justification and a presumptionist in questions of rationality. This distinction is further elaborated on pages 101-2.

The point about presumptionism being compatible with external evidentialism is important because advocates of postfoundational rationality refer to our pre-analytic concept of rationality as a reason why we should accept internal evidentialism. Brown writes, "perhaps the central idea included in our preanalytic concept of rationality is that we have reasons for our rational beliefs and can provide those on request" (Brown 1988: 183), while van Huyssteen says that "even on an everyday, preanalytic level, our judgments and beliefs are regarded as rational if we can appeal to good reasons for having them, and if we can provide those reasons on request" (van Huyssteen 1999: 132). Moreover, Shults maintains, "it is important [in epistemology] to capture our pre-analytic intuition that being rational includes having good reasons as a basis for our beliefs" (Shults 1999: 30). But all we take for granted in everyday life is that a rational person's beliefs are not completely groundless, simply taken out of the blue. We presuppose that they are the result of properly functioning biological belief-forming processes. But these processes do not (and more importantly should not, I have argued) necessarily involve careful deliberation and the capacity to provide good reasons on request. Rather, rational persons — who are finite beings with limited cognitive resources and time at their disposal — initially trust the deliverance of their cognitive faculties and what the latter automatically deliver unless there are good reasons to question those deliverances.

Moreover, I am inclined to advocate presumptionism both when it comes to actual belief-forming (first-order issues) and when it comes to thinking about *belief policies*, that is, the deliberation about the amount of effort and the means one should use when evaluating one's beliefs (second-order issues).[6]

When it comes to first-order issues my claim has been that in general we are rational in accepting the beliefs that our biological belief-forming processes automatically deliver, unless experience provides us with good reason not to do so. We do not have to start asking what evidence we have for these beliefs, submit them to peer evaluation, and so on. Deliberation is not a necessary condition for rationality. We can always start thinking about our belief policies, however, about ways of improving our cognitive performance. But in doing so we still have to use the same limited fund of cognitive resources and time at our disposal as when we are dealing with first-order issues. Thus, there is always a trade-off between, at least, three things:

(a) forming beliefs (or making decisions),
(b) evaluating one's beliefs (or decisions), and
(c) evaluating the belief (or decision) policies one uses in evaluating one's particular beliefs (or decisions).

Should we demand good reasons for the acceptance of a belief policy before it is rational to adopt it, as evidentialism seems to imply? I think the answer is no. Instead we are rationally entitled to use the belief policies we happen to have (for biological and social reasons), unless experience provides us with good reason not to do so. We should accept presumptionism also at this meta-level.

Take my son Jacob as our example. (He was five years old when I wrote this paragraph for the first time in a letter to Brown.) One of his belief policies is to ask his father about pretty much everything. On a presumptionist account he is rational in accepting both this belief policy and the particular beliefs that this policy delivers unless experience pro-

6. The notion of "belief policy" is developed in Helm (1994).

vides him with good reason not to do so. He does not have to consciously evaluate either of these two things to be rational in his cognitive performance. Jacob might even be rational in believing everything adult people tell him. This is an expanded version of the belief policy of asking your daddy! As he grows older counter-evidence against these belief-forming policies will arise. He will notice that sometimes there are inconsistencies between what other people and I say, and so forth. To stay rational he must then change or modify his original belief-forming policy. Jacob will also notice (pretty fast!) the limit of my knowledge and realize that if he wants to know these things he must find other ways to obtain information about them. In school and perhaps by asking other people and me, he will become aware of other sources of information: books, libraries, the web, and so on. Again he will notice inconsistencies between these sources of information and start to distinguish between more or less reliable sources.

In school Jacob will (I hope) learn the scientific belief policy, that is, judgment-based evidentialism. He will learn that scientists (ought to) actively collect adequate evidence for and against their theories, then estimate the combined strength of the evidence and submit these theories and the evidence to peer evaluation. And if he is rational, that is, taking into account all the inconsistencies of information he has experienced, he will understand that this is a good belief policy to use. He will not always use the scientific belief policy, however (it is probably more than one, actually), when forming and regulating his beliefs. The reason for this is sometimes simply that he is lazy or that he feels that the result would go against what he wants to believe — in both of these cases we can say that he is irrational. But the presumptionist idea is that at other times Jacob will not and more importantly should not use the scientific belief policy because it spends too much of his limited cognitive resources and is too time consuming. In other words, he will (I hope) realize without perhaps knowing it consciously that the scientific belief policy is merely a *local* belief policy, that is, a policy that beings like us can use only to a limited extent. To use it as a *global* belief policy would just leave him epistemologically paralyzed.

Scientific and Theological Rationality Reconsidered

My conclusion is that van Huyssteen's postfoundational model of rationality is still too much based on the sciences to apply to human life in general.

It does not work as general model. I have, nevertheless, suggested that it is useful as a local model of scientific and theological rationality. Let us now consider this issue in more detail.

As I pointed out, both scientists and theologians are people who have been paid to think eight hours a day on certain problems and to develop certain hypotheses to solve these problems. In doing this it seems reasonable to assume, as van Huyssteen does, that scientists and theologians, even though they have limited cognitive resources, still have the time to try to make informal judgments and to base their reasoning on the best available evidence. So it seems reasonable to assume that *deliberation* (that is, careful exercise of thought about what to believe and do) is a necessary condition not only for scientific rationality but also for theological rationality. Scientists as well as theologians ought to be engaged in careful deliberation about the evidence they have and its strength and about other possible alternatives to what they are inclined as scholars to believe to be rational. Here we have an overlap between science and theology, even though the evidence they consider may be of a different sort.

Nevertheless, we can have too idealized a picture not only of everyday belief formation and regulation: our picture of scientific belief formation and regulation can also be too idealized. The fact that we are finite beings with limited cognitive resources and time at our disposal applies even when doing science and theology. Also within these specific areas of human life every application of our cognitive resources has a certain cost. I therefore maintain that it is not really rational even for scientists and theologians to carefully check all the theories and methods in their field because if they were to try to do such a thing they would probably never get anywhere in their own research. For these reasons authority and trust play, as I pointed out in chapter 2, an important role in scientific practice (see p. 19). As a scientist one has to rely on the work of other scientists. Scientists do not have the time to clutter their heads with details of other scientists' subspecialties. Instead they learn to identify who the experts are in the field, and when they need information they go to people who are regarded as authoritative by the scientific community with respect to the question involved. So without trust in others, an individual scientist would neither be able to pursue his or her projects rapidly nor be capable of developing projects that are impossible for a single individual to accomplish.

Judgment-based evidentialists are to some extent sensitive to this since they realize that our ability to be rational (to make informed judgments) is limited by our expertise and that therefore in cases where we lack it, we can still be rational if we seek expert advice (van Huyssteen 1999: 146; cf. Brown 1988: 185). But it is nevertheless somewhat misleading to write, for instance, that "rationality . . . requires serious assessment of good reasons and available evidence" or that "being rational is . . . not just a matter of having some reasons for what one believes in and argues for, but having the best or strongest reasons available . . . within a concrete sociohistorical context" (van Huyssteen 1999: 161, 129). This is so because not even scientists within their own profession are actually able to meet this kind of evidential requirement. Scientists do not even have the cognitive resources for rechecking the scientific information that is already a part of their own memories. They are not able to trace the justification of these beliefs. This applies to all scholars. Many of us believe certain things to be true or false, plausible or implausible, in our particular field. But on reflection we realize that we cannot retrace the original source of these beliefs by using our memory or notes we have made on papers or files in our computers or elsewhere. I as a philosopher of religion hold a number of beliefs about ideas of revelation, religious diversity, metaphors, biblical scholarship, Christianity, Buddhism, Islam, and so on. But I am not able to state explicitly the evidence I have for holding all of these beliefs, even less show that this is really good evidence. Even if I were able to provide this I would maintain that I am not ready to invest that kind of time and cognitive resources on these issues, because I want to keep those resources for the things that really matter to me, for instance, my own research projects. Perhaps there was a time when I made an informed judgment about these issues; I have now just forgotten the grounds for this judgment. I do not wish to deny this possibility, but it is just as likely that I, after reading all the books and articles I have read, merely find myself believing these things without having gotten involved in any process of deliberation.

Although the details in the story would be different, I suggest that we would reach the same conclusion if our agent of rationality was an evolutionary biologist, a neuroscientist, or an anthropologist. Where does this leave us? What does rationality in science and theology amount to? The key is to understand that both science and theology are practices in which many people cooperate and in which we therefore can find a division of labor. For the practitioners (the agents of rationality) of these practices this means that the requirement of informed judgments typically kicks in when they develop their own theories and do their own research. As I pointed out earlier, it seems quite reasonable to demand that I as a scholar should carefully investigate the evidence for and against a particular model of rationality before I reject or propose it as an adequate model to be used in understanding and evaluating religious practice. So the rational thing to do for scientists and theologians is probably to limit one's deliberation to the theories one is working on and perhaps to those issues one is asked to participate in as an expert adviser. But other than that, the rational thing to do is to fall back on the more global presumptivist belief policy of questioning the scientific or theological theories one accepts only if there are good reasons to do so. If counter-evidence in the form of incompatible data or new theories emerges, then rational scholars get involved in a process of deliberation and critical assessment.

But what about the idea that peer evaluation is a necessary condition for scientific and theological rationality? Let us call this the "social requirement of rationality." As we have seen, van Huyssteen writes that "for a belief based on judgment to be a rational one, it must be submitted to the relevant epistemic community, a community of those who share the relevant expertise" (van Huyssteen 1999: 146). Moreover, "rationality . . . involves this capacity to give an account, to provide a rationale for what we believe, do or choose, and as such has an inescapable rhetorical dimension: through our persuasive discourse and action we try to demonstrate to *others* the reasonableness of our thinking, judgments, choices, values, and actions" (van Huyssteen 1999: 132; cf. Brown 1988: 187). The thesis is that people's actual belief formation and regulation processes are rationally governed only if what they deliver (beliefs) is (a) arrived at by an exercise of informed judgment and (b) exposed to peer evaluation.

But applied to everyday-life belief regulation the social requirement is unreasonable because we would again waste far too much of our limited time and limited cognitive resources. Must I test or submit every one of my beliefs in order to be rationally entitled to accept them? What about my belief that I now have a mild pain in my left knee, or that Anna loves me, or that the train leaves in ten minutes: do I have to ask other people their opinion before I am rationally justified in believing these things? Hardly. Moreover, the social requirement seems to have some problematic implications. Suppose, for instance, I am out traveling. As long as I meet and submit my beliefs to people I encounter I can be rational in what I believe, but as soon as I travel through nonpopulated areas I suddenly cannot be rational any longer. This is highly problematic. What I think van Huyssteen really has in mind is scientific and theological rationality. He would therefore probably admit that the scope of the social requirement is limited to these kinds of practices. I would, however, want to point out that it is problematic to apply without restrictions the social requirement even in this context.

First of all, the social requirement does not make sense in those cases in which it is unnecessary for theologians and scientists to make informed judgments in order to be rational in their belief regulation. If it takes too many cognitive resources and is too time consuming for scientists and theologians to engage in careful deliberation about the evidence they have for all the things they believe within the framework of their profession, then we can hardly demand that they must submit all of these beliefs to their colleagues in order to be rationally entitled to continue to believe what they believe. But what about their own research? I have maintained that when it comes to scientists' own theory construction, making informed judgment is a necessary condition of scientific and theological rationality. But is also peer evaluation a necessary condition? To see the problem, consider the following question: *is it rational for a scientist to believe her theory to be true even if she has not submitted it to peer evaluation?* To deny this would in my view be unduly harsh. It would mean that rationality within the scientific practice would be restricted to the context of justification and leave out the whole context of discovery. This actually goes against, I think, both Brown's and van Huyssteen's intentions. For instance, one of Brown's arguments for why we should prefer judgment-based evidentialism is that it makes more sense out of what is going on in the context of discovery than does rule-governed evidentialism (see Brown 1988: 30f., 142f.). I suggest that the best way out is to make a distinction either between subjective and objective rationality or, as I prefer, between rationality and justification.[7]

On this point we have to fall back on the question of what academic disciplines like theology and the sciences are all about. One of the aims of academic work is to produce knowledge or justified beliefs. This is (or at least should be) a collective epistemic goal that all academic disciplines share, although the methods used and the data appealed to might be of a very different sort (see again pp. 42-43). Once one accepts the role of an academic theologian or a scientist, it follows that one thereby consents to this

---

7. Van Huyssteen hints at this possibility when he makes a distinction between rationality and scientific objectivity (van Huyssteen 1999: 160).

collective epistemic goal. Scholars therefore have an obligation not only to make their theories accessible to other scholars (to avoid duplication of work), but to try to justify them, that is, to try to convince other scholars that their own theory better fits the evidence than rival theories in the field do. In other words, we must distinguish between:

(a) the question of scholars being rationally entitled to believe that their own theory is true or that it is better or more promising than the others in the field (the *question of academic rationality*); and

(b) the question of whether scholars have succeeded in justifying their own theory, that is, given an account that should convince their colleagues that they also ought to accept this theory (the *question of academic justification*).

Scientists and theologians have an obligation — given the epistemic goal of the academy — to get involved in a process of justification (or peer evaluation) and this is typically done by presenting one's research in academic journals and at scientific conferences. But scientists and theologians need not convince their colleagues that they are wrong in order to be rationally entitled to accept their own theories. This point holds more generally. We do not have to convince other people to accept our beliefs in order to be rationally entitled to them ourselves; at most we need to convince other people that we ourselves are rationally entitled to them — whether they are equally rational in holding those (that is, my) beliefs is another question. I therefore suggest that scholars' exercise of informed judgment is necessary for satisfying the demands of academic rationality, whereas this kind of exercise together with the social requirement (that is, peer evaluation) is necessary for obtaining academic justification.[8]

One of van Huyssteen's important insights is that the obligation of justification applies more widely than merely to one's own discipline or related subdisciplines. He writes that as a scholar one has an "obligation to reach beyond one's own immediate context in interdisciplinary conversation and deliberation" (van Huyssteen 1999: 174). What should unite all academic disciplines is the quest for intelligibility — our never-ending quest for optimal understanding (p. 115). We therefore need to relate and inte-

8. I actually argue in *Rationality in Science, Religion, and Everyday Life* (1995: 216-25) for a threefold distinction between rationality, justification, and knowledge.

grate the theories developed within our different disciplines and avoid a fragmentation of knowledge. As scientists and theologians we therefore cannot ignore our responsibility to become engaged in interdisciplinary conversation and assessment. What must be avoided in this dialogue are scientism (the view that the only way to establish this kind of unified perspective on reality would be in terms of the methods developed in the natural sciences) and the relativism of radical postmodernism or contextualism. Thus, the collective epistemic goal of the academy makes it necessary for scientists and theologians not only to present their theories to each other but to become engaged in a process of cross-disciplinary justification in which "shared resources of rationality" and the "overlap of beliefs and reasoning strategies" provide means "to step beyond the limitations and boundaries of our own local, disciplinary contexts" (p. 108).

Religious Rationality

We have seen that the postfoundational model of rationality (that is, judgment-based, internal evidentialism) should not be applied to everyday-life belief regulation and that it captures to a limited extent what scientific and theological rationality is all about. Now I want to address the issue of what it means to be rational (and irrational) in participating in religious practice, and I shall maintain that religious rationality resembles everyday-life rationality more than it does scientific rationality or theological rationality.

Science and theology, as I have pointed out, are academic disciplines. To be able to participate in practices of this sort requires a special training and a much higher degree of cognitive competence than is required for taking part in religion. No special cognitive competence at all is actually required to become a practitioner of some religions. To become a Christian, for instance, is taken to be an act of faith alone. So science and theology are theoretical or intellectual enterprises for the cognitively well trained, whereas religion is a practice in which anyone can, if they like, participate. In science, in contrast to religion, we therefore have nothing similar to ordinary religious believers, and merely a small subset of religious people are theologians. Therefore, it is better when evaluating what epistemic norms or standards of rationality should govern religious practice to compare religion with everyday living than to compare it with science.

For this reason presumptionism is to be preferred over judgment-based evidentialism in evaluating rationality in religion. Suppose, for instance, a group of religious believers hold that God is personal. According to presumptionism, they are rationally entitled to continue to believe what they believe as long as there is no special reason for them to do otherwise (call this the "principle of presumption"). To provide these people with a reason to abandon their personal conception of God, you have then to say something which (given they understand it) should persuade them that they can no longer rationally continue to believe what they believe or at least continue to believe it as firmly as before. Traditionally Christian believers have also held that God created human beings by a special act of creation, by taking up clay from the ground and forming creatures, including humans, out of it (Gen. 2). The sciences have shown, however, that this is probably not how life (human life included) came into existence. Instead they have given us powerful reasons to believe that life on earth came into existence through the gradual process of evolution from a primitive soup of matter by means of heritable variation in fitness. Hence, there exist good reasons for traditional believers to reconsider what they believe. How should they then revise the content of their faith? Obviously they need to modify their faith in such a way that it becomes compatible with evolutionary theory. But that could be done in a great number of ways. If they want to respond in a responsible and rational way, how should they think?

Suppose I believe that Peter is honest, but I discover that on one occasion he has told me a lie. Should I in such a situation believe that Peter is a dishonest person or should I revise my previous belief by formulating it more cautiously, so that I now believe that Peter is in general an honest person but that he sometimes lies? It seems to me that the more rational way of revising one's beliefs is the latter. Hence, if there is reason to change what we believe, then we should not revise our original beliefs more than is necessary. I suggest that we should accept not only the principle of presumption as a part of our model of rationality but also the "cautious principle of belief revision." The principle says, roughly, that *when revising something we already believe we should pick, among those alternatives that are available to us, the one that is nearest to our original conviction.*

I therefore suggest that traditional believers ought to interpret the Genesis account of the Creator's breathing of life into the dust of the earth to mean that God relied on the natural processes of the created world to form the first human beings and all other forms of life. But they are not rationally required to stop believing in God or in a personal God or anything similar because the evidence in this case does not require such a radical revision, and we should not, according to the cautious principle of belief revision, make more or bigger changes in our belief systems than is necessary. Gordon D. Kaufman, for instance, is not satisfied with this change of traditional believers' faith because he thinks that the acceptance of cosmic and biological evolution also requires that they abandon their conception of God as personal (Kaufman 2001: 401f.). If Kaufman is correct about this, he must offer good reasons why traditional believers should not merely revise what they believe (in accordance with the principle of presumption). He also needs to show that the alternative belief he proposes they adopt instead does not require a more radical revision of their faith than what is necessary or warranted by the evidence (in accordance with the cautious principle of belief revision). We shall assess Kaufman's argument in chapter 7; the point here is simply to exemplify and elaborate presumptionism a bit further.

Hence, I suggest that religious rationality should be explicated in terms of the principle of presumption and the cautious principle of belief revision. At least one more principle is of importance in understanding and evaluating religious rationality. The background to this principle is that everything we believe does not concern us to the same degree. Some of the things we believe are more peripheral than others, in that they do not to the same extent influence the constitution and coherence of the rest of what we believe. (Let us call everything we believe about reality our "belief-world" [cf. Jeffner 1981].) We can give them up without much happening. We could say that different things have a different "depth of concern." I believe that the name of Jacob's teacher is Anne, but if it turns out that that is wrong it does not matter all that much to my belief-world in general. If, however, it turned out that Elon and Alice are not my parents, as I believe, then this would have profound consequences. Suppose now that a Christian really believes that Jesus has died and been resurrected for her sake so that her sins could be forgiven and she could come into a right relationship with God, or suppose that a Muslim really believes that Mohammed is the prophet of God, who has mediated God's infallible revelation to us through the *Qur'an*. Presume now that these religious beliefs are undermined because both of them realize that there are certain reasons to doubt that what they believe is true. These changes would have profound consequences for their belief-world. It is, therefore, reasonable that these persons require stronger reasons for giving up these beliefs than they would for something which has less depth of concern in their belief-world. I suggest that for this reason we should accept the "principle of concern." The principle says, roughly, that *we should require stronger reasons for giving up something we believe which has greater depth of concern in our belief-world than for giving up something which plays a more peripheral role.*

Having said that, I nevertheless realize that a central problem when it comes to religious matters is that quite frequently religious practitioners adopt a dogmatic attitude toward what other people believe. We could say that one has a dogmatic attitude if one reasons and acts in such a way that it excludes the possibility that one could be wrong and somebody else right about a particular state of affairs. That is to say, one behaves in such a way that one shows that nothing whatsoever could count against one's religious (or moral, political, and so on) convictions. This "no-matter-what-happens-mentality" bothers philosophers and theologians. How should this problem be handled within the epistemology of religion?

Notice first that we hold some of our beliefs much more firmly than others. I am more convinced that my father was born and raised in Gränsgård than that he moved to Vännesby in 1949. I am more convinced that people have an intrinsic value than that animals have it. In a similar way, one can believe with greater firmness that God exists than that the Bible or the *Qur'an* is the infallible word of God, or believe with greater firmness that God is love than that God is omnipotent. Hence, we can talk about different degrees of conviction or strengths of belief. I suggest that we accept the idea that everything we believe can be placed on a scale where one extreme consists of those beliefs we hold with maximum conviction or strength and the other consists of those beliefs we hold with minimum conviction or strength.

Suppose now that everyone in my neighborhood shares a certain belief with me, for instance, that Uppsala is situated in Sweden or that it is now winter. In such a situation it must not even be permitted to think that one could be wrong; one must take what one believes as obviously and unquestionably true. But I maintain that a rational person's conviction about what he or she believes to be true ought to be affected in such a way that its strength decreases to some extent if many other apparently reasonable and honest people happen to believe something quite different. Suppose that I believe a certain thing about my grandmother, but when I talk about it with my parents and my sister it turns out that they do not share my view.

Or suppose that I in conversation with my colleagues express some of my political ideas, but it turns out that many of them have a very different opinion. In both cases it would be peculiar if I did not let this difference of beliefs affect my believing, at least in the sense that I realize that what I believe is not obviously or unquestionably true. The same, I believe, holds true for religious practitioners.

I therefore suggest that we should add a "strength-of-belief-principle" to our model of religious rationality.[9] It could be stated roughly as follows: *in a situation where I meet many other apparently reasonable and honest people who happen to believe something other than I do, this should affect the strength with which I hold onto my belief at least in such a way that I realize that there is a real chance that I actually could be wrong.* Therefore there exists no reason to ignore or show disrespect for what other people say and do. (A strength-of-belief-principle regulates the firmness with which we hold onto our beliefs, unlike the principle of presumption, which regulates the circumstances under which we are entitled to believe something.)

But why, then, do so many religious people often dogmatically accept their religious beliefs? Can we find some kind of explanation? I think that the nature of the intentional object of religious faith can give us a clue to why this is so. If the intentional object of religious faith is typically thought to be the most perfect possible reality (it is so great that we can conceive of nothing greater), then it is no surprise that religious people in experiencing this reality would be so overwhelmed by it that even the thought that this reality might not be real appears to be unthinkable. In fact this is what many religious believers report. Augustine says, "far off, I heard your voice saying *I am the God who IS*... and at once I had no cause to doubt. I might more easily have doubted that I was alive than that Truth had being" (Augustine, *Confessions* 7.10). Mahatma Gandhi reports, "Often in my progress I have had faint glimpses of the Absolute Truth, God, and daily the conviction is growing upon me that He alone is real and all else is unreal." Merold Westphal maintains that religious experiences of this sort "are based on a sense of the presence of something that is more real than myself and the world of my immediate experience. I become what is relative,

---

9. In fact, I believe this principle ought to be a proper part of any general model of human rationality, although it is of special relevance in respect to religious matters because of the widespread tendency of dogmatic thinking in that domain of human life.

and in relation to this something I find myself to be suddenly doubtful, less real and not definitely there."[10] Westphal characterizes these phenomena as experiences of "ontological inadequacy."

Could it then be rational to hold one's religion or belief in God in a dogmatic way? Although it will perhaps surprise some, I would like to give an affirmative answer to this question. But the answer depends on what kind of cultural situation the believer finds herself in. Suppose the believer lives in a purely monocentric culture, that is, a culture in which there is almost no knowledge of or acquaintance with other religions or worldviews. In such a cultural setting, where nobody or almost nobody has thought that these things could have been different, it could be rational to believe that it is unthinkable that one's own religious faith could be wrong. In such a situation it could be defensible not to take criticism of one's religion seriously and to adopt a dogmatic attitude. As I have hinted, I do not think that this is confined to religious matters. Some philosophers, for instance, question whether there is a world or reality that exists independent of us. They doubt that the world would still be there if we ceased to exist. Suppose that an "ordinary" person who takes the existence of an external world for granted and has never ever even thought about the matter comes in contact with these philosophical ideas, but merely shakes his or her shoulders and categorically rejects these ideas as weird and incomprehensible. The person is, in other words, not open to criticism of the idea that there exists a human-independent reality. Why could it be rational to proceed in this way?

The reason is that we have to take into account what is typically believed and questioned in the culture we investigate, in other words, its social plausibility structure, when we determine what it is rational to believe or disbelieve. If nobody or almost nobody in a particular cultural setting questions a certain set of beliefs then it should be intellectually permitted for human beings to not consider, at least initially, the reasons that are presented against these commonly and also personally accepted beliefs. It seems unduly harsh to assert that these people violate the requirements of rationality, in particular if we take into account their limited cognitive resources, the limited time at their disposal, and the other tasks they face every day as a properly functioning human being.

10. Westphal (1984: 27-28). The quotation from Gandhi is also taken from these pages.

This, however, would mean that this kind of epistemic situation ends as soon as these people meet and start to interact with other people with a different set of beliefs or religion. All that is needed for them to be irrational in how they conduct their cognitive affairs is frequent contact with people with other religious, political, or philosophical ideas. In such a situation they should start thinking about and taking into account that one actually could believe something different and that it is possible that one could be wrong. In other words, a pluralistic cultural situation makes a dogmatic attitude irrational.

So even if the nature of the intentional object of much religious faith helps us understand why a tendency to dogmatic thinking exists in many religions and the principle of concern allows rational people to require stronger reasons to give up their central religious beliefs, the strength-of-belief-principle nevertheless shows the irrationality of adopting a dogmatic attitude. According to this principle, having a rational attitude implies that when we discover that other apparently reasonable and honest people do not share our most central religious convictions, we make ourselves aware of the possibility that we could be wrong. Hence, we should keep in mind that it is not unquestionable that we are right and that therefore it is not completely obvious that others are wrong.

This does not mean that I suggest that religious practitioners must necessarily only *tentatively* affirm what they believe as soon they find themselves in a situation where other people disagree with them. We could say that a belief is *tentatively* accepted when one thinks there is a need to investigate it further, but one is willing to use it as a starting-point (a working hypothesis) for something one is doing because one thinks it is possibly true. (This further inquiry might be carried out in different ways — for instance, by actively looking for counter-evidence of one view, or by actively searching for evidence of it, or both.) The strength-of-belief-principle is compatible with *full* acceptance, that is, one thinks what one believes is true and that there is no need to investigate those beliefs further, or no need in this way to doubt its credibility.[11] Hence, we should not

11. I actually think that full acceptance of belief must typically be the stance we adopt toward our beliefs because the cognitive cost of tentative acceptance is much higher than that of full acceptance of beliefs, and this is probably the reason why people normally tend to accept what they believe fully rather than tentatively. The reason is that it takes a certain degree of sophistication and training to be able to investigate an issue by only tentatively accepting various beliefs. This is so because when one only tentatively accepts something one

think that the strength-of-belief-principle entails tentative acceptance, nor confuse full acceptance and dogmatic acceptance. Even if one thinks, at present, that continuing reflection on the truth of a belief is unnecessary, that does not mean that the belief cannot be revised or rejected. Full acceptance is compatible with openness to criticism. Hence, there is a crucial difference between full acceptance and dogmatic acceptance.

But does the strength-of-belief-principle, as I have defined it, really make any significant difference? I do not intend to deny that more could and should be said about religion and dogmatic thinking, but to see the relevance consider the following scenario. Suppose I am out walking in the street and meet a person who prevents me from going any further. The reason he offers is that just behind him is an invisible abyss. I shake my head and keep walking. If he tries to stop me, I first tell him to move out of the way, and if that does not work I perhaps simply push him aside so that I can keep on walking. What I maintain is that my way of treating this man is strongly affected by the fact that I can hardly imagine that I am wrong and he is right. This assumption justifies my way of treating him. In other words, we have a justified tendency to ignore fools and sometimes even take the liberty to lock them up. We also often assume that we know better than they what is in their interest, and do so even in cases when they object. My suggestion is now that it is likely that in the religious case things are similar. The way religious practitioners treat other people and what they believe is strongly influenced by whether they assume that it is almost totally out of question that these other people could be right and that they could be wrong. But the strength-of-belief-principle I propose blocks the possibility in a pluralistic culture of treating other people of other faiths or secular people as "fools" or as "not quite right in the head" (even if one does not say this) or something similar, which would have justified the view that one does not need to fully respect those people and what they believe. At least in this way there is a

---

needs to keep in mind which tentatively accepted claims depend on others. One must try to remember what evidence there is for or against various possible outcomes of the issue. Until the investigation is completed, one needs to keep a record of justifiers for various possible conclusions, possible defeaters of the justifiers, defeaters of those defeaters, and so on. So if we take into account the fact that we have limited cognitive resources there is nothing irrational or strange in finding it difficult in general to accept things only tentatively, and we quickly convert this type of acceptance of various beliefs into full acceptance. It is a matter of cognitive economy to adjust how one believes to one's resources.

connection between a theoretical rationality (what is rational to believe?) and practical rationality (what is rational to do?).

Of course, more than this needs to be said about religious rationality (and irrationality), but in this context I would like to add just one more component, which is especially important to keep in mind in a science-religion dialogue. Boldly stated, my claim is that religious rationality is a different species of rationality than both scientific and theological rationality. It is a kind of "agent-rationality," whereas rationality in science and theology is a kind of "spectator-rationality" (these forms of rationality are defined below).

A temptation for scientists is to treat the issue of religious rationality as a purely theoretical matter. The risk is that they will discuss the matter as if taking a stand on religious issues is not much different from making up one's mind about scientific issues. Thus Dawkins, as we have seen, tells us, "I pay religions the compliment of regarding them as scientific theories and . . . I see God as a competing explanation for facts about the universe and life" (Dawkins 1995b: 46-47). On the basis of these assumptions he discusses the rationality of religion. Peter Atkins talks about the different "styles for theistic and scientific explanations," about what science can explain and what religion cannot explain, and even about the "omnicompetence of science" and comes to the conclusion that contemporary religious believers are irrational, uninformed, and weak-minded (Atkins 1995: 124, 132). Richard Swinburne, on the other hand, draws exactly the opposite conclusion. He writes that the fact that "there is a God explains everything we observe, not just some narrow range of data" (Swinburne 1996: 2).

At least two problematic assumptions are often made in these kinds of reasoning about religion and rationality. First, what is presupposed is that a "rationally acceptable religious belief" is, essentially, a belief that is justified with respect to its truth-promoting function and explanatory scope. Since, however, the relevant goal of religious practice is then taken to be merely epistemic, the "religious believer" whose beliefs are examined in fact turns out to be a purely epistemic being (a being whose sole concern is believing as many truths and as few falsehoods as possible). But the problem is that actual religious believers — whether Christian or not — are not purely epistemic beings, and if they were trying to be, it would be irrational for them to do so! This is because they (and all of us) are beings who live in the world. Actual religious believers are the kind of creatures who live in a world that has dangerous surprises from which their well-being must be secured. In *that* kind of situation they need, and therefore value, beliefs and activities that do certain jobs for them. The job religion does is (among other things) to help them find a way of getting through the barriers of suffering and death, guilt and meaninglessness. It makes sense out of these experiences, diagnoses them, and helps believers find a way through these existential constraints. Hence religion has a practical goal as much as an epistemic one (see again the discussion on pp. 28-42).

Second, this means also that what is at stake in religious matters is not only whether some beliefs are true or what conclusions we should draw regarding certain arguments, but *how we actually should live our lives*. It is not just a matter of making up one's mind: it is also a matter of choosing or denying a *way of living*. This choice cannot be postponed for real human beings. We must live right now, one way or another. Hence, real people are rationally justified in taking risks, because of their predicament, that the "religious believer" in much scientific and religious literature would not be justified in taking. So what it is rational for such a being to believe about religious matters cannot help us, since we are in a radically different situation.

But the choice of whether or not to accept a religious faith, in the kind of reasoning that Atkins, Dawkins, and Swinburne (to somewhat different extents) exemplify, is essentially, if not completely, perceived as a *theoretical* choice: what conclusions should we draw, when it comes to certain arguments for or against the existence of God or something else religious practitioners believe? Are these arguments valid and sound? The paradigm for rationality is taken to be science. If we simplify somewhat, the scientific-choice situation could be characterized as follows. A scientist or group of scientists tries to explain a particular phenomenon, for instance, the speed of light or some fossils. They develop different hypotheses to explain this phenomenon. They carefully investigate the evidence supporting the different hypotheses. Should they accept hypothesis x or hypothesis y, or should they try to develop a third hypothesis z? The evidence is perhaps not unequivocal so they decide to postpone their decision. Instead they go home for the day or even take a vacation with the intention of deciding later which hypothesis should be accepted.

Do these scientists behave in a rational way? Well, there are many things that point in that direction. It seems foolish to take any unnecessary risks if one has time to wait and acquire better grounds for the decision before one makes up one's mind. Scientific rationality is thus to a great extent a species of *spectator-rationality,* in other words, an issue about how one as a human being should use one's cognitive resources in an intelligent way in a situation in which one is not required to make a decision about what to believe or do immediately, but can either postpone the decision to some point in the future or withhold judgment altogether.

Could then the religious and the scientific context of choice be equated in this way? There are strong reasons to doubt that. Is not the situation such that religious practitioners must do something, choose a way of living, try to handle existentially important experiences, and deal — one way or another — with death, guilt, and alienation, and create opportunities for forgiveness, friendship, and meaning? Is it not the case that the religious quest is an *unavoidable existential matter* and not a theoretical decision that could be postponed? A question such as, "Should I continue or stop believing in God?" is asked by somebody who is in a situation in which she must act and must come to a decision. People could not postpone this kind of choice. We must live right now, one way or another. If we do not choose with our head then we choose with our feet. The choice can neither be avoided nor, in reality, postponed. Hence an adequate evaluation of religious rationality must take into account that the people in question must do something, choose a way of living. Religious rationality is in other words essentially an example of *agent-rationality,* that is, an issue about how one as a human being should use one's cognitive resources in an intelligent way in a situation in which one must come to a decision about what to believe or what to do, and in which it is impossible (or at least very difficult) to postpone the decision to some point in the future or withhold judgment altogether.

What is the relevance of this difference between rationality in religious practice (theology excluded) and in scientific practice? Let me take an example from a different area of life to clarify this. Suppose that one late winter day I am out fishing on the ice of the river of Vindeln. For some reason the ice cracks and I suddenly find myself on an ice floe, which is slowly dissolving. I pass by an area where the ice looks good and solid, but realize that it is doubtful whether I can jump that far without ending up in the cold water. I am forced to make a decision, and fast. Should I jump or wait for a better opportunity? The point is that we cannot give an adequate answer to this question unless we take into account that I am forced to make a decision about what to do and believe. The answer would probably be a different one if I did not have to immediately make up my mind. In such a situation the rational way to proceed would very likely be to refrain from jumping if even the smallest reason of doubt existed that I would succeed and to instead take my time and consider the different options I have. In other words, it is rational, in a situation in which we must come to a decision about what to believe and do, to take risks that we in a situation without time pressure and constraints on our freedom of action would not be entitled to take. If you wait too long to make up your mind about what to do and believe, the drowning man would be dead, your marriage broken, and the job offered to somebody else. Therefore we cannot equate agent-rationality with spectator-rationality: the conditions when it is rational for someone to believe or do something are different in the two cases. Hence, an adequate evaluation of religious rationality must take into account that the religious quest concerns an issue that people cannot avoid and that is urgent.

As a result, an examination of religious rationality is inadequate if it does not take into account that religious practitioners must *do* something, choose a way of living, and instead treats the issue as a purely theoretical matter (as if a response or resolution need not be more or less immediately practically implemented within people's life). It is also inadequate if it does not take into account that religious practitioners also have other aims with their religious activities than epistemic ones. It is in fact assessing something other than what is at issue.[12]

IN THIS CHAPTER we have discussed whether religion exhibits a rationality that overlaps with or could be informed by the epistemology of science. We have done this by focusing on van Huyssteen's postfoundational model of rationality. The key idea is that while there is no universal rationality, we can still talk about a transversal rationality. The transversality between science and religion consists at least of (in my terminology) judgment-based, internal evidentialism. But even if a postfoundational model of rationality greatly improved our understanding of scientific and theological rationality, it still, as we have seen, offers a picture of what rationality in science, theology, and religion could and should be all about which is too glamorous and thus unrealistic. Instead presumptionism seems to give us the key

---

12. Of course, there is nothing wrong with working with a theoretical or idealized construction, but if participants in the science-religion dialogue want to say anything substantial about real religion, then this will not do. In particular, if they want to make claims about the intelligibility or rationality of *human beings'* religious faith, then they run the risk of getting a distorted picture if they proceed along such lines.

to understand human rationality, and should be our global belief policy; at the same time, as a local belief policy judgment-based, internal evidentialism may be appropriate to use, at least when it comes to scientists' and theologians' own research. This allows for a cross-disciplinary justification, which provides means to step beyond the limitations and boundaries of our own local, disciplinary contexts as scientists, theologians, or philosophers. When it comes to transversal rationality our account has not been comprehensive enough to draw any general conclusions beyond the one we reached in the previous chapter, namely, that everything we can learn in one area of life from another area which can improve our cognitive performance ought to be taken into consideration by rational people. We can, therefore, not exclude that there could and should be an overlap between science and religion in respect to epistemology or methodology. But whether an attempt to impose epistemic norms of one practice such as science on another practice such as religion will prove convincing depends on whether one has sufficiently understood what is going on not merely in the first but also in this second practice. This could turn out much harder than many scholars participating in the science-religion dialogue seem to think and might require more profound studies of both science and religion than those hitherto carried out. I hope that the multi-dimensional framework, the distinctions and the principles of rationality that I have tried to develop here, could prove to be helpful in such an inquiry.

Chapter 6

Theological Pragmatism
and Religious Rationality

W e have seen that scholars disagree on a number of issues in the discussion about scientific rationality and religious rationality, and
about the possibility of an overlap between them. In this chapter I shall try
to make explicit the different levels at which we can find this disagreement
(and also locate the model of rationality I have developed so far in that
context). Moreover, I have argued that other things than epistemic matters
are of relevance when understanding religious rationality. Religious practitioners are not to be understood to be purely epistemic agents because
religious practice has both epistemic and practical goals. In this chapter I
shall also address what I consider to be the opposite danger, that is, to neglect that rationality in religion is about truth and other relevant epistemic
aspects and focus merely on political and moral considerations.

Disagreements about Rationality

I suggest that there are at least four levels where conflicting assumptions
about rationality can be found in the religion-science dialogue. Scholars in
this context could (1) use different concepts of rationality (disagree about
the *nature of rationality*), (2) assume different epistemic norms or principles (disagree about the *standards of rationality*), (3) have different ideas
about the relevance or applicability of the epistemic norms or principles
(disagree about the *scope of rationality*), or (4) accept different kinds of ev-

idence (disagree about the *reasons of rationality*). These disagreements are, in turn, often related to differences in assumptions about the teleology of science and religion.

So far I have not said much about the first level of disagreement, the level about the nature of rationality. But we need to notice that the term "rational" can have different meanings. Aristotle is well known for claiming that "Man is a rational animal." His idea was that being rational is a property we have; it is essential for our species. Some philosophers have questioned Aristotle's view by pointing out that we sometimes, maybe very often, believe or do irrational things. Therefore it is wrong to say like Aristotle that man is a rational animal. What they fail to pay attention to is that the sentence can be interpreted in two different ways: It could mean that we are the kind of animal that can be either rational or irrational; that is, in contrast to other beings or entities, we have a capacity for reasoning or reason-governed activities. In this sense, rationality (or better yet, human reason, intelligence, or cognitive resources) connotes the power, skill, or ability we have to organize and interpret our experiences and to draw conclusions about things that go beyond our immediate experience. But, on the other hand, the fact that we have the resources of reason does not mean that we necessarily use these resources *wisely,* or exercise this capacity in a *proper* way. We can use our intelligence in an unintelligent way. Rationality in this second sense has to do with the proper exercise of human reason or intelligence.

In other words, two different ways to specify the concept of rationality are these:

(A) Rationality ultimately signifies a *particular ability* or *capacity* that humans possess, namely, their reason, intelligence, or cognitive resources.

(B) Rationality ultimately signifies a particular way humans should *use* or *exercise* their reason, intelligence, or cognitive resources.

For instance, when Peacocke talks about "the cognitive processes that evolution has provided us with" and says that "it warrants postulating the existence of a general rationality in *Homo sapiens,*" he seems to understand the concept of rationality in terms of (A) (Peacocke 2001: 26). But when he writes that "the theory of rationality expressed here is best understood in terms of the 'inference to the best explanation' model" (p. 29), he uses the concept in sense (B). Here he assumes that the proper way to use or exercise human cognitive resources is to treat our beliefs as hypotheses which explain certain data and which we should weigh against competing explanatory hypotheses and which we should seek to intersubjectively assess according to the criteria of comprehensiveness, fruitfulness, general cogency, and so on (p. 28). Making a stipulation could easily solve the conflict between these different understandings of the concept of rationality, however. Let us use the terms "reason," "intelligence," or "cognitive resources" when we have in mind (A) and reserve the concept of rationality for (B).

There is, however, a genuine conflict between models of rationality that presuppose (B) and those that presuppose (C):

(C) Rationality ultimately signifies a *property* a proposition, belief, or theory can have or lack.

J. L. Mackie, for instance, seems to presuppose an understanding of the concept of rationality in terms of (C) in his discussion of religious rationality. He thinks that the argument from evil can establish the irrationality of religious belief. He writes, "Here it can be shown, not that religious beliefs lack rational support, but that they are positively irrational . . ." (Mackie 1990: 25). If "God is omnipotent; God is wholly good; and yet evil exists" are logically inconsistent beliefs, as Mackie thinks they are, then this set of beliefs has the feature of being irrational. Hence it is not, or not just, that some religious practitioners are irrational in their beliefs, but that some religious beliefs have the property of being irrational. Therefore, rationality captures, for Mackie, not strictly speaking a relation between some real agents — actual religious practitioners — and some of what they believe, but a logical relation between beliefs or propositions. Obviously Mackie can still talk about rational persons, but "a rational person" must then be taken to refer to an *ideally rational person,* someone whose *beliefs* have the property of being rational.

Let me briefly mention why I think we should prefer option (B).[1] I maintain that we must accept that it was rational for most people two thousand years ago to believe that the earth was flat, but that it is not rational for most people today to believe that. But if rationality ultimately signifies a property a belief can have or lack then it does not matter who holds this belief. This would entail, however, that if the belief that the earth is

---

1. See Stenmark (1995) for a more extensive argument.

round is rational, it follows that people in ancient times were irrational in holding the belief that the earth is flat. But it is hardly reasonable to claim this because we would then demand far too much of these people. We would demand that they should have known facts that scientific research was able to give us convincing information about only much later. What is rational for people to believe therefore depends on what information they have access to.

Consequently, the notion of rationality is *person-related* in a way that, for instance, the notion of truth or the notion of consistence is not. To be able to determine whether two or more beliefs are *inconsistent* with each other, we need not know who the holders of the beliefs are. Or to be able to determine whether it is *true* that the earth is round we need not know if the person believing this is someone alive today or someone who lived two thousand years ago. It is sufficient to investigate the shape of the earth. But to know whether a person is *rational* in believing something we must know who that person is as well as his or her circumstances. We cannot ask in an abstract fashion if it is rational to believe that the earth is round, that God exists, or that salvation can be found in many different religions. We always need to first know what people we are talking about and in what circumstances they find themselves.

If the nature of rationality is understood in terms of (B) then not merely does it follow that rationality is conceptually different from truth and consistency (because it is person-related in a way that these latter concepts are not), but also that truth is not a necessary condition for rationality. Someone could be rational in believing *p* even if *p* happens to be false.

If we focus merely on this level of rationality, I do not think that there is any difference in respect to the nature of rationality between science and religion. On this issue I believe that van Huyssteen and I agree; the disagreement about evidentialism or presumptionism arises at the second level about the appropriate standards or principles of rationality. Moreover, how closely related the truth question and the rationality question are depends in its turn on *what* the proper standards of rationality are taken to be. So we now reach another level at which conflicting views about rationality can be differentiated.

When is it the case that people use their intelligence in an intelligent way? What conditions must be satisfied? In short, we have seen that van Huyssteen's postfoundational model of rationality includes the acceptance of the evidential principle (it is rational to hold a belief only if there are good reasons to think that it is true) developed in terms of informed judgment. It thus entails the rejection of the rule principle (it is rational to hold a belief only if it is obtained by following the appropriate rules) but the acceptance of the social principle (it is rational to hold a belief only if it has been exposed to peer evaluation), while being silent about, for instance, the proportionality principle (the firmness with which one accepts a belief ought always to be in proportion to the strength of the evidence for it). My model, on the other hand, includes the acceptance of the principle of presumption (it is rational to believe something as long as there are no good reasons to believe otherwise), which implies the rejection not merely of the evidential principle but also of the rule principle and the proportionality principle.[2] It also includes the acceptance of the cautious principle of belief revision (when revising something we already believe we should pick, among those alternatives that are available to us, the one that is nearest to our original conviction), the principle of concern (we should require stronger reasons for giving up something we believe which has greater depth of concern in our belief-world than for giving up something which plays a more peripheral role) and the strength-of-belief principle (in a situation where I meet many other apparently reasonable and honest people who happen to believe something other than what I do, this should affect the strength with which I hold onto my belief at least in such a way that I realize there is a real chance that I actually could be wrong). So here we have another possible area of disagreement concerning issues of scientific and religious rationality.

The third level concerns the scope of rationality, which is perhaps the most explicitly discussed level in the science-religion dialogue. Should rationality be the same in all areas of life, in all places, and at all times? Should the conditions for what it means to use one's intelligence in an intelligent way be the same in, for instance, science, religion, and everyday life, or are there significant differences? (I thus suggest that the issue about the scope of rationality is interpreted as a question about the range of the standards of rationality and not about the range of the nature of rationality [level one] or the reasons of rationality [level four].) We have seen that restrictionists such as Stephen Jay Gould and Vincent Brümmer reject the idea of rationality being the same in both science and religion. In fact, they reject the idea of an epistemological overlap between the two practices. Scientific expansionists such as Richard Dawkins and Edward O. Wilson,

---

2. These are things I have argued for in Stenmark (1995) and (1999).

on the other hand, believe that rationality is perhaps now not the same in science and religion, but that it ought to be the same; scientific rationality ought to be our guiding light in all things we do. Van Huyssteen and I have both instead suggested that that there could be an overlap between the rationality of science, theology, and religion (the idea of transversal rationality), but we have rejected the ideas of a universal rationality (Dawkins and Wilson) and of a contextual rationality (Gould and Brümmer). By accepting the idea of transversal rationality, one thereby endorses the idea of rationality not only as person-related but also as *practice-related.* That is to say, to know whether a person is rational in believing or doing something we need to know not merely who he or she is but also what kind of practice he or she participates in.

Van Huyssteen, however, believes that judgment-based, internal evidentialism provides this epistemological bridge between science and religion, whereas I deny this and maintain that it at best provides such a bridge between science and a subset of religion, namely, confessional theology. This does not mean that my view entails that there is no overlap or should not be any overlap; my discussion has been far too limited to reach such a conclusion. On the contrary, what I have suggested is that everything we can learn in one area of life (in one practice) from another area (yet another practice) that is such that it can improve our cognitive performance ought to be taken into consideration by rational people. But whether an attempt to impose the standards of rationality of scientific practice on another practice such as religion will prove to be convincing depends on whether one has sufficiently understood what is going on in this other practice. This condition is not always satisfied, and the reason for this might be that not enough attention has been paid to the social and teleological dimensions of science and religion.

Finally, there is also a fourth level at which people participating in the science-religion dialogue may disagree. The discussion at this level does not concern what standards of rationality should govern religious and scientific practice, and whether these are the same, but is about what constitutes good reasons (or evidence) for or against the beliefs, theories, stories, and the like which are part of these practices. We find at the fourth level disagreements about the *reasons of rationality.* For instance, it is probably not a good counter-reason to the acceptance of religious beliefs that they cannot predict a new empirical state of affairs, though that might be a good counter-reason to the acceptance of a theory in physics. It seems not to be a good argument against a theory in physics that it cannot help us become morally better persons; whereas, if the moral fruits of a religion are bad this is a valid objection against it. Why this might be so depends, I suggest, to a great deal on the fact that these practices have different ends or goals, because what counts as a good reason depends on what it is supposed to be a reason *for,* what the end or goal in question is. Again we can see the importance of the teleological dimension of a practice.

The question I shall in particular address is whether both epistemic and non-epistemic (or practical) reasons are relevant when assessing religious beliefs. Hitherto I have here and to a greater depth in *Rationality in Science, Religion, and Everyday Life* argued against the view that epistemic (or truth-promoting) reasons are the only relevant factors to take into account when assessing religious rationality. Here I want to argue against what I think is the opposite extreme, namely, the view that non-epistemic, pragmatic, moral, or practical reasons are the only reasons we really have to take into account within the epistemology of religion — a view that seems to be especially influential among certain groups of theologians today.

Notice, however, that levels three and four are very closely connected and that some ideas about rationality could be expressed in terms of either level three or level four. For instance, the view held by these theologians that we shall examine could be expressed as the idea that the essential standard used to assess religious beliefs and images should be pragmatic; that is to say, one ought to accept those religious beliefs and images that have, for instance, the best moral and political consequences. Or it could be expressed as the view that these theologians accept the evidential principle in the sense that to be rational one has to have good reasons for what one believes, but that they add that what should count as good reasons in religion are moral and political considerations. Let us now take a closer look at the way in which these theologians argue.

Theological Pragmatism

What is interesting and worth reflecting on is that an influential group of contemporary Christian theologians do epistemology of religion in a way that is significantly different from the way it is typically done by philosophers of religion and participants in the science-religion dialogue. In their discussion about what one should, as a Christian, believe about God and what images one should use to express one's religious faith, a number of influential contemporary theologians employ a kind of epistemology that can be classified as a form of pragmatism (although one could of course develop pragmatism in a quite different way).[3] I shall refer to this epistemological standpoint as *theological pragmatism*. I shall not try to define it at this point. Rather, I shall illustrate this form of pragmatism by quoting some of its advocates.

Mary Daly applies what she calls a "pragmatic yardstick" to God-language:

> In my thinking, the specific criterion which implies a mandate to reject certain forms of God-talk is expressed in the question: Does this language hinder human becoming by reinforcing sex-role socialization? Expressed positively . . . the question is: Does it *encourage* human becoming toward psychological and social fulfillment, toward an androgynous mode of living, toward transcendence? (Daly 1973: 21)

Likewise, Gordon D. Kaufman writes,

> We must critically examine our religious symbolism and attempt to reconstruct it in ways that will more likely assure, so far as we can see, that it will function to good effect in human affairs. (Kaufman 1985: 32)

In addition, Sallie McFague claims that

> the main criterion for a "true" theology is pragmatic, preferring those models of God that are most helpful in the praxis of bringing about fulfillment for living beings. (McFague 1987: 196 n. 13)

> The question we must ask is not whether one [image of God] is true and the other false, but which one is a better portrait of Christian faith *for our day.* (McFague 1987: xiii)

Finally, and perhaps most blatantly, Rosemary Radford Ruether maintains that

3. See, for instance, Herrmann (1995), Ochs (1998), and Zackariasson (2002).

Our criterion for what is truthful is, finally, what is most ethically redemptive. (Ruether 1991: 277).

The general idea articulated by each of these four theologians is that moral
and political considerations are the crucial ones to take into account when
evaluating religious beliefs or images. The God we should believe in and
the kind of images we should use to express our religious faith should be
evaluated primarily on the basis of the *consequences* they have for the
maintenance of certain political or moral values:

(a) Which are most helpful in the praxis of bringing about fulfillment
    for living beings (McFague)?
(b) Which are ethically redemptive (Ruether)?
(c) Which are most helpful in building a humane world (Kaufman)?
(d) Which encourage an androgynous mode of living (Daly)?

According to such theologians, the effects that religious beliefs and images
have in the lives of religious practitioners and for society as a whole should
be at the center of concern when determining what constitutes rational belief in religious matters. The key question for epistemology of religion
seems to be whether a religious belief p or a religious image q promotes a
humane world, a nonsexist society, and a responsibility for all life. The relevant category of reasons of rationality is non-epistemic or practical.

Let me give a more detailed illustration of this way of arguing. Sallie
McFague's concern in her book *Models of God*[4] is what views of God
Christians should maintain in an ecological, nuclear age: what beliefs and
images about God are rational for them to accept and use while living in a
postmodern world? She claims, as we have seen, that "the main criterion
for a 'true' theology is pragmatic, preferring those models of God that are
most helpful in the praxis of bringing about fulfillment for living beings"
(McFague 1987: 196 n. 13), and that "The question we must ask is not
whether one [image] is true and the other false, but which one is a better
portrait of Christian faith *for our day*" (p. xiii). McFague maintains that we
should try to determine which beliefs or which images are better "by asking what attitudes each encourages" (p. 78), and by asking whether they are
"helpful or harmful" (p. ix).

4. In 1988 McFague received the American Academy of Religion Award for Excellence
for this book.

Christians have traditionally believed that God is the creator of the world, and that the world and God are separate, but that God is nevertheless the sustainer of the world. Christians have also used different metaphors to express these beliefs. One influential metaphor is to regard God as the King of Kings and Lord of Lords, which McFague refers to as the "metaphor of the world as the king's realm," or simply the "monarchical model." McFague is very critical, however, of this way of understanding the relationship between God and the world: "The monarchical model is dangerous in our times: it encourages a sense of distance from the world; it attends only to the human dimension of the world; and it supports attitudes of either domination of the world or passivity towards it" (p. 69). She also asks, "Is this understanding of God's presence in and to the world, and hence, by implication, our presence in and to the world, one that is appropriate and helpful for a holistic, nuclear age?" (p. 62). McFague believes it is not appropriate and suggests instead that we consider the world as God's body.

Elsewhere she states the pro and con of these two images of God in the following way:

> The monarchical model encourages attitudes of militarism, dualism, and escapism; it condones control through violence and oppression; it has nothing to say about the nonhuman world. The model of the world as God's body encourages holistic attitudes of responsibility for and care of the vulnerable and oppressed; it is nonhierarchical and acts through persuasion and attraction; it has a great deal to say about the body and nature. (p. 78)

Since the key standard of rationality that religious beliefs and images must satisfy is that they should be helpful in bringing about fulfillment for living beings, McFague's conclusion is clear: Christians should no longer imagine the world as being separate from God. Rather, we should instead imagine it as God's body.

Some Critical Remarks

What should we say about this way of approaching theology and indirectly epistemology of religion? Should, as these theologians maintain, moral

and political considerations be allowed to play such a crucial role in determining what it is rational to believe about God and God's relationship to
the world? At first glance this way of reasoning seems rather awkward in
comparison with the way in which we typically argue. I think, however,
that theological pragmatism can be qualified in certain ways that would
make it less counter-intuitive. Let me start, nevertheless, by ignoring these
possible qualifications, just to make clear the contrast between these theologians' way of arguing and how we typically argue in ordinary life and the
sciences.

The logical structure of McFague's argument seems to be as follows:

(1) (A group of people) C believe (or imagine) p.
(2) Belief (or image) p has negative political and moral consequences for
S.
(3) S is very important and valuable.
(4) Belief (or image) q, on the other hand, has positive political and
moral consequences for S.
(5) Therefore, C should not believe (or imagine) p but q.

That is to say, C, traditional Christians, believe (or imagine) p, that God
and the world are separate. The belief (or image) that God and the world
are separate, however, has negative consequences for S, the creation of an
ecologically sound, egalitarian, and nonsexist society. It encourages attitudes of militarism, dualism, and escapism. But the creation of S, an ecologically sound, egalitarian, and nonsexist society, is politically and morally important and valuable. On the other hand, the belief (or image) q,
that the world is God's body, has positive consequences for S. It encourages
holistic attitudes of responsibility toward and care for vulnerable and oppressed people.

Given the pragmatic standard of rationality — that we ought to accept those religious beliefs or images which are most helpful in bringing
about fulfillment for living beings[5] — Christians, C, should therefore not
believe (or imagine) p, that God and the world are separate, but q, that the
world is God's body. The latter is a belief or image that portrays better the

5. Or, alternatively, that we ought to accept those religious beliefs or images which are
ethically redemptive (Ruether), which are most helpful in building a humane world
(Kaufman), or which encourage an androgynous mode of living (Daly).

Christian faith for our day. Thus, the rule of inference justifying the transition from the premises to the conclusion is the pragmatic standard of rationality.

What seems deeply problematic is that we do not ordinarily think that the truth or the rationality of a belief, model, or theory is undermined by its coming into conflict with certain political or moral values. This is presumably because we think that there is no automatic connection between the nature of reality, on the one hand, and our political visions and moral aspirations, on the other hand. Let me give one counter-example from the sciences to bring this out. Scientists believe, for example, that atoms can be split into parts. They also know that this belief was crucial in the construction of the atomic bomb. Some of us think that atomic bombs and other nuclear weapons are evil things and constitute a massive threat to the creation of an ecologically sustainable and peaceful society. Hence, believing that atoms can be split in parts could be regarded as "dangerous" in our time. It would also be seen as "encouraging" attitudes of militarism, control, and oppression and undermining our moral aspirations and political visions. According to these theologians, the question we now should ask is not "whether this belief is true or false" but whether it is "helpful in the praxis of bringing about fulfillment for living beings."[6] If it is not, it would follow that scientists should try to believe something that has positive consequences for the creation of an ecologically sustainable and peaceful society.

By arguing in this manner, however, we mix in an awkward way factual matters with moral and political considerations. Contrary to the above example, it can still be rational to believe that atoms can be split in parts, even though this belief does not promote a humane world, a non-sexist society, and a care and responsibility toward all life. The fact that it would be politically or morally desirable that *p* is the case does not entail that it is true or probably true that *p* is the case.

Moreover, similar counter-examples can be construed by taking beliefs from ordinary life. For instance, if we use the belief "Men are in general physically stronger than women" instead of "Atoms can be split in parts" in the previous example, we would end up with pretty much the same result.

But perhaps religion is, in this respect, different from ordinary life

---

6. Or whether it is ethically redemptive (Ruether), helpful in building a humane world (Kaufman), or useful in encouraging an androgynous mode of living (Daly).

and the sciences? Or to put it somewhat differently, are there any considerations we have failed to take into account when discussing theological
pragmatism and construing these counter-examples? I certainly think so.
Hence, it remains to identify such considerations and to determine how
they affect the credibility of theological pragmatism in general and of
McFague's expression of it in particular.

Let me start by listing some of the possible conditions or restrictions
for the use of the pragmatic standard and thus for non-epistemic reasons.
These can be found in the writing of these theologians. The idea that the
main standard of rationality for assessing (religious) beliefs and images
should be whether they promote or hinder certain political and moral values applies only

(1) to metaphorical expressions;
(2) to beliefs whose truth-value we cannot know or determine (that is, in
    situations of epistemic uncertainty);
(3) to non-factual claims (for example, when religious beliefs are inter-
    preted only in moral terms); and/or
(4) to mythological projections (such as, for instance, those beliefs about
    God that are assumed to be merely projections of people's power
    ambitions or fears).

I shall here focus on (1) and (2) and presuppose that the *prima facie* justification given in chapter 3 for understanding religious practice as containing
factual elements is correct, which — if true — would undermine but not
falsify (3) and (4) because of the plurality of religious practices.

Metaphorical Expressions

One thing that clearly seems to be relevant in assessing theological pragmatism is that, whereas I have been talking about beliefs, these theologians
tend to talk about metaphors, models, or symbols. Is this an important
distinction? McFague maintains that the metaphor of the world as the
king's realm is dangerous in our times; it is not appropriate because it is
not helpful for a holistic, ecological, and nuclear age. What we need instead is "an imaginative vision of the relationship between God and the
world that underscores their interdependence and mutuality, empowering

a sensibility of care and responsibility toward all life . . ." (McFague 1987: 60). According to McFague this is what the metaphor "the world is God's body" can provide us with. Hence, we should use this metaphor and not the monarchical metaphor when expressing God's relationship to the world. Consequently, as McFague also argues, we ought to talk about God *as* mother, father, lover, and friend, instead of God *as* king, lord, ruler, and patriarch.

How does this approach fit with how we typically argue in the sciences and in ordinary life? Phrased differently, if we add this restriction — that we are not talking about beliefs in general but about metaphoric expressions — how does it affect the credibility of theological pragmatism? McFague gives an example that we can use to determine the answer to this question. She writes that a metaphor,

> such as the remark that "war is a chess game," immediately sparks our imaginations to think of war, a very complex phenomenon, as viewed through a concrete grid or screen, the game of chess. Needless to say, war is not a chess game; hence, a description of war in terms of chess is a partial, relative, inadequate account that, in illuminating certain aspects of war (such as strategizing), filters out other aspects (such as violence and death). (p. 33)

Suppose now the metaphor "war is a chess game" were to become in our culture a common way of expressing what war is all about. Under these circumstances many of us would think that this metaphor is a dangerous one. The metaphor would be regarded as dangerous because it does not encourage the right attitudes toward war. It is, moreover, not appropriate for an ecological, nuclear age. Our argument would proceed as follows: We, *C*, generally express our beliefs about war by using *p*, the metaphor "war is a chess game." The metaphor *p*, that war is a chess game, has negative consequences for *S*, the creation of an ecologically sound, egalitarian, and nonsexist society. But the creation of such a society is, both politically and morally, important and valuable. On the other hand, the alternative metaphor *q*, that "war is a slaughter," has positive consequences for *S*, the creation of an ecologically sound, egalitarian, and nonsexist society. Therefore, we should not imagine *p*, that war is a chess game, but *q*, that war is a slaughter.

At this point we are certainly on to something. Metaphors can certainly affect our beliefs about the world to a certain extent. By highlighting some things and suppressing others, they can direct or influence our perception. The idea behind theological pragmatism would then be that people who mainly use the metaphor that war is a chess game would probably have a different attitude toward war than people who use the metaphor that war is a slaughter. The theologians discussed above assume that the same is true of religious metaphors. Hence, the theologian's task (or a part of it) is to guide religious people by influencing their choice of metaphors, so they can develop appropriate attitudes toward God, God's creation, and other human beings. It is perhaps in this way that we should understand, for instance, McFague's claim that the main criterion for a "true" theology is pragmatic: We should prefer those models (that is, metaphors) of God that are most helpful in the praxis of bringing about fulfillment for living beings.

I write "perhaps," however, because there are certain problems with approaching theological pragmatism in this way. These problems arise because McFague *also* maintains that "all [linguistic] constructions are metaphorical" and that "[a]ll renderings of reality are metaphorical (that is, none is literal) . . ." (McFague 1987: 26). Furthermore, she claims that "what a metaphor expresses cannot be said directly or apart from it, for if it could be, one would have said it directly" (p. 33). This view that all talk about reality is irreducibly symbolic or metaphorical and that, as a result, no distinction between literal and figurative speech can be upheld consistently seems to be endorsed not only by McFague but also by many other theological pragmatists.

It means that such theologians maintain that metaphorical thinking constitutes the basis of human thought and language. McFague argues that "metaphor *is* ordinary language. It is the *way* we think" (McFague 1982: 16). Nothing can be known or thought literally. In saying these things we are, moreover, recommended to use "metaphorical" in a new and different way. Traditionally we have thought, for example, that a sentence such as "John is a chicken" can be interpreted both metaphorically and literally, and if it can be interpreted metaphorically it can at least partly be translated into literal words. If the sentence is interpreted literally, it says something about a certain animal with feathers and wings which somebody — say a farmer — calls "John." If the sentence is interpreted metaphorically, as when I claim that my old classmate John is a chicken, it says something (true or false) about his character. Furthermore, we imagine that we can partly translate my claim that "John is a chicken" with the claim that "John is a coward." On this view, a metaphor's central thrust can be literally translated, but its ramifying overtones, emotional colors, and perhaps also some of its cognitive content are lost in such translation.

But according to McFague also the farmer's sentence "John is a chicken" and my claim that "John is a coward" are metaphorical expressions. Her argument for this seems to be that nothing can be known or thought of directly (that is, we can never experience reality uninterpreted); therefore, all speech is metaphorical: "If . . . *all* thought is indirect, then all concepts and theories are metaphorical in the sense that they too are constructions; they are indirect attempts to interpret reality, which never can be dealt with directly" (p. 26). The same kind of justification of the thesis that all talk about reality is irreducibly metaphorical appears in her book *Models of God.* She writes, "To claim that all [linguistic] constructions are metaphorical is to insist that one never experiences reality 'raw' . . ." (McFague 1987: 26). Hence, only agents that have direct access to reality, beings such as God, can utter literal statements; all the rest of the inhabitants of the universe must be satisfied with less.

I would certainly agree with theological pragmatists such as McFague that we have no direct access to reality, at least in the sense that (as we say in philosophy of science) all observations are to some extent theory-laden. But why think that this undermines the traditional distinction between metaphorical and literal speech? Indeed, you need no direct access to reality to be able to understand the differences between my two speech acts, "John is a chicken" and "John is an old classmate." Even if you were never able to determine whether these statements were true or false, such an inability would not be of relevance when determining whether these statements are to be understood metaphorically or literally. McFague thus seems to confuse semantic issues with epistemic issues.[7]

Of course, theologians like McFague have a right to stipulate the term "metaphor" in the way they want. The problem, though, is that if all speech is metaphorical, the term "metaphorical" itself no longer has any meaning, since it is incapable of marking any such semantic distinction. It seems to me more useful to retain the two terms, with their different meanings.[8]

---

7. See Stenmark (1997a) for a more detailed criticism of McFague on this point.

8. See Ward (1996b, chap. 6) for a more detailed criticism of the idea that language is irreducibly metaphorical.

Be that as it may, the problem nevertheless remains that *if* all talk about reality is irreducibly metaphorical, then the belief considered above in the counter-example concerning atoms and the atomic bomb is *also* to be understood as a metaphorical expression. The statements "atoms can be split in parts" and, further, "people get killed in wars," "women are oppressed," and "we can destroy the earth with our nuclear weapons" are all examples of metaphors. But if "atoms can be split in parts" or if *any* of these other statements is a metaphorical expression, these statements also could, and, indeed, should, be rejected if they are not helpful in bringing about fulfillment for living beings or in creating an ecologically sound, egalitarian, and nonsexist society. We are, as a result, back where we started, and the counter-example already given shows that this is not a promising way of developing the epistemology of religion.

So it seems that theological pragmatists like McFague are thus forced to make a choice. Either they have to admit that not all talk about reality is metaphorical and that the pragmatic standard applies only to metaphors, or they have to give up the whole idea that the main standard of rationality is pragmatic in the sense that they understand the term. (It is, of course, still possible to develop pragmatism within theology or philosophy of religion in other ways.)

Epistemic Uncertainty

Another consideration that should be taken into account in assessing theological pragmatism is that many of these theologians embrace a kind of *religious agnosticism*. For example, McFague writes, "I begin with the assumption that what we can say with any assurance about the character of Christian faith is very little and that even that will be highly contested" (McFague 1987: x). In fact, a key motive why she argues that the main criterion of theology ought to be pragmatic is her endorsement of this kind of agnosticism. McFague also maintains that

> how the [God] metaphor refers we do not know — or indeed, even if it does. At the most one wagers it does and lives as if it does, which means that the main criterion for a "true" theology is pragmatic, preferring those models of God that are most helpful in the praxis of bringing about fulfillment for living beings. (p. 196 n. 13)

Thus, when she maintains that Christians should believe or imagine that the world is God's body, this is "not to say that the world is God's body or that God is present to us in the world. Those things we do not know" (p. 61). Instead, it is to say that Christians should live as if it were true that God exists and is a personal power, as well as that the world is God's body.[9]

Accordingly, she maintains that only in certain situations should moral and political considerations be decisive in determining what to believe and how to express these beliefs. The idea, then, is that in a situation of *epistemic uncertainty*, people ought to accept those beliefs and images that have positive consequences for the fulfillment of the moral and political values that should be embraced — that is, those beliefs or images which are most helpful in bringing about fulfillment for living beings (McFague), are ethically redemptive (Ruether), are most helpful in building a humane world (Kaufman), or encourage an androgynous mode of living (Daly). Consequently, since we cannot know whether God exists and is personal, almighty, loving, the creator of the world, eternal, incarnated in Jesus Christ, and so forth, we ought to *reconstruct* these beliefs or images in such a way that they encourage, rather than hinder, the creation of an ecologically sound, egalitarian, and nonsexist society. When we cannot know whether religious beliefs are true or false, political and moral considerations should determine whether we should accept, reject, or modify them.

It remains to ask whether these considerations about epistemic uncertainty make theological pragmatism more plausible. It may be the case, but let us once again see what happens if we use this line of reasoning in ordinary life and in the sciences. Suppose, for example, that we could never know whether the special theory of relativity is true or false. What we know is that, if it is true, this theory will endanger people's safety in that it threatens the creation of a peaceful and humane society because the theory describes the release of large amounts of energy. It would then follow that, for moral or political reasons, scientists should avoid that theory and try to come up with alternative theories that are more helpful in our situation, encourage the right attitudes, and are ethically redemptive.

But many of us would not be happy with this kind of scientific epis-

---

9. That God exists seems to mean for McFague at least that it is true that "the universe is neither indifferent nor malevolent but that there is a power (and a personal power at that) which is on the side of life and its fulfillment" (McFague 1987: x).

temology — or, for that matter, everyday-life epistemology — because it seems, again, to fail to take into account that there is no automatic fit between our moral aspirations and political visions, on the one hand, and how the world is structured, on the other. We know this because we have on many occasions experienced things to be true, even though we, because of our political and moral convictions, have *wished* them not to be true. I really wish it were not true, for example, that John was unfaithful to Sarah, that the Holocaust took place, that men beat and rape women, that not everyone believes in God. These things are, nevertheless, true, and this is the case regardless of whether or not it fits my ideological profile, so to speak. Hence, this form of pragmatism can easily become a matter of wishful thinking.[10]

In her argument for religious agnosticism, McFague also makes a big and, I think, unjustified leap. She goes from the claim that (1) we cannot know anything about God to the conclusion that (2) we should, therefore, reconstruct our beliefs about God in such a way that these beliefs become helpful in bringing about fulfillment for living beings. Although at least some — but, of course, not all — Christians would agree that they do not really know that God exists, they would, nevertheless, maintain that certain things that have happened in their lives indicate that it is true that God exists. They have experienced glimpses of what they think is God, and other people have also confirmed that they have had similar experiences. Perhaps these Christians also think that they can see God's footprints in the cosmos, that God is somehow speaking to them through the Bible, and so forth. Hence, even if these people would accept that they do not really know anything — or, at any rate, not much — about God, it would not be rational for them to change their religious beliefs *merely* because these are not the most helpful things to believe in bringing about fulfillment for living beings. It is not rational for them to do so, because they would probably have to ignore previous experiences they have had about who God is and about God's relationship to the world.

The political and moral considerations on which theological prag-

---

10. But this does not matter, of course, if one thinks of religion as nothing but wishful thinking. (On this point see the fourth condition above.) Then it is better to at least develop "useful" wishful thinking. Ruether writes, for instance, that a "feminist reconstruction of the images of God . . . assumes that all of our images of God are human projections. . . . The question is: what are worse projections that promote injustice and diminished humanness, and what are better projections that promote fuller humanness?" (Ruether 1991: 277).

matists like McFague focus their attention are, nevertheless, relevant in assessing the rationality of religious practice. This is so because, for many Christians, belief in God is primarily a matter of trusting and loving God, that is, presupposing that God is good and therefore also worthy of worship. For them God is of supreme value. But would it then also follow that those who confess that they worship and serve God, the locus of supreme love and justice, do not care about the Earth, and oppress women and poor people? Ought not the transformation of human existence, that is, salvation, show itself in its spiritual and moral fruits? The answer to these questions must be, I think, "yes." But it is clear that a one-sided focus on moral and political reasons of belief will not do when it comes to issues about religious and theological rationality.

The difficulty, however, is to determine what conclusion should be drawn from these observations. Does it merely mean that the moral character of these religious practitioners is weak, that these people do not understand fully what moral commitments are hooked up with their religious beliefs, or, more fundamentally, does it mean that there is something seriously wrong with their conception of God? These issues deserve to be taken seriously also by philosophers of religion and by participants in the science-religion dialogue.

WE HAVE SEEN that it is possible to distinguish at least four levels where conflicting assumptions about rationality arise in the religion-science dialogue or in any account about scientific or religious rationality. We could (1) use different concepts of rationality (disagree about the nature of rationality), (2) assume different epistemic norms or principles (disagree about the standards of rationality), (3) have different ideas about the relevance or applicability of the epistemic norms or principles (disagree about the scope of rationality), or (4) accept different kinds of evidence (disagree about the reasons of rationality). We have also seen that these disagreements are in turn often related to differences in assumptions about the teleology of science and religion.

We have in this chapter, moreover, evaluated the tendency among a number of theologians to understand religious rationality in terms of moral and political considerations. This means that they focus all their attention on non-epistemic reasons and neglect epistemic reasons in their discussion about what rationality amounts to in religious practice. Theological pragmatists like Daly, Kaufman, McFague, and Ruether claim that the God we should believe in and the kind of images we should use to express our religious faith should be evaluated primarily on the basis of the consequences they have for the maintenance of certain political or moral values: Which are most helpful in the praxis of bringing about fulfillment for living beings (McFague)? Which are ethically redemptive (Ruether)? Which are most helpful in building a humane world (Kaufman)? Which encourage an androgynous mode of living (Daly)?

I have in this context tried to show that these theological pragmatists focus too exclusively on political and moral considerations in their discussions about religious and theological rationality. Even if it is true that reasons other than epistemic ones are of importance when developing a model for religious rationality, we cannot focus as one-sidedly on moral and political reasons as they do. The key difficulty is that their pragmatic epistemology seems to fail to take into account that there is no automatic fit between our moral aspirations and political visions, on the one hand, and how the world is structured, on the other. We know this because we have on many occasions experienced things to be true even though we, because of our political and moral convictions, have wished them not to be true. These theologians' strong emphasis on political and moral considerations is, therefore, most plausible when restricted to the evaluation of metaphors. On the other hand, many philosophers of religion and participants in the science-religion dialogue tend to ignore political and moral considerations and other practical considerations by focusing too exclusively on epistemic issues. But if we take into account the teleology of religious practice, it seems difficult to avoid the conclusion that both epistemic and non-epistemic reasons for and against the output of this practice are of relevance.

Chapter 7

The Inquiries of Science and Religion: Overlapping Concerns?

We have come to see that the relationship between science and religion is a multilevel or multidimensional relationship. So far we have focused on the social, teleological, and epistemological aspects of the relation between these two human practices. Hence the logically possible models — the unity view, the independence view, and the contact view — could be expressed differently depending on which one of these three levels of engagement between science and religion we are talking about. It is now time to move on to the fourth and perhaps most obvious level of interaction between science and religion. This fourth level, which has certainly been at the center of contemporary science-religion dialogue, concerns the *theoretical content* of religion and science. Do the theories of science and the beliefs and doctrines of religion have the same, similar, or totally different subject matters? This level of engagement has typically been understood in terms of the relevance of the content of particular scientific theories for religious belief (see, for instance, Barbour 1997: 165f.). If there is any interaction, it is assumed to be a one-way interaction from science to religion. But this engagement could, of course, also be understood in terms of the relevance of the content of particular religious beliefs or values for scientific theory construction. In our discussion of religious expansionism in chapter 8, we shall come back to this second possibility.

Because the focus in the religion-science dialogue has been so heavily directed toward this fourth level of interaction between science and religion, I shall in this chapter merely offer two illustrations about the possible unity, intersection, or separation of the theoretical content of science and religion. This is sufficient since my overall objective is to offer a model of how to relate science and religion and for this reason I have given priority to the other levels of interaction because they are less well known or even neglected in much of the writing about science and religion.

First, I shall evaluate Gordon D. Kaufman's argument that the acceptance of modern science (especially the account of cosmic and biological evolution) is not compatible with a belief in a personal God who is the creator of the world. Second, I shall return to some of the claims made by biologists about the relevance of evolutionary biology for a religious understanding of the meaning of life. Is it the case that evolutionary theory undermines the religious belief that there is a purpose behind the emergence of human beings in natural history?

Science and a Personal Conception of God

In a recent essay in the *Journal of the American Academy of Religion* (Kaufman, 2001), Gordon D. Kaufman has argued that if one accepts the scientific account of the emergence of life, one cannot any longer believe that God is personal and the creator of the world.[1] Therefore, we need to develop a new conception of God that is compatible with modern science. Kaufman's own proposal is that we should think of God in terms of the metaphor "serendipitous creativity," that is, roughly, in terms of the coming into being of something new conditioned by an inscrutable mystery of surprise (Kaufman 2001: 412f.). The question I shall address is whether Kaufman has given Christians, Jews, and Muslims who believe that God is personal and the creator of the heavens and the earth any good reason for abandoning this view and for starting to understand God in terms of creativity instead. (Let us call these people "traditional believers.") In particular, is a personal conception of God really incompatible with the scientific idea of cosmic and biological evolution?

"Traditional believers," as I shall understand the term, hold that God

---

1. Parts of this section are a reprint of an article published in the *Journal of the American Academy of Religion* (71, 2003). For editorial reasons the article was reduced to roughly half of its original size. I have, however, decided to include the other sections in this book as well.

is personal and is the creator of the world. God is such that God can have knowledge and awareness, can perform actions, can enter into a loving relationship with humans, can respond to prayer, and can be morally good; God is also believed to be responsible for the world's existence. The idea of a personal God is very important for traditional believers, or so it seems, because for them worship and religious life in general are understood in terms of a personal relationship with God. Some of them, nevertheless, have a fairly naive or crude picture of God. God is assumed to be a "Big person" or a kind of superhuman being. They have an anthropomorphic conception of God. Others, and certainly a great number of theologians and philosophers working within this religious tradition, have a view that is more nuanced. According to them, even if we cannot adequately describe God with human concepts it is nevertheless the case that the propositions "God is personal" and "God is love" are closer to the truth than the propositions "God is impersonal" and "God is hate" or the propositions "God is neither personal nor impersonal" and "God is neither love nor hate." They are aware of the analogical nature of religious language, but they nevertheless hold on to a personal conception of God and reject the other two possibilities, namely, an impersonal conception of God or a beyond personal-impersonal conception of God. (These are the options we have, and whether or not we want to call the first of them "anthropomorphic" does not in this respect make any difference.) Perhaps we could say that traditional believers hold that God is not a person, but that God is more like a person than like anything else, since God has (they believe) entered into a loving and caring relationship with human beings.

Kaufman's Argument

Is it rational for traditional believers to hold a personal conception of God? Kaufman thinks that earlier people were rational in understanding God in such a way or at least that it "was not implausible" for them to do so, but he claims that this is no longer the case because such a conception is incompatible with a central scientific view of the world (pp. 410-11). Kaufman maintains that "as far as we know, personal agential beings did not exist, and *could not have existed*, before billions of years of cosmic evolution of a very specific sort and then further billions of years of biological evolution also of a very specific sort had transpired." How, then, he asks rhetorically, "can we today think of a person-like creator-God as existing before and apart from any such evolutionary developments?" (p. 410). The answer is that it seems to Kaufman "increasingly impossible" (whatever that means) to make sense of such an idea of God as "creator of the heavens and the earth" (p. 410).

He maintains that among theologians and others involved in the current religion-science dialogue "who otherwise seek to take modern evolutionary biology and cosmology seriously, there is a failure to come to terms directly with [this] problem" (p. 411 n. 1). He takes the well-known scientist and theologian John Polkinghorne as an example of someone who makes this mistake. Polkinghorne wants to take science seriously, but he assumes that one can hold a personal conception of God and at the same time accept the results of contemporary science. Kaufman claims that Polkinghorne is mistaken on this point. Why? Because Polkinghorne fails to consider "a *central* scientific understanding," namely,

> that complex features of the world such as conscious intention, purposive action, deliberate creation of artifacts, loving attitudes and behaviors, and the like — all attributed to God from the "big bang" onward in the anthropomorphic model in terms of which his notion of God is constructed — *can come into being only after* billions of years of complex cosmic, biological, and historical development have provided the necessary conditions for their emergence to occur. (p. 411 n. 1, emphasis added)

Kaufman's argument seems thus to be:

(1) Traditional believers hold that God is personal (that is, God has intentions, can act, create, love, and the like).[2]

(2) But science has shown us that human beings (that is, creatures who have intentions, can act, create, love, and the like) *came into existence* after billions of years of cosmic and biological evolution.

(3) Moreover, science has also shown that personal beings of *any* sort

---

2. This means, I have suggested (see again p. 139), that they believe that the proposition "God has intentions" is closer to the truth than the propositions "God does not have intentions" or "God neither has nor lacks intentions," and so forth, with all of these personal attributes.

could come into existence only after billions of years of cosmic and biological evolution.

Therefore, traditional believers should no longer hold that God is personal.

What we need to assess is whether the premises of Kaufman's argument are true or likely to be true and whether the conclusion follows logically from the premises.

It is self-evident that premise (1) is true given my definition of traditional believers. If we turn to the second premise of the argument it is clear that Polkinghorne accepts it, and as I have maintained, other traditional believers should also do so. But a difficulty is, of course, that the conclusion does not follow merely from premises (1) and (2) because (2) says something only about humans and *we need scientific information that also applies to a personal conception of God.* So I suggest that premise (3) (see again the long quotation above) expresses what Kaufman takes to be "a central scientific understanding," besides the content of premise (2) about which he and Polkinghorne agree. If science put restrictions on what kind of personal beings can possibly come into existence then this information seems to have some bearing on an understanding of God as personal.

The problem we face in assessing this argument is, however, that Kaufman *merely tells us* that science has shown that personal beings of any sort could come into existence only after billions of years of cosmic and biological evolution. He does not explain *why* this is so nor does he specify the scientists who hold this view. This would have been extremely helpful, because it is after all something that a scientist of Polkinghorne's credentials has failed to notice.

Hence, the issue is about whether science has shown us that personal beings can come into existence only after billions of years of cosmic and biological evolution. There are good reasons to doubt this. Science is typically understood to be able to discover *contingent truths,* that is, states of affairs that obtain as a matter of fact, but which could have been different. Scientists have as a matter of fact discovered that there exists a planet we call Neptune, that metal expands when heated, and that Darwin was right and Lamarck was wrong. But it did not necessarily have to be this way. It could have been the case that there was no planet Neptune and that metals did not expand when heated. It is logically possible that only eight planets move in an ellipse around our sun and that metals expand when exposed to water. It would be a different world from the one we inhabit, but it is a possible world. In this world scientists could also have discovered that Lamarck was right and Darwin was wrong. A *necessary truth*, on the other hand, is a state of affairs that obtains and could not have been otherwise. Examples of necessary truths are that no one is taller than himself or herself and that all bachelors are unmarried men.

The trouble with premise (3) is, however, that it seems to presuppose that science gives us necessary truths, because it tells us that it is possible that personal beings can come into existence *only* after billions of years of cosmic and biological evolution. On this reading, Kaufman assumes a very controversial idea indeed, and it is little wonder that Polkinghorne has failed to take it into account. But the case seems instead to be that if, for instance, the natural laws had turned out radically different than they did, it would have been quite possible that it would not have had to take billions of years of cosmic and biological evolution before personal beings turned up. Perhaps they might have come into existence after a week. They might also have looked quite different from *Homo sapiens,* but they could still, of course, have been personal beings. Nothing in science contradicts these kinds of possibilities. There is also a possible world in which Christian fundamentalists are right about the creation of life and Darwin is wrong! It is logically possible that God could have created Adam and Eve in a special act of creation in such a way that they would not share a common ancestry with other life-forms on earth. But as a contingent truth that is not what science has discovered happened in this, the actual world.

Things are, however, still more problematic than this because even if Kaufman was right in that science has shown that personal beings of any sort could come into existence only after billions of years of cosmic and biological evolution, this would still not imply that traditional believers should no longer hold that God is personal. The argument, even if we grant that its premises are true, does not entail the conclusion or even make it probable. The reason is that the argument tells us about what conditions must be satisfied for something *to come into being* with the properties that are necessary for being personal. But of course traditional believers do not believe that God came into existence. Rather, they believe that God has always existed. They believe that God is *eternal.* This is understood either to mean that God is everlasting (God has always existed as God and always will) or that God does not in any way exist in time but outside of it (there is no past, present, or future in God's own unique form of existence). Either way, traditional believers — in contrast to, perhaps, process theists — do not hold that God has come into being, and this makes God different from God's creation. So even if it is true (which it probably is not) that science tells us that personal beings of any sort could come into existence only after billions of years of cosmic and biological evolution, this is not relevant when it comes to evaluating the personal conception of God held by traditional believers because God's existence, *ex hypothesi,* is taken not to be of that kind.

But could not Kaufman reply that his point is really that, because of what the sciences have discovered about the origin of personal beings that come into existence, we can no longer meaningfully think about or make sense of a God who is believed to not have come into being? After all, he asks rhetorically, "What could *we possibly be imagining* when we attempt to think of God as an all-powerful *personal* reality existing somehow before and independent of what we today call 'the universe'?" (p. 410, first emphasis added).

The difficulty is that Kaufman clearly maintains that it is something *in the development of science* that undermines the idea of an eternal and a personal God. But what is this new piece of data that science has discovered? It cannot simply be that we and all other living things are — in contrast to God — contingent beings, since that is something people have known or believed for ages. I have suggested that it is (2) and that Kaufman mistakenly believes it also to be (3). But my point is that even if (3) were true, the conclusion that traditional believers should no longer hold that God is personal would still not follow (because God is believed by them to be eternal). Kaufman could, of course, introduce *positivism* here, claiming that we can meaningfully talk only about what is scientifically verifiable or falsifiable. The idea would then be that since scientists have discovered only personal beings that emerge out of a process of cosmic and biological evolution and *it makes no sense to talk about anything that the sciences cannot discover (verify or falsify)*, the personal conception of God lacks cognitive meaning, and, therefore, traditional believers should no longer believe that God is personal. But I take it that Kaufman does not want to embrace positivism. It follows that this is hardly the path he wants to follow.

In my view, the most reasonable interpretation of Kaufman is that he thinks that the idea that personal beings of any sort could come into existence only after billions of years of cosmic and biological evolution is part of the body of scientific knowledge. But since this is not the case, his argument fails.

Does Kaufman Accept Scientism?

There is, however, another way in which we could interpret Kaufman's argument. Maybe his argument is not really about the limits set by science for possible states of affairs, but about the limits set by science for our knowledge and what we are rationally entitled to believe. It would then be about epistemology and not really about metaphysics. Recall that Kaufman writes that "*as far as we know,* personal agential beings did not exist, and could not have existed, before billions of years of cosmic evolution of a very specific sort and then further billions of years of biological evolution also of a very specific sort had transpired" (Kaufman 2001: 410, emphasis added). Perhaps we have the key to his argument in the phrase "as far as we know." What Kaufman writes here is, of course, not quite right since traditional believers think they know that a personal God exists or at any rate think that they are rationally entitled to believe this. So let us, therefore, interpret "as far as we know" as "as far as *scientists* know" and do this also because the argument is, after all, about the relevance of science for a particular conception of God.

Kaufman's argument would then in this version contain at least the following premises:

(4) Traditional believers hold that God is personal.
(5) But as far as scientists know, personal beings did not exist before billions of years of cosmic and biological evolution.

There is reason to believe that Polkinghorne accepts both of these premises and — I have argued — so should traditional believers. But the problem is that the conclusion that "traditional believers should no longer hold that God is personal but start to think of God in terms of creativity instead" does not follow from merely these two premises. Something more is needed. After all, traditional believers do not claim that they base their belief in a personal God on what scientists have (or have not) discovered, and they would not even, I expect, be surprised if that is something which science cannot discover anything at all about.

As far as I can see, only if Kaufman assumes the truth of *scientism,* or something akin to it, can he validly derive his conclusion. That is to say, if we accept (4) and (5) and

(6) the only reality we can know anything about is the one science has access to,

then the conclusion seems to follow that

Therefore, traditional believers should no longer hold that God is personal.

Or perhaps that is not quite right. Because it does not really follow from the premises that it is impossible that a personal God exists. It merely follows that even if such a God exists, we can never know it because our knowledge is limited to what can be known through the sciences. Thus what follows is not that traditional believers cannot *believe* that God is personal; rather, what follows is that they cannot any longer claim (if they were aware of this argument) that they *know* that God is personal. This would clearly make a difference for some traditional believers. Note, however, that at least some of them do not claim that they know that God is personal but merely maintain that it is rational for them to believe so. Religion for them is about faith and not about knowledge.

This is worth stressing because Kaufman has a tendency at this point in his argument to present us with merely two alternatives:[3] either we know that God is personal or we have to be agnostic about it. For instance, he contrasts the talk about God-as-mystery with talk of God-as-creator and maintains (as a historical remark) that "this latter concept seemed to imply that we knew the ultimate mystery (God) was really a person-like, agent-like being," but he thinks that it is important to preserve the notion of God as the ultimate mystery of things (p. 413). But many things we believe, we do not consider we know (or completely know). For instance, I do not think I know that my wife parked our Audi at my department today. But since she told me this morning that she in-

---

3. I am well aware that Kaufman elsewhere has developed a more nuanced view, which of course does not contradict that the interpretation I suggest is the most plausible one to offer in this context.

tended to, I maintain that I am *rationally entitled* to believe this; and so with many other things in life (religion included). So we can either claim that (a) we know (or partially know) something, or that (b) we are rationally entitled to believe it, or that (c) we withhold judgment (remain agnostic) about it, or that (d) we reject it. Hence, traditional believers who have, for example, experienced God's presence in their life as the presence of a Divine Thou (in Martin Buber–inspired terminology) can claim that they are rationally entitled to believe in a personal God. They are thus *not* rationally entitled to believe that God is impersonal or that God is neither personal nor impersonal or to be agnostic about it, or, for that matter, to believe that God is a complete mystery.

This last option seems to be Kaufman's own view. He maintains that

> God is, in the last analysis, utterly unknowable. As German hymn writer Gerhard Tersteegen (d. 1769) put it, "A God comprehended [that is, successfully captured in, and thus mastered by, our human concepts and images] is no God." Pseudo-Dionysius, Maimonides, Thomas Aquinas, Eckhart, Luther, and others all understood this, though unfortunately they often compromised this insight by claims about special "experiences" of God or "revelations" from God. . . . (pp. 413-14)

But how could these theologians possibly have "compromised" this idea? Is not the most reasonable interpretation that they actually thought that they had in these experiences and revelations encountered God as a Divine Thou? Therefore, they would in fact have been *irrational* if they did not reject the idea of God as utterly unknowable because of these experiences (given, of course, that they did not have good reasons to question the validity of these experiences). This does not mean that they were right. Truth is, after all, not a necessary condition for rationality. It is, therefore, quite possible that Kaufman is right (although we might wonder how — if that is his claim — he could know that God is utterly unknowable).[4] But what it means is that these theologians were not engaged in any compromising

---

4. Here we actually need to distinguish between two claims, namely, between "I do not know anything about God" and "No one knows or can know anything about God." Kaufman may very well be rationally entitled to embrace the first claim, but whether he also knows that the latter is true or at any rate is rationally entitled to believe it to be true, is a different issue.

activities. Rather, they were very likely rational in believing what they believed on this point. Moreover, is it not so that these theologians never actually claimed that we can "comprehend" God in the sense that Kaufman gives this term, namely, "successfully captured in, and thus mastered by, our human concepts and images" (p. 414)? Did they not rather maintain that we merely know *some* things about God and that our knowledge of God is very much limited and fragmentary? If so, they might have actually agreed with Tersteegen.

Let us now go back to the argument. If Kaufman wants to argue also against those traditional believers who maintain that they are rationally entitled to believe in a personal God, then he needs a stronger premise than (6), for instance,

(7) The only things we are rationally entitled to believe are those that are scientifically knowable.

But again, by employing this strategy Kaufman cannot refute or show the increasing improbability of the existence of a personal God. To do that, he would need an ontological and not an epistemological premise, such as

(8) The only reality that exists is the one science has access to.

Let us, however, focus our attention on premise (6), since premises (7) and (8) cannot be true if (6) is false. What Kaufman then needs to demonstrate is that the claim that "the only reality we can know anything about is the one science has access to" belongs to the stock of scientific knowledge or that science implies scientism (so if you have the first you have to have the second).

But here he would run into deep problems. The difficulty is that the scientistic belief that we can know only what science can tell us seems to be something that science cannot tell us. How can one set up a scientific experiment to demonstrate the truth of that claim? What methods, for instance, in chemistry, biology, or physics are suitable for such a task? Well, hardly those methods that make it possible for scientists to discover and explain electrons, protons, genes, survival mechanisms, and natural selection. Furthermore, it is not because the content of this belief is too small, too distant, or too far in the past for science to determine its truth-value (or probability). Rather, it is that beliefs of this sort are not subject to scientific inquiry. We cannot come to know (6) by appeal to science alone. Premise (6) is, rather, a view in the theory of knowledge and is, therefore, a piece of philosophy and not a piece of science. But if it is a piece of philosophy, then we cannot know it to be true because we would then have *extra-scientific* knowledge. Thus, the claim undermines itself. This is a very serious problem for the defenders of scientism, because if premise (6) is self-refuting then it is not even possible for it to be true. The claim would be necessarily false in the same way as it is logically impossible for the propositions "Some married men are bachelors," "There are no truths," and "There is a human being who is taller than himself" to be true and to constitute knowledge. So no matter how successful science turns out to be in the future, it will not make the slightest difference for the truth of (6).

But it is not merely that (6) is self-refuting and thus cannot possibly be true. We also know, I would claim, that we have extra-scientific knowledge. In fact, if we did not have that we would not be able to have any scientific knowledge. Think, for instance, about beliefs of memory, that is, those beliefs which are about things we have previously experienced or thought about. For instance, I remember that I am married to Anna and fell in love with her in 1986, and that I am now writing about Kaufman. Furthermore, I do not merely believe these things, I also think that I know these things. But I do not think that the beliefs of memory can be scientifically proven. Rather, to be able to develop and test a scientific hypothesis against a certain range of data, scientists have to be able to remember, for instance, the content of the hypothesis, the previous test results, and more fundamentally that they are scientists and where their laboratories are located. Their scientific knowledge presupposes memory. The truth is that unless we could trust our memories (and obtain knowledge), we could never reason at all or do any science whatsoever, because in any inference we must remember our premises on our way to the conclusion.

Is the belief that *I* exist — and thus am a locus of feelings and thoughts — a scientific belief, and if not, can it still constitute knowledge? We have experiences of personal identity over time. We are aware that we are individual centers of consciousness, who now exist and also existed ten years ago. With us matter has become aware of itself. It is furthermore very difficult to doubt that I exist, and that I am the one who is feeling a pain in the stomach and who is now thinking about scientism. It is hard to question that I *know* that *I* exist. Is this belief that there is an "I" or a "self" a scientific belief? No, I certainly have neither acquired nor tested that belief by using scientific methods. In fact, it seems very hard to do such a thing. Must I not assume my own existence at the outset of such a scientific inquiry, in order to believe that I was the one collecting and examining the relevant evidence? The answer must be yes, thus making the whole process hopelessly circular. I would have to assume at the outset what I intended to prove (or disprove).

Moreover, only a self-conscious being knows that he is a knower, that is, someone who is capable of being aware that he knows certain things. One cannot have self-reflective knowledge if one does not know that it is oneself who has this knowledge. Hence, the advocates of scientism can consciously know that the proposition "Scientific knowledge is the only kind of knowledge we can have" is true only if they also know that *they* are the ones who know this. But then they have to admit that they know at least one thing that is not scientifically knowable (namely, that they have a self). So if they know that they know that the only things we can obtain knowledge about are the ones science has access to, they cannot know it because it is false. This point holds with respect to all self-reflective knowledge we have (and that is a lot!), for example, my knowledge that *I* am writing this chapter on scientism, that *I* am married to Anna, that *I* am looking at the tree outside my window, and that *I* am a philosopher of religion.[5]

Hence, there are two serious problems with this second possible version of Kaufman's argument. First, it contains an extra-scientific premise and cannot for this reason be part of a central scientific understanding. Second, this premise is also self-refuting, and therefore the argument cannot possibly be true.

I am not going to develop this next point fully because it seems unnecessary to do so. But let me point out anyway that *even if* one or both of Kaufman's arguments were successful or others like them, traditional believers should still probably not follow his advice and stop thinking about God as personal. The reason is that there seems to be an alternative that is closer to the view that traditional believers hold than is Kaufman's own view, and according to the cautious principle of belief revision (which we discussed on p. 104) this is something rational people should take into account. According to process theists, God is personal but not — as tradi-

---

5. See Stenmark (2001b, chap. 2) for a more extensive argument for the existence of nonscientific knowledge and the way in which scientific knowledge is possible only if we first assume the existence of certain forms of nonscientific knowledge.

tional believers hold — ontologically distinct from the world: instead the world constitutes a part of God. God is, therefore, affected by the world, but God alone is everlasting and does not perish. God is within, but not totally within, the temporal order, and nothing comes into being apart from God. But God nevertheless needs a body (a world) in order to exist.[6] My tentative suggestion is that this opens up a possibility (if one thinks that is necessary) for connecting more closely the idea of a personal God to the evolutionary processes that scientists have discovered and could discover. Hence, in his argument Kaufman needs not merely show that traditional believers' personal conception of God lacks credibility today, but that the same is true about process theism: only then is it rational for traditional believers to reject a personal conception of God and endorse Kaufman's conception of God as creativity.

What have we achieved? Our starting point was that there are traditional believers who hold that God is personal. Our model of rationality, presumptionism, entails that they are rationally entitled to believe this as long as there are no special reasons to believe otherwise. Kaufman, however, maintains that there is such a reason. Christians (who are his main concern) and other believers who have a personal conception of God should, therefore, abandon this view and instead develop a different conception of God based on the idea of creativity. This reason, Kaufman argues, is provided by the sciences. But it is not obvious, because Christian scientists including Polkinghorne (as Kaufman is aware) have failed to notice it and so have many other participants (myself included) in the contemporary science-religion dialogue. This assumed central scientific understanding is, as far as I can understand, that science has shown that personal beings of any sort could come into existence only after billions of years of cosmic and biological evolution. Science has thus established that a necessary condition for any form of personhood to exist is to come into being after a very long period of natural development. But this, I have tried to show, is no part of science, but a metaphysical interpretation of it. There is no problem in doing science, accepting the contemporary established scientific theories, and denying this simply because it is an extra-scientific claim. I also develop another possible version of Kaufman's argument which focuses on the limits of our scientific knowl-

6. Within the science-religion dialogue these ideas have been developed by, for instance, Ian G. Barbour (1990) and John F. Haught (2000).

edge. To derive the conclusion, however, Kaufman needs to presuppose scientism (that the only kind of knowledge we can have is scientific knowledge). But since this claim that the only kind of knowledge we can have is scientific knowledge is not a scientific claim and moreover is self-refuting, his argument fails also in this second version.

We cannot be certain that any of these interpretations do justice to Kaufman's view since he is not as clear as one would like on this point. Our conclusion must, nevertheless, be that it is not rationally required of traditional believers that they give up their belief in a personal God for the reasons that Kaufman gives. Note, however, the limitation that applies to our conclusion. Kaufman's discussion of a conception of God as creativity (which he understands to exclude a personal conception of God) is intriguing and brilliant, and it could very well be rational for many religious believers to think about God along these lines. All I am saying is that it is not rational to do so if you are a traditional believer and encounter Kaufman's arguments. Hence, there might be other reasons (including scientific reasons) why it is not rational for traditional believers to think that God is personal, but our conclusion must be that the ones supplied by Kaufman fail.

Kaufman's Rejoinder

Kaufman has been kind enough to respond to my criticism and it is therefore necessary to consider what he writes, to see whether my conclusion still holds (Kaufman 2003). The issue concerns whether recent developments in science (especially in biology and ecology) undermine a belief in a personal God who among other things is taken to be the creator of the world. Kaufman thinks that this is the case, and therefore suggests that we should no longer hold a personal conception of God but instead think of God in terms of the metaphor of serendipitous creativity. The argument that we should reconstruct religious belief in this way is stated at the beginning of his essay, and then he spends most of his time developing this alternative conception of God (a conception I did not discuss). To put it bluntly, I attempted to undermine his whole project by pointing out that none of the scientific information (the data or theories) he offers us actually supports or entails the conclusion that such a change of conception of God is for *scientific* reasons required of those who believe in a personal God taken to be the creator of the world (I refer to these people as "traditional believers"). (This is of course the reason why I do not explore the main point of Kaufman's essay, thinking of God as serendipitous creativity.)

What, then, is the content of the premises which entail or make Kaufman's conclusion probable? I suggested, on the basis of Kaufman's reference to "a central scientific understanding" that he thinks Polkinghorne and others in the science-religion dialogue have failed to take into account, that the most likely candidate is this premise:

(3) Moreover, science has also shown that personal beings of *any* sort could come into existence only after billions of years of cosmic and biological evolution.

Premise (3) together with the nondisputed premises —

(1) Traditional believers hold that God is personal (that is, God has intentions, can act, create, love, and the like); and
(2) Science has shown us that human beings (that is, creatures who have intentions, can act, create, love, and the like) *came into existence* after billions of years of cosmic and biological evolution —

seems to entail the conclusion:

Therefore, traditional believers should no longer hold that God is personal.

The content of premise (3) was primarily based on Kaufman's claim that

Polkinghorne takes "with all seriousness all that science tells us about the workings of the world" with the exception of a *central* scientific understanding: that complex features of the world such as conscious intention, purposive action, deliberate creation of artifacts, loving attitudes and behaviors, and the like — all attributed to God from the "big bang" onward in the anthropomorphic model in terms of which his notion of God is constructed — can come into being only *after* billions of years of complex cosmic, biological, and historical development have provided the necessary conditions for their emergence to occur. (p. 411 n. 1)

In his rejoinder, Kaufman responds by saying that "no such absolutistic statement concerning what science has shown about 'personal beings of any sort' is to be found in the essay" (p. 183). On this point he is of course absolutely correct. Premise (3) expresses rather what I thought (on the basis of the things he wrote) he *would have to maintain* to justify his conclusion, namely, that there are good scientific reasons why we should no longer hold a personal conception of God but instead start to think of God in terms of creativity. That is to say, the scientific discoveries must be such that they would be of relevance not merely for beings of our kind but also for God (hence, the phrase "personal beings of *any* sort"). So, as I have previously remarked, if science put restrictions on what kind of personal beings can possibly come into existence then this information seems to have some bearing on an understanding of God as personal. But if premise (3) is wrong, how should it then be formulated? Kaufman writes,

> I suggest something like this: 3. Humans are the only beings (of which we know) that possess qualities such as intentions and being able to act, create, love, and the like. It was only in the course of a long, complex, distinctive evolutionary and historical process that these qualities appeared, and we have no reason to suppose that qualities of this sort would be likely to appear elsewhere apart from a quite similar process. (p. 184)

Is the premise in this version more convincing? Let us call Kaufman's own statement of the disputed premise (3′). The obvious problem with the first sentence of (3′) is that it begs the question. Many traditional believers claim that they know that God is personal or at any rate are rationally entitled to believe this (because they believe, for instance, that they have experienced the presence of a divine Thou in their lives). This is what Kaufman should give reasons for rejecting: it should not be something that he already presupposes to be false. Moreover, what "we know" must ultimately be derived from what scientists know if it is going to be a "central scientific understanding" which requires this change of religious belief. So the solution is perhaps to formulate the premise (or the first part of it) as

(3′) the only kind of beings that scientists have discovered possess qualities such as intentions and being able to act, create, love, and the like are human beings, and the second part of it as,

(4) scientists *qua* scientists have no reason to believe that qualities of this sort (that is, personal qualities) would be likely to appear elsewhere apart from a long, complex, and distinctive evolutionary process.

Should we accept (3') and (4)? Kaufman admits that (4) is a debatable point, but let us for the sake of argument accept both of these premises. The difficulty is, however, that the conclusion that traditional religious believers should no longer hold that God is personal does not follow and is not made probable by this line of argument. It says something only about the limits of scientific knowledge or scientifically entitled rational belief but nothing about the limits of religious knowledge or religiously entitled rational belief. It is therefore possible that traditional believers know things or are rationally entitled to believe things that scientists in their professional role cannot know or be rationally entitled to believe. This problem is, of course, quickly solved if we introduce scientism by, for instance, adding this premise:

(5) Our knowledge or what we are rationally entitled to believe is limited to what can be known or justified through the sciences.

The difficulty with this argument — besides the fact that formulations like (5) are self-refuting as we have seen — is that Kaufman explicitly says in the rejoinder that he rejects scientism: "I also agree with Stenmark that it is a mistake to suppose (as some 'scientistic' types perhaps do) that 'our knowledge is limited to what can be known through the sciences'" (p. 184 n. 4). My mistaken assumption that Kaufman does his "theological work completely within scientific bounds is a major source of the confusions in his discussion," he continues (p. 185). I have of course not made any comment about Kaufman's theological work, but merely suggested that one way in which he could justify his conclusion is by adding a scientistic premise to the argument. It is a proposal offered to make his (in my view) incomplete argument valid. The problem with his rejoinder is, however, that he *also* writes thus:

> Now surely a God with humanlike qualities of the sort we are considering here would be at least as complex as we humans are. So to posit a

God of such complexity at the beginning of the whole world process does go directly counter to the basic thrust of evolutionary thinking, though it is certainly not logically impossible. . . . The more we are persuaded that evolutionary/ecological patterns of thinking are the most appropriate ones now available for understanding the realities with which we humans have to do, the more questions we will have when we try to think about God in an anthropomorphic way. (pp. 184-85)

But this way of arguing sounds scientistic! Kaufman assumes that evolutionary/ecological patterns of thinking are the most appropriate ones now available for understanding the realities which we humans have to understand, *including even God.* But why should we believe this, if we do not presuppose that there is something privileged about science and the scientific way of knowing even when it comes to religious issues? Evolutionary biologists in their scientific work should of course not "posit a God of such complexity at the beginning of the whole world process," but why think that traditional believers would be limited in this way? (Recall also the problem, discussed in chapter 4, that arises from thinking that religious people see or should see belief in God as a hypothesis.) Kaufman himself does not seem to accept such limitations because he writes, "In the picture of evolution that I draw, I certainly go — in many respects — beyond what can be scientifically established (as theology always should be free to do)" (p. 185). But why should not those theologians and others who hold onto a personal conception of God be allowed to do the same thing? Moreover, I am not at all convinced that evolutionary patterns of thinking are the most appropriate ones now available for understanding, for instance, love, altruism, or morality in general. I have in *Scientism* (2001b) tried to show how such unique human features can be seriously misconstrued if one takes categories from evolutionary biology as one's basic frame of reference. This could be just as true when it comes to conceptions of God.

Whether or not what Kaufman says entails the acceptance of some form of scientism, the premise which together with (3') and (4) makes the conclusion of this new version of his argument probable is lacking. Hence, my overall conclusion still holds that Kaufman has not given traditional believers any good *scientific* reason for abandoning a personal conception of God and that, therefore, there is no reason why they should understand God in terms of serendipitous creativity. But this is, of course, not to deny that "today's scientific pictures of the world and its evolutionary development must be taken very seriously as we pursue our thinking about God" (p. 185). On this we can certainly agree. It is just that it might not be as relevant as Kaufman thinks.

Notice further that also in this version of the argument Kaufman fails to take into account one of the objections I previously raised. Also understood in this way the argument tells us merely about what conditions must be satisfied for something to come into being or to be "likely to appear" (p. 184). But, of course, traditional believers do not hold that God came into existence. Rather, they believe that God has always existed. They believe that God is eternal. So even if not merely scientists *qua* scientists but all of us have no reason to believe that personal qualities such as being able to create and love would be likely to appear elsewhere in the universe apart from a long, complex, and distinctive evolutionary process, this is not relevant when it comes to evaluating the personal conception of God held by traditional believers because God's existence, *ex hypothesi*, is not understood to be of that kind.

Biology, Religion, and Ultimate Meaning

A number of biologists maintain that recent developments in evolutionary biology have profound implications for religion, morality, and our self-understanding in general.[7] Richard D. Alexander, for instance, maintains that these recent developments have such an impact that "we will have to start all over again to describe and understand ourselves, in terms alien to our intuitions" (Alexander 1987: 3). These developments, such scholars maintain, are going to change every concept of relevance for our self-view, concepts such as rationality, consciousness, guilt, meaning, unselfishness, and egoism. In this section I focus on one of these issues, namely, the *impact of evolutionary biology on a religious understanding of the meaning of life*. If we take the recent developments in evolutionary biology seriously, how is it likely to affect our religious beliefs about the meaning of life?

7. The first version of this section was published in Stenmark (2001a) and reprinted in Stenmark (2001b). In this new version I have extended some of the argument and added new material. It has been available online in *Metanexus: The Online Forum for Science and Religion* (www.metanexus.net).

The challenge posed by science is that evolutionary theory seems to undermine the religious belief that there is a purpose or meaning to the existence of the universe and to human life in particular, and therefore people should reject such a belief or perhaps even abandon their religion as a whole.

Let me give some examples of scientists holding this view. Gould tells us that "Darwin argues that evolution has no purpose. Individuals struggle to increase the representation of their genes in future generations, and that is all" (Gould 1977: 12). Provine asserts, "Modern science directly implies that there . . . is no ultimate meaning for humans" (Provine 1988: 28). Dawkins maintains, "The universe we observe has precisely the properties we should expect if there is, at bottom, no design, no purpose, no evil and no good, nothing but blind, pitiless indifference. . . . DNA neither knows nor cares. DNA just is. And we dance to its music" (Dawkins 1995a: 133). Wilson writes, "no species, ours included, possesses a purpose beyond the imperatives created by its genetic history" (Wilson 1978: 2). Finally, George Gaylord Simpson claims, "Man is the result of a purposeless and natural process that did not have him in mind" (Simpson 1967: 345).

But many Christians, Jews, and Muslims, for instance, believe that the universe is created by God and that God intended to bring into being creatures made in God's image, and that therefore the universe and also human life have a purpose. So there seems to be a serious clash between science and religion on this point. The theologian John F. Haught thinks that if these evolutionary biologists are right then the conflict is so serious that "although theology can accommodate many different scientific ideas, it cannot get along with the notion of an inherently purposeless cosmos" because such an idea is so central to a theological and religious concern (Haught 2000: 26). He does not think this is true about merely the major theistic religions but of most religions of the world. Haught writes,

> Since for many scientists today evolution clearly implies a meaningless universe, *all religions* must be concerned about it. Evolutionists raise questions not only about the Christian God but also about notions of ultimate reality or cosmic meaning as these are understood by many of the world's other religious traditions. . . . Almost all religions, and not just Christianity, have envisaged the cosmos as the expression of a transcending "order," "wisdom," or "rightness," rather than as an irreversibly evolving process. Most religions have held that there is some

unfathomable "point" to the universe, and that the cosmos is en-
shrouded by a meaning over which we can have no intellectual control,
and to which we must in the end surrender humbly. (Haught 2000: 9)

So there are good reasons why many religious practitioners ought to take
seriously these claims made by scientists and in particular by evolutionary
biologists. The key claim seems to be that evolutionary theory implies that
there is no purpose or meaning to be found behind the emergence of human beings in natural history. In other words, we are not here for a reason
and, in particular, we are not planned by God or anything like God. (I
think there are more claims involved but I will not consider them in this
context.)

The Scientific and the Scientistic No-Purpose Argument

Even if the key claim is not difficult to identify it is not so easy to determine what exactly the argument is that these biologists appeal to, to justify
it. The conclusion is more often stated than the premises that warrant such
conclusion. But it seems to have something to do with the fact that evolutionary biologists have discovered that central to the development of life is
chance or randomness. Dawkins writes that "natural selection, the blind,
unconscious, automatic process which Darwin discovered, and which we
now know is the explanation for the existence and apparently purposeful
form of all life, has no purpose in mind" (Dawkins 1986: 5). But, of course,
Christians, Jews, and Muslims (in short, theists) are not committed to believe that natural selection had any purpose in mind, because natural selection is not an agent and as far as we know only agents can have purposes
in mind. What they seem to be committed to believing is rather that *God
had a purpose in mind in using natural selection as a means to create human
beings and that we, therefore, exist for a reason.* The question is then
whether science undermines such a religious belief. To be able to argue
that that is the case, it seems as if one must show that natural selection (or
any other relevant biological process) and the belief "God brings us intentionally into existence" are or probably are incompatible; in other words,
they cannot both be true at the same time.

What Gould writes may prove to be a good starting-point for such a
"no-purpose argument" because he maintains that evolutionary biology

has shown that "we are the accidental result of an unplanned process . . . the fragile result of an enormous concatenation of improbabilities, not the predictable product of any definite process" (Gould 1983: 101-2). In other words, evolutionary biologists cannot find any propensities in the organic material they investigate which make the development of human beings likely. Therefore, human life lacks a meaning in the sense that we were planned by God or anything like God to appear in natural history. Gould writes, "*Homo sapiens* . . . ranks as a 'thing so small' in a vast universe, a wildly improbable evolutionary event, and [therefore] not the nub of universal purpose" (Gould 1999: 206). The argument then seems to be that all biological events taking place in evolutionary history, including the emergence of our species, are random with respect to what evolutionary theory can predict or retrospectively explain. Therefore, there is no ultimate meaning to human life. Humans are not planned by God or anything like God to be here.

Before assessing this argument let me try to clarify in what sense we are talking about purpose or meaning in this particular context. First, we need to distinguish between the meaning or purpose of (a) the universe, of (b) human life in general, and of (c) a particular individual's life. Such a distinction is of importance because it seems possible that an individual life, for instance, can have meaning even if the universe as a whole were to lack meaning. What we primarily focus on is the second issue, the one about the meaning or purpose of the existence of the human species. Second, we also need to distinguish between whether something (e) exists for a reason, (f) serves some particular end, or (g) chooses to achieve some particular end. For instance, there is a purpose to my children's lives in the sense that they exist for a reason because my wife and I intended that they should come into existence (sense e). But we did not intend that they should serve some particular end, at least not in the way that our new car is intended to make it easier for us to travel between different places (sense f). We hope, however, that they in their lives would strive toward some particular end or strive to realize some particular values (sense g), so that their lives will have a positive meaning. So it is possible that we can exist for a reason without ourselves serving a particular purpose, and other combinations of these different senses might be possible as well.

The question "What is the meaning or purpose of life?" is, in other words, ambiguous in a twofold way. In asking it we can mean "Why does the universe exist?" or "Why do humans, that is, our species, exist?" or

"Why do I exist?" Moreover, in asking, "What is the meaning or purpose of life?" we can also mean, "Do humans in general or I in particular exist for some purpose?" or "What values or interests should we (or I) structure our lives (or my life) around to give them (or it) meaning?" Our focus, however, is merely on the question whether the human species exists for some purpose, that is (b) and (e) combined (not denying of course that the answer we give on this issue may have implications for the others).

So what about the "scientific" no-purpose argument — is it a valid and sound argument? The argument appears to be thus:

(1) The human species came into existence through the process of evolution.
(2) But all individual species that come into existence through the process of evolution are random (i.e., have a low probability) with respect to what evolutionary theory (or more broadly, the sciences) can predict or retrospectively explain.

Therefore, the existence of human beings is an accidental event; that is, their existence as a species is not a result of God's purposes, intentions, or plans (given that such a being exists).

Let us grant, for the sake of argument, that it is true that the existence of human beings is a wildly improbable event given the information that is accessible to scientists through the use of biological methods; but how can we from this information alone conclude that we are not intended by God or something like God to be here? This does not seem possible and consequently there is a logical gap between the premises and the conclusion. The scientific no-purpose argument is an incomplete argument. We need an extra premise to make the argument valid because it is quite possible that things could exist for a purpose even if evolutionary biologists were unable to discover it.

Does perhaps the argument presuppose the all-sufficiency of biology or that the scientific account is exhaustive? That what science cannot discover does not exist or at least that we cannot know anything about it? If so we would, it seems, have the extra premise needed for the argument to be valid: If evolutionary theory implies that our existence is a widely improbable event and *the only source of knowledge we have is science (or more specifically evolutionary biology, in this case)* then it follows that we ought to believe that our existence is the result of pure chance, that is, it is not a part of anyone's plan and it serves no one's end. (Thus a "chance event" is in this context taken to be something that is not a part of anyone's plan and serves no one's end.)

Let us call this version of the argument the "scientistic" no-purpose argument (since it presuppose the acceptance of scientism):

(1) The human species came into existence through the process of evolution.

(2) But all individual species that come into existence through the process of evolution are random (that is, have a low probability) with respect to what evolutionary theory (or more broadly, the sciences) can predict or retrospectively explain.

(3) *The only things we can know anything about or rationally believe anything about are the ones science can discover.*

Therefore, the existence of human beings is an accidental event, that is, their existence as a species is not a result of God's purposes, intentions, or plans, given that such a being exists.

But the problem with such an argument is that the extra premise appears to contain a *non-scientific* claim. For how can one set up a scientific experiment to demonstrate the truth of (3)? What methods in, for instance, biology or physics are suitable for such a task? Well, hardly those methods that make it possible for scientists to discover and explain electrons, protons, genes, survival mechanisms, and natural selection. Furthermore, as we have earlier discussed, it is not because the content of this belief is too small, too distant, or too far in the past for science to determine its truth-value. Rather, it is that beliefs of this sort are not subject to scientific inquiry. We cannot come to know (3) by appeal to science alone. Premise (3) is a view in the theory of knowledge and is, therefore, a piece of philosophy and not a piece of science. But, again, if it is a piece of philosophy then we cannot know it to be true because we would then have nonscientific knowledge, which the premise denies the possibility of. Thus, the more profound problem with the premise is that it seems to undermine itself. If it is true, then it is false. So what we have here is a version of the no-purpose argument which contains a controversial nonscientific premise (scientism) and, moreover, appears to be self-refuting.

The "Not Purely Scientific" No-Purpose Argument

Is there any other, more promising way in which the no-purpose argument could be developed so that those of us who take evolutionary theory seriously may after all have to reconsider at least some of our religious beliefs? I think so. These biologists could, instead of maintaining (3), add a premise about the *conditions that must be satisfied for something to exist for a reason or to be something that is intended or planned by someone.* Thus they could claim that it is this premise together with premises (1) and (2) that entails the conclusion.

Remember that the religious belief under consideration is that we — as a species — are here in accordance with God's plan, that there is in this sense a meaning or purpose to our existence. We are not merely accidental because God intended to create us and did so, we have discovered, not by a direct act of creation but by the process of evolution. It seems, however, as if a requirement for a plan, purpose, foresight, or intention to be involved in an object coming into being is that this object is not the result of mere chance but has a certain likelihood of obtaining. That is to say, we cannot *attribute purpose* to a thing without implying that someone did something intentionally, that someone had a purpose in mind in bringing about the thing. But that is not sufficient. I might have the intention to bring about a state of affairs, say to plant some red roses in my garden, and as a result I take away the grass and in its place put some topsoil from a bag that I have bought. Three weeks later, even though I have not planted some seeds in the flowerbed, red roses start to grow. Under these circumstances we would not say that there is a purpose why these red roses grow in my garden merely because I had such a general intention. Even though I had the intention to bring about this state of affairs this is not in itself sufficient, because the likelihood that my action, given what I actually did, would have this outcome is too low.

If the advocates of the no-purpose argument from evolutionary biology apply these observations about purposive actions of human agents to God, they would, it seems, have a complete argument, and one that would not presuppose the acceptance of scientism. The argument would then be as follows:

(4) The human species came into existence through the process of evolution.

(5) *The existence of the human species is planned by God (or something like God) only if (a) the species' existence is intended by God and (b) it is probable that its emergence by means of evolution will take place for that reason.*

(6) But all individual species that come into existence through the process of evolution are random (that is, have a low probability) with respect to what evolutionary theory (or more broadly, the sciences) can predict or retrospectively explain.

Therefore, the existence of human beings is an accidental event, that is, their existence as a species is not a result of God's purposes, intentions, or plans (given that such a being exists).

Is this a good argument? Perhaps, but notice that it is not a *scientific* argument because premise (5) contains an extra-scientific or philosophical claim. So this argument could not be used to support Provine's claim that "Modern science directly implies that there . . . is no ultimate meaning for humans" (Provine 1988: 28). Evolutionary biology alone cannot establish that the universe and humans are not here for a reason. What seems true is that scientific theories such as evolutionary theory can *in conjunction with* an extra-scientific or a philosophical claim like (5) undermine such a religious belief.

Let us assume that the argument in this version is valid and sound. What would then follow, for instance, for Christians who take evolutionary theory seriously? It would imply that they had to accept that God did not have the human species in mind when creating the world and that therefore our existence is without purpose in the sense that it is not part of anyone's plan. Our existence would then be due to chance because it was not a part of God's plan for the creation. Is this a modification that Christianity can undergo without losing its unique identity?

I think, perhaps surprisingly, that the answer is "yes," and to see why consider the following analogy. Jacob is my firstborn child. My wife and I did not plan to have Jacob, however; our plan was simply to have a child. But as things turned out, Jacob happens to have been born.[8] Jacob's existence, then, is due to chance, because when we decided to have a child he

---

8. This in contrast to my sister and her husband who decided to adopt children. They decided to adopt *those* particular children, Victor and Victoria.

was not part of our plan. I suggest that Christians and other religious believers can understand their relationship to God in a similar way, and just
as my wife and I love our son, God could love people in the way Christians
believe that God loves them, even though the human species was not intended to exist. (Here is in fact an opportunity to get away from the strong
form of anthropocentrism that, I think, has been too closely associated
with traditional Christianity.)

What Christians (and of course Jews and Muslims as well) seem to
be committed to is rather the belief that central to God's purpose is, as
Keith Ward puts it, the "generation of communities of free, self-aware, self-
directing sentient beings" (Ward 1996a: 191). On such an account the purpose of genes is to build bodies, the purpose of bodies is to build brains,
and the purpose of brains is to generate consciousness and even self-
consciousness, and with it there appear for the first time in natural history
reflective and critical thinking, experiences of meaning, love and forgiveness, and a capacity to choose between good and evil. This development is
something that was part of God's plan with creation, although the specific
development of human beings was not part of that plan.

But does perhaps evolutionary biology also undermine this belief
that God brought the universe into being in order to realize a set of values
or worthwhile states, including, in particular, the emergence of a complex
self-conscious life-form, a life-form that due to chance happens to become
Homo sapiens? It is more difficult, I think, for evolutionary biologists to argue successfully for such a conclusion because in their profession they typically focus on the evolution of a particular lineage of animals — which
they have shown could have developed in a number of quite different ways
from the way it actually developed — and not on the *types* of life-forms
and *functions* served. Holmes Rolston has provided at least some reasons
to doubt the credibility of such a version of the no-purpose argument. He
writes,

> Assuming more or less the same Earth-bound environments, if evolu-
> tionary history were to occur all over again, things would be different.
> Still, there would likely again be organisms reproducing, genotypes
> and phenotypes, natural selection over variants, multicellular organ-
> isms with specialized cells, membranes, organs; there would likely be
> plants and animals; photosynthesis or some similar means of solar en-
> ergy captured in primary producers such as plants, and secondary

consumers with sight, and other sentience such as smell and hearing; mobility with fins, limbs, and wings, such as in animals. There would be predators and prey, parasites and hosts, autotrophs and heterotrophs, ecosystemic communities; there would be convergence and parallelism. Coactions and cooperations would emerge. Life would probably evolve in the sea, spread to the land and the air. Play the tape of history again; the first time we replayed it the differences would strike us. Leigh Van Valen continues: "Play the tape a few more times, though. We see similar melodic elements appearing in each, and the overall structure may be quite similar. . . . When we take a broader view, the role of contingency diminishes. Look at the tape as a whole. It resembles in some ways a symphony, although its orchestration is internal and caused largely by the interactions of many melodic strands." (Rolston 1999: 20)

The biochemist Christian de Duve agrees with Rolston and Van Valen on this point. He writes, "Life was bound to arise under the prevailing conditions, and it will arise similarly wherever and whenever the same conditions obtain. There is hardly any room for 'lucky accidents' in the gradual, multistep process whereby life originated. . . . I view this universe [as] . . . made in such a way as to generate life and mind, bound to give birth to thinking beings" (Duve 1995: xv and xviii). So perhaps it is true that the development of the human species is not likely given the scientific theories we have, but the development of *some* form of intelligent life might still be. If we play the tape again and again, it seems likely that something *like* us will reappear.

I have suggested that Christians and other theists may, as a response to what we have come to know through evolutionary biology about the development of life on earth, modify their religious faith in such a way that they admit that the existence of the human race was probably not planned by God. Instead of believing that God had a *particular species* in mind, they should (or at least could) believe that what God had in mind was the emergence of a generation of communities of free, self-aware, self-directing sentient beings. The benefit of thus revising our beliefs is that the likelihood that such a life-form would appear in evolutionary history is much higher than that a particular instance of this type of life, *Homo sapiens*, would emerge.

But why think even that this development had to take place on

Earth? Why believe that part of God's plan or intention was to create on *a particular planet* a complex self-conscious life-form by means of evolution? I see no reason why Christians (or Jews and Muslims, for that matter) should think that they are committed to believe that the creation of the Earth was essential for God's plans. If we accept this line of thought, however, then surely the likelihood that free, self-aware, and self-directing sentient beings would appear *somewhere* in the universe is higher than the likelihood that this form of life would emerge on the planet that we call "Earth." So it seems to be compatible with theism not merely that our existence is due to chance, but also that it was due to chance that the evolution of a complex self-conscious life-form did take place on this particular planet.

The Complete No-Purpose Argument

But suppose that evolutionary biologists like Dawkins, Gould, and Wilson succeeded in developing an argument that could show even that the emergence of communities of free, self-aware, self-directing sentient beings in natural history is not probable on Earth or anywhere else in the universe, given what evolutionary theory (or more broadly, the sciences) can predict or retrospectively explain. Does it really follow then, as we have assumed so far, that the existence of a complex self-conscious life-form (which has by chance been actualized in the form of the human species) is not, or is probably not, a result of God's purposes, intentions, or plans? I do not think so for the following reason.

It seems to me that the relevant issue is not, strictly speaking, what is likely given the scientific information or theories we possess (premise 6), but what is probable given what we could assume that *God's* knowledge would be about the outcome of the evolutionary process that science investigates, if certain initial conditions are initiated at the beginning of the universe. Theists agree that such a being's cognitive capacity would far outrun our capacity. They disagree, however, whether God's knowledge includes merely what *has* occurred and *is* occurring, or also all that *will* occur. Some theists even think that God possesses "middle knowledge." In other words, God also knows what *would* in fact happen in every possible situation or possible world (see Basinger 1996 and Hasker 1989).

Moreover, where theists stand on this issue depends at least partially on whether they think God is best understood as a temporal or as an atemporal being. Ernan McMullin, like St. Augustine and Thomas Aquinas, believes that the most appropriate way to describe God's relationship to time is to say that God is an atemporal being or that God exists "outside of" time. This means that God knows the world in the act of creating it, and thus knows the cosmic past, present, and future in a single unmediated grasp. But if this is so, McMullin points out, it does not seem as if it matters whether the emergence of the human species or any other complex self-conscious life-form is an inevitable product of the evolutionary process or whether it is a widely improbable event given what evolutionary biologists can predict or retrospectively explain (McMullin 1998: 410). This is so because God would then not anticipate the future by extrapolating from knowledge of the present, as we do, but would know the outcome of evolution in the direct way that we know the present. For God to plan means on such an account that the outcome occurs; there is no gap between decision and completion.

But even if God is understood to be a temporal being and God's knowledge is limited to everything that is or has been and what follows deterministically from it, it seems as though God's ability to predict with great accuracy the outcome of future natural causes and events is enormous. We cannot, therefore, automatically assume that what is probable, given such divine knowledge, is the same as what is probable given the scientific knowledge that we happen to have.

Thus if God planned to create us or more specifically a complex self-conscious life-form, and if it is likely that we or such a life-form actually came into existence, then, given what God can know about the future of the evolving natural processes, one could reasonably claim that we are here for a reason, although the human species was perhaps not an explicit part of God's plans, purposes, or intentions, just as I could maintain that my daughter Beatrice exists for a reason, although she was not an explicit part of our plan when my wife and I decided to have a second child.

To establish the opposite conclusion seems to require more than basing one's calculation of probable outcomes on current scientific theories. The argument would have to show that the evolution of human beings or any complex self-conscious life-form is unlikely given (a) what we know through biology or any other science about evolution and (b) what we could assume God would know about the outcome of the process of evolution, and that the existence of human beings or of a complex self-conscious life-form, therefore, has not occurred for some purpose, that is, is not a result of God's intentions or plans. The argument would then be as follows:

(4′) A complex self-conscious life-form, that is, the human species, came into existence through the process of evolution.

(5′) The existence of a complex self-conscious life-form is planned by God (or something like God) only if (a) its existence is intended by God and (b) it is likely that its emergence by means of evolution will take place for that reason.

(6′) But the development of any complex self-conscious life-form through the process of evolution is random (that is, has a low probability) with respect to what evolutionary theory (or more broadly, the sciences) can predict or retrospectively explain.

(7) *Moreover, the development of a complex self-conscious life-form through the process of evolution is unlikely given what we can assume that God (given that such a being exists) would know about the outcome of the process of evolution.*

Therefore, the existence of a complex self-conscious life-form is or is most likely an accidental event, that is, its existence is not or is probably not a result of God's purposes, intentions, or plans, given that such a being exists.

(Notice that the old premises [4], [5], and [6] and the conclusion are modified in this argument because the focus is no longer on the human species in particular but on complex self-conscious life-forms. This change is motivated by the fact that, as I have suggested, it is possible that Christians and many other theists could accept without any misgiving that the human race is not a specific part of God's plan.)

But we have seen that there are good reasons to question premise (6′) and premise (7), and that the argument therefore is simply unconvincing. Moreover, a successful elaboration of the no-purpose argument takes us far outside the domain of science and into philosophy and theology. Hence, any inferences from evolutionary biology that a self-conscious life-form, actualized in the human species, does not exist for some purpose cannot be categorized as scientific, at least not along the lines we have investigated.

A number of scientists maintain, then, that evolutionary theory undermines the religious belief that there is a purpose or meaning to the existence of the human race, that — in other words — we as a species were planned by God to emerge in natural history. We have seen that the problem with their argument is that the conclusion that "the existence of human beings is not a result of God's purposes, intentions, or plans (given that such a being exists)" does not follow merely from the scientific information they offer as evidence. What is also needed is some kind of extra-scientific or philosophical premise or premises. But then it follows that evolutionary biology (or the sciences in general) alone does not undermine a religious understanding of the meaning of life, in the interpretation we have given to the idea, and to pretend anything else would be misleading.

There are, however, at least some reasons to doubt that God had the human species in mind when creating the world, given that we add to the evolutionary or scientific premises a premise about what the conditions are for being justified in attributing meaning or purpose to a thing, process, or event. Therefore our existence may be without purpose in the sense that it is not part of anyone's plan. In this way evolutionary biology *in conjunction with* certain plausible philosophical ideas about purposive action may convince religious people to reconsider their religious faith. But such a modification of Christianity, Judaism, or Islam is, contrary to what it perhaps seems, not something devastating but rather something that makes these religions less anthropocentric and thus perhaps more interesting.

WE HAVE EXAMINED two ways in which it has been claimed that the content of particular scientific theories is of great relevance for the content of religious faith. The first claim contained the idea that the scientific understanding of cosmic and biological evolution undermines the conception of a personal God, who is the creator of the universe. The second claim was that evolutionary theory implies that we, *Homo sapiens,* are not here for a reason, in particular, we are not planned by God or anything like God to be here. The theoretical overlap between science and religion (at least as regards the classic theistic religions Christianity, Islam, and Judaism) is such that scientific theory development forces or makes possible — depending on whether or not we think these changes would improve religion — a reevaluation and reconstruction of a key element in the content of religious faith. Although I have argued that both of these arguments fail because they rely on the truth not merely of scientific premises but also of extra-scientific or philosophical premises, they could (more successfully in the second case) in conjunction with premises of this second sort force or make possible changes in the content of religious faith. This state of affairs paves the way for a contact view in respect to the theoretical level of engagement between science and religion.

Chapter 8

A Science Shaped by Religion

O ur discussion has led us to question many of the claims made by scientific expansionists such as Peter Atkins, Richard Dawkins, and Edward O. Wilson. Their ideas, I have argued, typically presuppose the acceptance of extra-scientific or philosophical claims. In particular, such individuals fail to see that their views are not really science but disguised naturalism. They presuppose (consciously or unconsciously) the acceptance of a particular worldview, in terms of which they then interpret the data they have access to as scientists. It is on exactly this point that people who are not scientific expansionists but *religious expansionists* agree with me. But they are ready to go one step further than what I have taken so far. According to them science cannot and should not be thought of as religiously neutral at all. They believe, rather, that the boundaries of religion can and should be expanded in such a way that religion in some important way becomes a part of the scientific enterprise — this to the extent that it is appropriate to talk about a "theistic science," "faith-informed science," "religious science," or "sacred science."

They do not stand alone on this issue. A number of philosophers, sociologists, biologists, and other academics have expressed similar ideas, although the system of thought they want to incorporate into science is not necessarily Christianity or Islam or any other religion, but feminist, Marxist, gay, postmodern, or African-American ideas. They have taught us to ask questions such as "Science for whom?" "Who is served by science and who is ignored?" "Why do we know this and not that?" "How might science look different were its methods or personnel or priorities to change?" These issues about the "ideologies of science" have to do with how and to what extent political parties, industry, gender, class, and race influence scientific practice, encourage or discourage research, and lend bias to scientific results.

We could also classify these views as religious if we wanted to, but since these views are typically understood to be political or ideological rather than religious (although no sharp distinction can be upheld), I shall classify them as versions of "ideological expansionism" and call their defenders "ideological expansionists." The term "worldview expansionists" will be used as an umbrella term, covering both religious and ideological expansionists (not denying thereby that there could be a significant overlap between these kinds of expansionists). Thus, the concept of worldview will be taken to refer to religions and their secular counterpart, naturalism, as well as to political ideologies such as environmentalism, feminism, and Marxism.[1]

The "official" view under attack is the idea that proper science is independent (or at least should be carried on independently) of religious or ideological concerns. What the scientists are trying to do — often successfully but not always — on such a view, is to figure out the truth about the earth, cosmos, and us without either presupposing or advocating a particular ideology or religious faith. Science is therefore taken to be religiously or ideologically neutral.

But who is right? Moreover, if science is not (and should not be)

---

1. Notice that there is a fundamental ambiguity in the way the concept of worldview is used within the science-religion discussion. On the one hand, scholars talk about the scientific worldview and by that mean the picture of the universe that emerges if we bring together the different theories of physics, astronomy, biology, sociology, and so on into a systematic whole. On the other hand, we can find scholars making statements about the embeddedness of science within a particular worldview, for instance, within feminism, Christianity, Islam, or naturalism. It is in this second sense that the term "worldview" is used in this book. The function of a worldview in this sense is primarily to help people to deal with their existential concerns, that is, their questions about who they are, why they exist, what the meaning of their life is, and what stance they should take toward experiences of death, suffering, guilt, love, forgiveness, and so forth. A worldview is thus the constellation of beliefs and values that (consciously or unconsciously) guides people in their attempt to deal with their existential concerns. A religious worldview affirms that we can adequately deal with our existential concerns only if we let our lives be transformed or enlightened by God or a divine reality, whereas a secular worldview denies this.

ideologically or religiously neutral, what is the alternative? *Should we not question not merely scientific expansionism but also scientific restrictionism, and thus accept worldview expansionism?* Here we face a crucial choice. We can see this if we consider what answers we could give to the question of whether the proposed expansions of the domain of science we have examined are a genuine part of science. Let us call these expansions simply "scientific naturalism." We can answer this question in any of the following ways:

(1) Scientific naturalism is proper science.
(2) Scientific naturalism is not proper science because it is shaped by ideological or worldview elements.
(3) Scientific naturalism is not proper science because the religious or ideological elements it is shaped by are not made explicit.
(4) Scientific naturalism is not proper science because it is shaped by the wrong kind of religious or ideological elements.

I have suggested that there are good reasons to reject (1), that scientific naturalism is proper science, because many of the things the advocates of scientific naturalism think are scientific statements are not warranted but are in fact speculative claims or extra-scientific ones, and these things cannot, therefore, be put forward in the name of science.[2] Thus, I seem to have taken for granted position (2). But perhaps this is premature. Could it be the case that (2) cannot really be maintained, or, even if it can, perhaps (3) or (4) is to be preferred anyway? Views (3) and (4) are examples of positions that religious expansionists maintain. Since they believe that science and worldviews either cannot or should not be kept apart, their criticism of scientific naturalism cannot be that it contains worldview elements. Instead it must consist of the idea that advocates of scientific naturalism either hide their worldview, which is wrong, or do not tie science to the right worldview. Thus to be able to defend position (2) successfully, it seems as if one must not only show why we should reject this form of scientific expansionism but also why worldview expansionism ought to be rejected. But recall that if we accept the *dynamic* model that I have proposed, we cannot once and for all reject any of these two forms of expansionism even if we find good reasons to reject them at the present time. This is so be-

2. This is more extensively done in Stenmark (2001b).

cause the development and transformation of either science or religion/ideology (or both) could be such that it warrants in the future one or the other of the two forms of expansionism. Moreover, the model of science and religion we have developed is a *multidimensional* model, and therefore overlap between science and religion could be found or advocated at different levels. Religion, as we shall see, could shape science (and vice versa) in many different ways; some of these might be more acceptable (or even more desirable) than others.

Next I shall introduce some distinctions and concepts that I hope give us the conceptual tools we need to be able to analyze and eventually evaluate the interrelated issues of worldview expansionism and worldview-neutral science, before we consider the case for religious and ideological expansionism in more detail.

Worldview-Neutral and Worldview-Partisan Science

Terms such as "neutral" and "biased," which are central to the debate about religiously or ideologically neutral science, are terms we frequently use in other areas of life with a similar meaning. I shall therefore take my starting-point in a different context which is less complicated but which can nevertheless shed light on the former.

I am one of the coaches of my eleven-year-old son's soccer team. Imagine that one day his team is playing against another team, but the referee does not turn up. We decide to play the game anyway and the other team agrees that I shall be the referee of the game. My hope is that although I cannot and will not deny that I want my son's soccer team to win the game, I nevertheless can avoid being biased, that is, avoid unfairly favoring his team over the other. This might be difficult but not, it seems, impossible. The game starts and I make the calls, and after the game (which my son's team wins) the coaches of the other team thank me and tell me that I did a great job because in their judgment all my calls were fair and unbiased. They tell me, however, that I made one big mistake. By the end of the game their team should have had a penalty kick that I failed to see. But they still do not think that I was biased or unfair. Why? They are aware of the fact that the game at that point turned very quickly from one side of the field to the other, and for that reason I was too far away from the ball to be able to really see what happened. So I made an error, a serious error, but I was nevertheless not biased because the most reasonable explanation of my behavior was not that I really wanted my team to win and therefore unfairly favored them, but something else, my lack of speed and sight.

Here we have several important distinctions that I think we can apply also to our discussion about worldview-neutral science and worldview expansionism. One is that although I wanted my team to win, it was still possible, but difficult, to avoid being biased, that is, to avoid favoring my son's team unfairly over the other. The other is that the difference between the referee who did not turn up and me was that he did not beforehand favor any of the teams whereas I did. He was in this regard neutral whereas I was partisan. My first suggestion is that we use the terms "neutral" and "partisan" in the same way in the debate about worldview expansionism. We could then say the following:

(1) Science (or some part of science) is *religiously* or *ideologically neutral* if it is not aligned with or does not support a particular ideology, religion, or worldview over another.

(2) Science (or some part of science) is *religiously* or *ideologically partisan* if it is aligned with or supports a particular ideology, religion, or worldview over another.

Given the definitions (1) and (2), Helen Longino's feminist science, Michael Root's perfectionist science, and Alvin Plantinga's theistic science are examples of worldview-partisan science. Longino writes, "the neo-Marxists are understood as advocating an alternative vision of nature and natural processes largely on moral and sociopolitical grounds. . . . In this regard the neo-Marxists stand on the same ground as the feminist scientist. In order to practice science as a feminist, as a radical, or as a Marxist one must deliberately adopt a framework expressive of that political commitment" (Longino 1990: 197). Root maintains that "the practices of the science should include or be grounded on a view of the kinds of life worth pursuing" (Root 1993: 2); science ought to be designed to push or pull citizens in a direction that reflects and sustains a particular set of values or traditions. Plantinga writes that "in doing Augustinian science, you start by assuming the deliverances of the [Christian] faith, employing them along with anything else you know in dealing with a given scientific problem or project" (Plantinga 1996b: 377).

Statements such as the following ones could, on the other hand, be read as a defense of a worldview-neutral science:

> Ethics and science have their own domains, which touch but do not interpenetrate. The one shows us to what goal we should aspire, the other, given the goal, teaches us how to attain it. So they never conflict since they never meet. There can no more be immoral science than there can be scientific morals. (Poincaré 1958: 12)

> *In my view, science, as such, has no social responsibility.* In my view it is society that has a responsibility — that of maintaining the apolitical, detached scientific tradition and allowing science to search for truth in the way determined purely by its inner life. Of course, scientists, as citizens, have responsibility, like all other citizens, to see that science is *applied* to the right social and political ends. This is a different, independent question. . . . (Lakatos 1978: 258, italics in original)

What we will see, however, is that often defenders of the idea of a worldview-neutral science have particular aspects of scientific inquiry in mind. Max Weber, for instance, maintains that scientific results are "value-free" (in the terminology he preferred) if they do not contain any judgments of personal, cultural, moral, or political value. In this sense science is value-free or worldview-neutral. But values cannot, he believed, be eliminated when it comes to what scientists choose to investigate. In this sense science is value-partisan or worldview-partisan (Weber 1969). John O'Neill holds a similar position. He writes, "the core normative claim [of the value-freedom doctrine] is that the only values that a scientist should employ in deciding the truth or falsity of scientific propositions and theories are the internal cognitive values of science — consistency, explanatory power, simplicity and so on" (O'Neill 1993: 156). The definitions (1) and (2) include the phrase "Science (or parts of science)" for this reason, to indicate that defenders of the idea of a worldview-neutral science have particular aspects of scientific inquiry in mind. This is an issue we shall discuss in much more detail in the following chapter.

Moreover, we must distinguish between science that is explicitly and science that is merely implicitly worldview-neutral or worldview-partisan. *Implicitly* neutral or partisan science is any science (or part of science) that is not directly declared as either worldview-neutral or worldview-partisan, but which nevertheless in the way it is conducted presupposes an acceptance of either neutral science or partisan science. *Explicitly* neutral or partisan science, on the other hand, is openly presented as either worldview-neutral or worldview-partisan. Purported neutral science might, of course, turn out to be implicitly partisan science, if it actually turns out that it is aligned with or supports a particular ideology, religion, or worldview over another.

The soccer game analogy also shows that we need to distinguish between, on the one hand, this neutral-partisan aspect of the debate and, on the other, the issue of whether science is biased or unbiased. We must, in other words, also in this debate be able to capture the difference between, on the one hand, my situation and that of the referee who did not turn up and, on the other hand, the issue of whether I was fair or unfair in my calls. Hence we need to distinguish (1) and (2) from the following:

(3) Science (or some part of science) is *biased* if it unfairly or in an unjustified way represents the way things are or seem to be.

(4) Science (or some part of science) is *unbiased* or *objective* if it fairly or in a justified way represents the way things are or seem to be.

(5) Science (or some part of science) is *wrong* (or in error) if it misrepresents the way things are.

So (3) states that bias is a part of science if, for instance, something besides the evidence acceptable to scientific inquiry influences either what theories are accepted by scientists or to what extent they are taken to be warranted by scientists.[3] The soccer game analogy makes this clear. Suppose I had instead given my son's team more free kicks than the other team and I did this not because the other team violated the rules of the game more than my son's team did, but because I sympathized with his team and wanted them to win. If that was the case then something besides the evidence of violations of the rules of the game influenced what calls I made. Where this was the case, such calls were therefore biased.

If a claim, theory, or call is correctly classified as biased, which entails that something has gone wrong, this does not, however, entail that the claim, theory, or call is necessarily false or mistaken. It gives us merely a *prima facie* reason to think it is false or mistaken. For instance, the only

---

3. What kind of evidence would be acceptable might, of course, be an issue on which the participants in the debate could disagree.

reason why a scientist who is a Christian proposes a theory about human nature or altruism might be that it is what should be true if his or her understanding of Christianity is correct. Thus the theory is biased. But it is still possible that good scientific evidence might in the end be found which shows that the theory is true or the best-supported one among competing alternatives. This is very important to keep in mind because when it comes to ideology and religion, one person's truth might be another person's bias. Moreover, the charge of ideology in science is often a charge of bias and not of partisanship. That distinction is not always clearly upheld, however, and thus we can find cases of "guilt by association" in the literature. If you are partisan then you must be or probably are biased. So you get the impression that if you can show that person A is a member of z then that undermines his or her claims, given the assumption, of course, that it is a bad thing to be member of z.

Not all forms of bias that we could find in science are of an ideological or a religious sort. If a scientist accepts a theory merely or at least partly because of the personal profit gained, it would not be an instance of the kind of bias we are investigating because profit in this sense is not typically associated with ideologies or religions. Hence not all forms of bias fall within our scope of inquiry.

What is the logical relationship between, on the one hand, (1) and (2) and, on the other hand, (3), (4), and (5)? Both (1) and (2) are compatible with (4); that is to say, whether science is religiously neutral or partisan it could, for instance, generate scientific results that are unbiased. It might be more difficult for worldview-partisan science than for worldview-neutral science to be unbiased,[4] but if some participants in the debate are right that worldview-neutral science is impossible then this is important to keep in mind. So being partisan or unneutral is not equivalent to being biased.[5]

4. All participants in the debate do not accept this, of course. They could instead believe that there is a privileged religious or ideological perspective. Feminist standpoint epistemology is a good example of such a view. According to feminist standpoint epistemology a more objective and transformative knowledge is to be found in the perspective of women than in other perspectives (Harding 1986: 26).

5. One could, of course, by "bias" mean the very same thing as "being partisan." A particular scientist would then be biased simply if he or she is aligned with or supports a particular ideology or religion such as Islam. My suggestion is, however, that we use the term only in the first way because "bias" indicates that something has gone wrong, and there is nothing wrong or illegitimate in a scientist adhering to a particular ideology or religion.

It is therefore important to understand that in (4) "objective" is used as a synonym for "unbiased." People are *objective* in this sense when they try to understand things as they are, not simply as they would like them to be because of partisanship, prejudices, distorted or irrelevant emotions, and the like. "Objective" could, however, also mean, among other things, that one is impartial or neutral in respect to a conflict or controversy. Thus partisan science (science designed to serve certain ideological interests) could be objective only in the first sense because it would fail by definition to be it in the second sense. As Robert N. Proctor points out, geologists might have developed more theories and collected more data about oil-bearing shales than about many other rocks, but their claims are thereby no less objective (in the first sense) or reliable (Proctor 1991: 10).

Whether (1) or (2) is the case, it is of course possible that scientists could be wrong, that is, (5). But scientists could be biased — that is, the state of affairs specified in (3) could obtain — only if they adhere (consciously or unconsciously) to (2), because it follows logically that if you are neutral, you could not be biased but only mistaken or in error, that is, (5). If you are not merely in error but also biased then you are by definition not neutral. So (1) is incompatible with (3) and compatible with (4) and (5), whereas (2) is compatible with (3), (4), and (5).

We should not confuse being biased with having a preconception. People have a preconception if on a given topic or in a particular situation they have an inclination one way or another. People are biased (or not objective) if they see things not as they are but as they want them to be because of partisanship, prejudices, distorted or irrelevant emotions, and the like. I had, for instance, a preconception that the other team should be much better than my son's team, but as the game proceeded I realized that that was wrong. But that is something different from being a supporter of my son's team (being partisan) or unfairly favoring his team in my calls (being biased). In most cases it is probably impossible not to have a particular preconception, but that does not entail being partisan or biased.

Moreover, by drawing the parallel between the soccer game and science we can also see that even if science is worldview-neutral, its outcome could be such that it could benefit one worldview more than another. To see this, consider again the soccer game. By making the calls I made, all fair ones, one team might have benefited more than the other. Moreover, even if I was unbiased but made some wrong calls, it could have benefited one team more than the other. In fact, if I had not missed the penalty kick the other team would probably have scored and equalized. Hence we could make these statements:

(6) Science (or some part of science) is *religiously* or *ideologically rele-vant* if what it does or contains could either support or undermine ideologies, religions, or worldviews.

(7) Science (or some part of science) is *religiously* or *ideologically irrele-vant* if what it does or contains could neither support nor undermine ideologies, religions, or worldviews.[6]

It is important, as we shall see, that we do not confuse the worldview-neutral and worldview-partisan aspects of the debate with the worldview-relevant and worldview-irrelevant aspects. As we shall see, Alvin Plantinga, for instance, maintains that "in [Herbert] Simon's account of altruism we have an example of a scientific theory that is clearly not neutral with re-spect to Christian commitment; indeed, it is inconsistent with it" (Plan-tinga 1996a: 184). Here Plantinga assumes that science is religiously neutral only if it does not refute or undermine religious beliefs and values. But since that is not the case science is religiously partisan. This is certainly a possible way to interpret the claim that "science is not religiously neutral." I suggest, however, that we should avoid doing so, simply because science has over the centuries refuted or undermined numerous religious and ideological beliefs which people have held. Science has, for instance, dis-covered that the earth is billions of years old and thus refuted the religious belief that the earth was created by God around six thousand years ago. Religious people have held (and advocates of the Flat Earth Society still do) that the Bible teaches that the earth is flat and that we therefore ought to believe this. Science has refuted this idea and replaced a geocentric with a heliocentric worldview.

In fact, science has the potential to undermine (or support, for that matter) *any* religious or ideological idea that has *empirical content*. Here lies also the key to understanding why we cannot expect that science is (or should be) worldview-neutral in this sense, because investigating empiri-cal claims and developing theories about empirical states of affairs is what science is all about; it is its proper domain. If religious or ideological ideas

6. See Weber (1969: 21f.), Root (1993: 34f.), and Helgesson (2002: 74) for a discussion of value-relevance/irrelevance, to which my distinction is related.

either contain an empirical element or presuppose the truth of it, these ideas could be undermined or refuted by scientific theories and data (and they can, of course, also be supported or verified by scientific theories and data). So this could not be what the debate is all about. Therefore, we should grant that science could be worldview-relevant in respect to religions or ideologies *x, y,* or *z,* while at the same time being worldview-neutral in respect to them. Worldview-relevance does not imply worldview-partisanship. Science, if worldview-neutral, would (on such an account) belong to neither side in a controversy, say between theism and naturalism or liberalism and socialism, but could obtain research results relevant for the truth-claims and value judgments involved in such a controversy. Science would, on the other hand, be worldview-irrelevant in my terminology if that were not possible. If so, all scientific research that might yield results which are ideologically or religiously controversial in any way would need to be abandoned.

Two other things we need to take into account are, first, that the idea of a religiously or an ideologically neutral science could be understood either in a descriptive or a normative way, and, second, that religiously or ideologically neutral science is a matter of degree rather than an either/or case (one could have a science that is more or less neutral or partisan and more or less biased or objective).

First, the term "science" can be used either descriptively or normatively. Either we mean by "science" the activities that scientists are actually engaged in when developing, for example, theories and explanations (call this *actual science*), or we mean the activities that scientists *ought* to be engaged in when doing science (call this *good science*). Although, for instance, it may be taken for granted that theories, at least sometimes, receive acceptance by the scientific community because of politics, religion, and gender, we may equally wonder whether that should be the case. Should we in doing science really accept political, religious, or gender preferences as valid reasons for accepting or rejecting theories or explanations? The answer is not of course obviously "yes." From the fact that actual science is not always good science, it does not necessarily follow that good science should be identical with actual science. Therefore we must distinguish between the issues of whether science *is* (given of course that it could be) worldview-neutral and whether science *should be* worldview-neutral.

Second, the questions about worldview-neutral/partisan and worldview-biased/objective science are not necessarily either/or issues, but could be more-or-less issues. To see this, consider again the soccer game. Let us start by focusing on the neutral-partisan aspect. It seems quite possible that one could find a referee who is partisan, but less so than I was. Suppose, for instance, a coach for one of the teams other than my son's had been around. We would expect him to be partisan but less so than I because he would not have had a son playing on one of the competing teams. One could then argue that it would have been better that he was the referee because he would be less partisan and therefore, everything else being equal, would have had a tendency to be less biased and more objective than I would. The same seems to be possible in respect to science: in other words, science could be more or less value-free/loaded or worldview-neutral/partisan.

Let us now turn to the bias-objective aspect. Suppose I was the referee, but I was not completely unbiased or objective as a referee because my partisanship clouded my judgment in certain situations. Someone could still have thought that I should have done a better job, even if that person acknowledges that it would have been impossible for me to be completely unbiased in my calls. Objectivity would on such an account be the *regulative ideal* even if I or somebody else who was partisan could not fully achieve it. The goal would be to approximate the ideal as far as possible for people in my predicament. Again, the same seems possible in respect to science. Even if science always was partisan and never fully unbiased, the goal of scientists could still be to strive to be as objective as they could, given their partisanship, abilities, and social context, and they could succeed in this to a larger or smaller degree.

This is crucial for our discussion because it matters considerably, for instance, not merely whether a biological account of human nature and behavior (such as Dawkins's or Wilson's) is motivated by ideological considerations but also, if this is so, to what extent that is the case. Do the advocates of this theory (or cluster of theories) of human nature and behavior accept it for purely nonscientific, ideological reasons, so that there is not a shred of scientific evidence that can be cited in its favor? Or is there actually some evidence that supports it, but because of ideological reasons its defenders present as established truth something which in fact should be regarded as sophisticated but not completely unwarranted speculation?

Thus, we have to distinguish between two related but different issues in debate:

(a) To what extent (if any) is science (or some part of science) actually religiously or ideologically neutral/partisan and biased/objective?

(b) To what extent (if any) should science (or some part of science) be religiously or ideologically neutral/partisan and biased/objective?

If science is worldview-neutral then it follows that science cannot at the same time be worldview-partisan; these claims are mutually exclusive. If we want to understand the debate, however, it is crucial that we take into account that by "science" we could mean a number of different things. In fact, some disagreements between participants in the debate about ideologies in science can be explained in terms of the different meanings they give to the term "science." I have tried, as I have already pointed out, to indicate that we could mean a number of different things by "science" by including in (1) to (6) the qualifier "science (or some part of science)." But this is a topic we will have to come back to in more detail later on in our discussion.

With these distinctions and clarifications in mind, we are ready, I believe, to consider the issue. In the following section I shall first present the ideas of religious expansionism (as found among Christians and Muslims) and then turn to two versions of ideological expansionism (those of Marxists and feminists). In the next chapter we will evaluate the arguments for worldview expansionism and try to reach a conclusion on the following issue: to what extent (if any) could or should science (or parts of science) be religiously or ideologically partisan?

Religious Expansionism

As participants in the discussion about science as a part of a larger culture (whose thought patterns, ideologies, and values influence the questions scientists ask, the concepts they use to interpret data, and the assumptions they make in the formulation and the justification of theories and explanations) we can find, as one voice, Christians, Muslims, and members of other religions who maintain that in much contemporary science we can find naturalist bias of a different sort. In their view, the presence of this kind of bias challenges the whole idea of a religiously neutral science. This idea, they maintain, must be rejected, and we ought instead to accept that worldviews (religions or ideologies) always shape science and that therefore the only form of science we reasonably can have is a worldview-partisan science. I have suggested that we call this view "religious expansionism" and its advocates "religious expansionists" because they, in contrast to scientific expansionists (who believe that the boundaries of science should be expanded in such a way that ethics and religion are subsumed under science), claim that the boundaries of *religion* should be expanded in such a way that religion shapes science. In the next two sections I shall give two examples of religious expansionism, one which is based on Christianity and the other on Islam.

Christian Faith and Augustinian Science

A number of influential thinkers working mainly within the Reformed tradition of Christianity have recently raised serious objections to the way science is conducted and to the bias they think exists within the academy against Christian beliefs and values and in favor of what is called "naturalism," "secular humanism," "secularism," or "nonbelief." This criticism has also led some of them to propose an alternative way of doing science, a so-called "faith-informed science," "theistic science," or "Augustinian science." I shall not be able to take all of this writing into account, but will instead focus on the ideas developed by Alvin Plantinga and to some extent also by George M. Marsden.

According to Plantinga, a view that has been popular ever since the Enlightenment is that "science (at least when properly pursued) is a cool, reasoned, wholly dispassionate attempt to figure out the truth about ourselves and our world, entirely independent of ideology, or moral convictions, or religious or theological commitments" (Plantinga 1996a: 178-79). But although this view has received widespread acceptance, he thinks it is wrong; the truth is instead that science is not religiously neutral. This in a way comes as no surprise for Plantinga because he, following Augustine, believes that human history is the arena of a great struggle between the city of God *(civitas Dei)* and the city of the world *(civitas mundi),* between "the Christian community and the forces of unbelief" (Plantinga 1991: 30; 1996a: 178). Therefore, science, just like any other human endeavor, cannot be expected to be wholly neutral with respect to this clash between opposing worldviews. It is even excessively naive to think that contemporary science is religiously and theologically neutral, standing serenely above this battle and wholly ir- relevant to it. Perhaps *parts* of science are like that: mathematics, for example, and perhaps physics, or parts of physics. . . . Other parts are obviously and deeply involved in this battle: and the closer the science in question is to what is distinctively human, the deeper the involve- ment. (Plantinga 1991: 16)

Much of contemporary science is, he believes, on the side of the city of the world and does not serve God's purposes. More specifically, it proceeds from the assumption of metaphysical naturalism. By "metaphysical natu- ralism" Plantinga means, roughly, the view that "nature is all there is: there is no such person as God or anyone at all like him" (Plantinga 1996b: 369). He does not think that there is a neat recipe for telling which part of sci- ence is neutral and which is not in this contest. But the rule of thumb, Plantinga suggests, is that its involvement depends upon how closely that part of science is engaged in the attempt to try to understand ourselves as human beings. Hence, we can expect that much of what goes on in eco- nomics, psychology, sociology, and also in biology, especially in socio- biology, proceeds from the assumption of metaphysical naturalism. Chris- tians must not, therefore, uncritically accept what the scientific experts say, because of the naturalist partisanship and bias that is present in much contemporary science. Such views might be completely wrong seen from a Christian perspective.

Plantinga gives a number of examples from scientific practice to jus- tify his claim that science is not religiously neutral. In an article in *Science,* the Nobel Prize winner Herbert Simon takes for granted that the rational way to behave is to try to act in such a way that one increases one's per- sonal fitness, that is, to act so as to increase the probability that one's genes will be widely disseminated in the next and subsequent generations (Si- mon 1990). The problem for biology is, however, that quite a few people do not act so as to maximize their personal fitness. They behave in an altruis- tic way. Simon therefore tries to develop a theory of bounded rationality to explain this nonrational way of behaving. Plantinga asks if this scientific theory is religiously neutral. His answer is no. Perhaps this is the rational way to behave if one presupposes naturalism, but it certainly is not if one adopts instead a Christian point of view. According to Christians, altruistic people, such as Mother Teresa, behave in the most rational way since they actually reflect the unselfishly loving character of God. Therefore, "in Simon's account of altruism we have an example of a scientific theory that is clearly not neutral with respect to Christian commitment; indeed it is inconsistent with it" (Plantinga 1996a: 184).

Moreover, Richard Dawkins and Stephen Gould, for instance, maintain that evolutionary theory is not merely the best-supported theory of the origin of life, but an established fact. In other words, they believe it is virtually certain that the theory (or at least something approximating it) is true. But the epistemological probability of evolutionary theory depends in part on what you think about naturalism and theism. Its probability given the empirical evidence is lower according to the views that theists hold than it is according to the views naturalists typically hold. This is so because evolutionary theory is the only game in town for naturalists, whereas theism is compatible with it but allows the possibility that God could have created the world in a different way. Plantinga concludes that "the way in which the theory of evolution is not religiously neutral is . . . that the view in question is much more probable with respect to naturalism and the [empirical] evidence than it is with respect to [Christian] theism and that evidence" (Plantinga 1996a: 186).

Plantinga quotes Dawkins, Futuyma, Gould, and Simpson claiming that evolutionary theory has shown or given us reason to believe that our species is merely accidental, that there was no plan or mind or foresight involved in it coming into existence. But Plantinga believes that "of course no Christian theist could take that seriously for a moment," because he or she knows that human beings are created in the image of God and, therefore, their existence cannot be merely accidental but is a part of God's plan (Plantinga 1996a: 187). Again, science is not religiously neutral because it is inconsistent with what Christians know to be true.

Simpson, furthermore, in answering the question "What is man?" maintains that "all attempts to answer that question before 1859 [the year Darwin's *Origin of Species* was published] are worthless and that we will be better off if we ignore them completely" (Simpson quoted in Dawkins 1989: 1). But this also is incompatible with Christian belief. According to Christians, the Bible teaches us that we are created in God's image, that we are sinners who need God's love and redemption, and so forth. So here again we have evidence that science is not religiously neutral.

Hence it is evident that we can find examples of naturalist bias within contemporary scientific practice. But how should Christians respond to this? What should they say in the public debate about what science is and should be?

Plantinga is not satisfied with merely a Christian criticism of contemporary science and a disclosure of hidden or unreflected presumptions of naturalism. He wants to go one step further and maintains that "a Christian academic and scientific community ought to pursue science in its own way, *starting from* and taking for granted what they know as Christians" (Plantinga 1996a: 178). Christians should develop what he sometimes calls "theistic science," at other times "Augustinian science." What then is Augustinian science? Plantinga writes that "in doing Augustinian science, you start by assuming the deliverances of the faith, employing them along with anything else you know in dealing with a given scientific problem or project" (Plantinga 1996b: 377). Christians should in doing science appeal, when appropriate, to what they know about God or God's activity or to what they know by the testimony of the Bible, and should take these beliefs as part of the background with respect to which the plausibility and probability of scientific theories are to be evaluated.

Christians can employ the basic tenets of Christianity in scientific practice in different ways:

> (1) stating and employing hypotheses according to which God does things directly, of course, but also (2) stating and employing hypotheses according to which he does something indirectly; further, there is (3) evaluating theories with respect to background information that includes Christian theism; still further, there is (4) employing such propositions as *human beings have been created in God's image,* either directly or as background, and (5) doing the same for such doctrines as that of original sin, which do not involve any direct mention of God at all, and (6) deciding what needs explanation by way of referring to that same background. (Plantinga 1996a: 212)

Hence, the appropriate response to the naturalist bias we can find in contemporary science is to develop a specifically Christian way of doing science. According to this view of science, it is acceptable that Christians start by assuming the truth of their religious beliefs and employ them together with everything else they know or at any rate think that they know in dealing with a given scientific problem. We would thus have within the academy at least a *naturalist science* and a *theistic science*. Practitioners of naturalist science and theistic science would sometimes say and do the same thing. But at other times they would not, because their research is shaped by the prior acceptance of different worldviews. We might have thought that there could and should be one common science, but instead Plantinga urges us to accept different forms of worldview-partisan sciences within the academy.

George M. Marsden holds a similar view. The Enlightenment rule we have inherited and which is taken to guide proper scientific procedure says that "to be part of the mainstream academic profession one had to lay one's religious faith aside" (Marsden 1997: 28). One should, it says, adopt a stance of neutrality with respect to the implications of beliefs such as that God exists, that God created the world, that God might reveal himself to humans, or that God may have instituted a moral law (p. 35). Marsden writes,

> University culture is not necessarily hostile to religion; but the norm for people to be fully accepted in academic culture is to act as though their religious beliefs had nothing to do with education. Scholars are expected to analyze subjects such as the nature of reality, beauty, truth, morality, the just society, the individual, and the community as though deeply held religious beliefs had no relevance to such topics [other than as objects of study]. (Marsden 1997: 23-24)

But what this means is that scholarship is built around a tradition that operates as though it was the case that physical reality is all there is. Such a "scientific naturalism" is meant perhaps to be methodological in character, but it easily slips into an ontological position: "Once we have a convincing explanation at the level of empirically researched connections we are inclined to think we have a complete explanation" (p. 75). But of course Christians "do not believe that empirically demonstrable explanations are the only, or even the most important, explanations" (p. 74).

The solution to this is that Christian scholars should cease being Christians merely in private, as though their faith were no more than a hobby, unrelated to their scholarly activities. Rather than being scholars who just happen to be Christians, they should be "Christian scholars." It is not that he wants to turn back the clock to those days when Christianity dominated the academic mainstream.

> Rather, whatever I propose by way of making a place for Christian scholars should apply, *mutatis mutandis,* to Jews, Muslims, Buddhists,

Hindus, and persons of other religious faiths or of no formal faith. In fact, in some pluralistic settings it may be best not usually to use "Christian," "Jewish," "Islamic," and so forth as an adjective in reference to one's scholarship. "Faith-informed scholarship" might be preferable. (Marsden 1997: 10)

All kinds of scholarship presuppose some form of faith in this sense. Marsden's claim is that religious faith should in principle have equal standing with other forms of faith (p. 10). If this is accepted a better balance among faiths or ideologies could obtain and we would not anymore unduly favor research based on purely naturalistic presuppositions (p. 24). Scholarship (he is not merely talking about scientific research) could and should be shaped by religion or ideology, but this must be done in an open way (p. 67). Marsden is therefore an advocate of an explicit worldview-partisan science.

Islamic Science

We can find among Muslims a similar discussion as the one provided by Christians such as Plantinga and Marsden. The idea of an "Islamic science" or a "sacred science" in contrast to a "secular science" or "Western science" was first developed in the 1960s but has subsequently been defended and developed by a number of scholars, among them Seyyed Hossein Nasr (1976, 1993), Ziauddin Sardar (1989), and Mehdi Golshani (2000). In 1977 the first World Conference on Muslim Education was held in Mecca and at this conference the Islamization of various scientific disciplines was emphasized. A similar conference but on the topic of the scientific miracles of the *Qur'an* and *Sunnah,* inaugurated by president general Mohammed Zia-ul-Haq, was held in Islamabad in 1987. Several centers or institutes such as Institute of Islamic Thought and the Centre for Islam and Science have come into existence. Journals such as *Journal of Islamic Science* and *The American Journal of Islamic Social Sciences* have been started and made available around the world. There is not space to survey all this literature and its religious, social, and political roots, so I shall therefore focus merely on the writing of Mehdi Golshani and his ideas about Islamic science.[7]

7. See Stenberg (1996) for such a survey of some of the key thinkers in contemporary Islamic science.

The idea of Islamic science has generated a lot of controversy both inside of and outside of the Muslim world. For instance, Mohammed Abdus Salam, the 1979 Nobel prize winner in physics writes, in the foreword to Pervez Hoodbhoy's *Islam and Science,* that "there is only one universal science, its problems and modalities are international and there is no such thing as Islamic science just as there is no Hindu science, no Jewish science, no Confucian science, nor Christian science" (Hoodbhoy 1991: ix). In a reply to the question, "Can there be an Islamic science?" Hoodbhoy himself writes, "No, there cannot be an Islamic science of the physical world, and attempts to create one represent wasted effort. This is in no way a discredit to Islam — as Sir Syed Ahmed Khan has argued, the purpose of religion is to improve morality rather than specify scientific facts" (p. 77).

Golshani is aware of this kind of criticism but maintains that the idea of Islamic science can and ought to be defended and further developed. He writes that some people deny that "the idea of Islamic Science" makes any sense. "They argue that science is an objective and universal enterprise, and it does not depend on any creed or ideology." But Golshani maintains that "this is a naïve interpretation of scientific activity" and that "'Islamic Science,' or for that matter, 'religious science,' has relevance at . . . [both] the theoretical level and the practical level" (Golshani 2000: 1). At the same time, however, he questions certain views of Islamic science, rejecting, for instance, the ideas that it involves the discussion of miracles of the *Qur'an* or the Islamic tradition; that it refers to the attempt to find ways of proving God's existence, attributing the origin of science to the Muslim scholars; that we could leave aside experimentation and observation; or that all knowledge is directly deducible from the *Qur'an* and the *Sunnah* (pp. 3-4, 15).

By "Islamic science" we should mean instead, Golshani writes,

> a science that is framed within an Islamic worldview and whose main characteristics are that it considers Allah as the Creator and Sustainer of the universe; does not limit the universe to the material world; attributes a telos to the universe; and accepts a moral order for the universe. (Golshani 2000: 4)

Since these characteristics are more or less present in both Judaism and Christianity it is possible to talk also about a "theistic science." Islamic (or theistic) science should be contrasted with the "secular science" that dominates the scene today, that is, a science that "neglects God, limits existence to the material world alone, denies any purpose for the universe and is negligent about values" (p. 4). The main difference between Islamic science and secular science is that within the former the metaphysical presuppositions of science are rooted in a religious worldview (the theoretical level) and religious considerations direct the proper orientation of the applications of science (the practical level).

Let us start by focusing on the relevance of Islamic science at the *theoretical* level. In developing his argument Golshani points out that it is naive to believe that science is an objective and value-free enterprise, and he supports this claim both by referring to the research other scholars have done on this issue and by giving examples of how religious or ideological considerations influence the making, selection, and evaluation of theories in science. For instance, he quotes and agrees with Robert Young, the editor of the journal *Science as Culture,* who writes that "recent work has made it clear to those with eyes to see that there is no place in science, technology, medicine and other forms of expertise where you cannot find ideology acting as a constitutive determinant" (Golshani 2000: 6).

One example offered of how what Golshani sometimes calls "religion" and at other times "ideology," "worldview," or "metaphysical presuppositions" shapes science is when Richard Dawkins maintains that natural selection alone is what causes the evolution of species and that there is, therefore, no need for God or a divine designer. Dawkins writes that while "evolution, the blind designer, using cumulative trial and error can search the vast space of possible structures, blind chance on its own is no kind of watchmaker. But chance with natural selection, chance smeared out into innumerable tiny steps over eons of time is powerful enough to manufacture miracles like dinosaurs and ourselves."[8] Golshani points out that we here have a clear case of secular science because acceptance of natural selection does not entail atheism or that there is no divine designer.

Golshani also believes that the popularity of the steady state theory or the oscillatory model of the universe among physicists can be explained at least partially by the fact that this theory or model provides grounds for an atheistic interpretation of the universe. Golshani refers to Steven Weinberg to justify this claim. Weinberg writes, "the idea that the universe had

---

8. Dawkins quoted in Golshani (2000: 10).

no start appeals to many physicists philosophically, because it avoids a supernatural act of creation."[9]

Moreover, examples of atheistic bias also come to the surface when questions about the purposefulness of nature arise. Golshani refers to Atkins and Dawkins, who both deny a telos to nature. Peter Atkins, for instance, writes, "A gross contamination of the reductionist ethic is the concept of purpose. Science has no need of purpose. All events at the molecular level that lies beneath all our actions, activities, and reflections are purposeless, and are accounted for by the collapse of energy and matter into ever-increasing disorder."[10] Golshani asks in response, "Can one, on the basis of data obtained from chemistry or molecular biology at the level of molecules or atoms, claim that there is no telos to nature? The answer is no, because this conclusion is not drawn directly from science, rather it is rooted in the metaphysical prejudices of the scientist" (p. 12).

Golshani gives more examples of how metaphysical presuppositions shape the content and results of science, but this is sufficient for our purposes. It is at this level that religions or ideology shape science in an important way, because if science were merely the collection of simple observations or facts, then there would be no difference between Islamic science and secular science. It is primarily in the process of making comprehensive theories that metaphysical presuppositions come into play. Golshani's conclusion is therefore that

> Recent studies have shown that religious ideas have been influential in the making, selection and evaluation of theories. It seems obvious that if one is not denying other kinds of knowledge besides scientific knowledge, then there will be room for the revealed knowledge and its effect on scientific knowledge. It is on this basis that we want to elaborate on the relevance of religious science, and in particular Islamic science. (p. 4)

Thus Golshani, just like Christians such as Plantinga and Marsden, is not satisfied with a religiously motivated criticism of science, which aims at the disclosure of hidden or unreflected presuppositions of naturalism or atheism. Instead he argues that since science without theories is not desir-

---

9. Weinberg quoted in Golshani (2000: 8).
10. Atkins quoted in Golshani (2000: 12).

able and scientific theories without metaphysical, ideological, or religious presuppositions are impossible, Muslims should in doing science let what they know as Muslims shape the content and results of science. We have here, then, a clear case of worldview-partisan science.

Moreover, Golshani maintains that religious considerations should also on the *practical* level direct the proper orientation of the applications of science. He points out that the history of science has demonstrated that value systems affect the orientation and application of science. In the words of John Brooke, whom Golshani refers to, "The direction and application of scientific research clearly can be different under different value systems. And since human values are often organically linked with religious beliefs, the latter can still be presented as relevant to the orientation of science and technology."[11] Since scientific research clearly can be altered under different value systems, advocates of Islamic science ought to claim that scientific research should be directed by Islamic or theistic values. This is so because "if scientific work is done within a theistic framework, its practical results are supposed to secure human felicity and welfare. But, if it is pursued within a secular matrix, then there is no guarantee for its being immune from destructive results" (p. 14). Religion could and should give science direction when it comes to both research priorities and the application of scientific results. Once upon a time science and values were united in an organic whole, Golshani writes, and we desperately need to come back to a united view again:

> In the past, ethical considerations were a concern of all faithful scientists, both in the Islamic world and in the Western world. This perspective has been dramatically changed in our era. The development of science and technology under the secularist-materialist world view has led to grave consequences for humankind. In this world view, the ethical, philosophical and religious dimensions of science and technology are neglected and humankind's physical comfort is confused with real happiness, though even this one is not achieved. (Golshani 2002: 8)

Hence, science could be done both in a religious and in a nonreligious framework. Sometimes Islamic science and secular science would say and do the same thing because they have common elements — for instance, in

11. Brooke quoted in Golshani (2000: 15).

experimentation or data collection — but Golshani writes that "in the long run they are bound to lead to different results both at the practical level and at the theoretical level (e.g., in the construction of universal theories)" (Golshani 2000: 18).

Ideological Expansionism

Christians and Muslims (or religious practitioners in general) are by no means alone within the contemporary academy in arguing for a conception of scientific practice shaped by extra-scientific beliefs and values. A number of scientists, sociologists, and philosophers have argued for a politicization of science on the basis of gender, class, or conceptions of the good. I have called these people "ideological expansionists." "Ideology" is, however, a term used in a number of different and incompatible ways. I shall therefore start by clarifying how the term should be understood in this context before we consider two versions of ideological expansionism, namely, left-wing science and feminist science.

In the material analyzed, "ideology" is essentially used in three different ways, and sometimes these senses are conflated. In the first sense "ideology" is used to connote a set of false beliefs and values that someone else's political views contain. An ideology is the false consciousness or false conviction shared by the members of a particular social class. In other words, the term is used in a disparaging way. It actually hides an accusation. This is the way Marxists typically have used the term. This gives us a first definition of ideology:

> An *ideology*$_1$ is a system of false or unjustified beliefs and values which are held in common by a group and which have a sociopolitical function.

Thus, ideology$_1$ is held, not because there are any good reasons for believing that it is true, but merely because it gives support to a particular group of people or a social institution of some sort.

It is sometimes added to the first sense of "ideology" that the term also signifies a set of ideas that are used to control or manipulate other people, as well as to hide what is really true. An ideology prevents people in a society from correctly understanding their true situation and real interests. It serves only the interests of the dominant groupings of society. Thus, an ideology is necessarily oppressive in nature:

> An *ideology$_2$* is a system of false or unjustified beliefs and values which are held in common by a group and which are used to control and oppress other people.

There is yet another way in which one could use the term and this is how I shall use it. "Ideology" is then employed in such manner that no judgment about truth or falsehood and a possibly oppressive character is included in its definition. Thus,

> An *ideology$_3$* is a system of beliefs and values which are held in common by a group and which have a sociopolitical function.

I prefer this last interpretation of the term because I see no reason why we should not allow that an ideology could be true or justified or rationally acceptable. Why should we define the term so that it is impossible to have true ideological ideas? Moreover, an ideology *can* of course be used in an oppressive way, as an instrument to control and manipulate other people; but I do not see that it *must* be used in such way. Thus, I do not want to exclude from the start the possibility that at least one ideology — say feminism, liberalism, or Marxism — can be non-oppressive in character. So in this sense the term "ideology" does not involve any evaluation of whether the beliefs or values in question are true or justified or whether they are oppressive or not. In what follows I shall use the word "ideology" exclusively for ideology$_3$.

Notice that I have already built into these definitions two requirements that Anders Jeffner thinks are necessary for calling something an ideology (Jeffner 1988). The first is that a set of ideas must be held in common by a group of people to classify as an ideology. There is then no such thing as an ideology embraced by one single person. The second is that it is not sufficient that certain ideas are held in common; they must also have a sociopolitical function, for instance, to secure the existence of a political organization or leadership or define a social order. An ideology then necessarily has some kind of social impact. This sociopolitical function can, like that of Islam in Iran, be strong, or it can be weak like the influence of Christianity in Sweden today. Hence, there could be an overlap between ideology and religion, but for practical reasons "ideology" and thus "ideological expansionism" will in this discussion refer to advocates of views such as feminism and Marxism, and "religion" and thus "religious expansionism" to defenders of views such as Christianity and Islam.

Left-Wing Science

Steven Rose, R. C. Lewontin, and Leon J. Kamin argue, in *Not in Our Genes: Biology, Ideology, and Human Nature* (1990), against the biological determinism they maintain can be found among many biologists and its claim to define human nature. By "biological determinism" they mean the view that (a) the behavior of organisms (including human behavior) is the inevitable consequence of the biochemical properties of the cells that constitute the individual organism, and that (b) the constituents of the individual's genes in turn determine these traits. According to this view, "all human behavior — hence all human society — is governed by a chain of determinants that runs from the gene to the individual to the sum of the behaviors of all individuals. The determinists would have it, then, that human nature is fixed by our genes" (Rose et al. 1990: 6). Defenders of biological determinism have claimed to locate the causes of the inequalities of status, wealth, and power between classes, genders, and races in society, and have defended human universals of behavior as natural traits of these societies.

Rose, Lewontin, and Kamin reject this biological theory of human nature; they talk about it as "science as ideology" and write about the "oppressive forms in which [this] determinist ideology manifests itself" (p. ix), claiming that these determinist ideas are false, a form of pseudoscience, and serve the interest of the dominant groups in society (pp. 9, 28). Thus, their use of the term "ideology" is in line with the Marxist-influenced definition of ideology. Rose, Lewontin, and Kamin define ideology as "the ruling ideas of a particular society at a particular time. They are ideas that express the 'naturalness' of any existing social order and help maintain it" (p. 3 n. 4). What, then, would the phrase "science as ideology" mean? Lewontin has in another context explicitly answered this question. He writes, "It is this dual process — on the one hand, of the social influence and control of what scientists do and say, and, on the other hand, the use of what scientists do and say to further support the institutions of society — that is meant when we speak of science as ideology" (Lewontin 1993: 4).

If we accept their definition of ideology, however, no ideas other than those of the ruling class can be an ideology, and as long as the establishment in society does not accept Rose's, Lewontin's, and Kamin's own political ideas, these ideas cannot be classified as ideological. But of course if they were accepted, their political ideas would become the new ideology of science. As a matter of fact, they never call their own standpoint an ideology, although they are careful to state explicitly their own political commitments. Concerning their own standpoint, they write,

> We share a commitment to the prospect of the creation of a more socially just — a socialist — society. And we recognize that a critical science is an integral part of the struggle to create that society, just as we also believe that the social function of much of today's science is to hinder the creation of that society by acting to preserve the interests of the dominant class, gender, and race. (Rose et al. 1990: ix-x)

Rose, Lewontin, and Kamin thus believe in "the possibility of a critical and liberatory science" (p. x).

Although we must keep their understanding of ideology in mind, their own socialist-influenced liberatory science, just as much as the biological determinism they critically scrutinize, counts as ideology (or a version of "science as ideology") as I have defined the term. I shall also on a second point diverge from their terminology. It is understandable that they would consider their alternative form of science a "critical and liberatory science." Critics of socialism would, however, of course reject such a characterization and probably maintain that in the end it is the socialist form of science that would turn out to be really oppressive and uncritical. Be that as it may, I shall nevertheless use a less value-loaded name for their form of science. Let us simply call it "left-wing science."

What is that Rose, Lewontin, and Kamin think is especially problematic about the kind of biological science that they criticize (other than that it could be wrong, just as any other scientific theory could be)? Why do they, in particular, think that it is appropriate in this context to talk about "biology as ideology"? What worries them are, I think, two things: (1) These biologists' scientific work serves the ideological interests of the dominant groups in society and not their own ideological interests, and (2) These biologists give a false appearance of being politically disinterested parties.

Let us start with the latter worry. Rose, Lewontin, and Kamin write, "time and again, despite their professed belief that their science is 'above mere human politics' (to quote Oxford sociobiologist Richard Dawkins), biological determinists deliver themselves of social and political judgments" (p. 8). More to the point, what is problematic is the dishonest strategy these biological determinists often use:

> To legitimize their theories they deny any connection to political events, giving the impression that the theories are the outcome of internal developments within a science that is insulated from social relations. They then become political actors, writing for newspapers and popular magazines, testifying before legislatures, appearing as celebrities on television to explicate the political and social consequences that must flow from their objective science. (p. 28)

Hence the complaint is not really, as the first quotation indicates, *that* the biological determinists are engaged in making political and moral statements about human society, but that they move from scientific claims to political and evaluative claims *without saying this explicitly* and that by doing so they use the authority of science in advocating their own ideological commitments. Accordingly, "they understand that, although there is no logical necessity connecting the truth of determinism to its political role, their own legitimacy as scientific authorities is dependent upon their appearance as politically disinterested parties" (p. 28). Rose, Lewontin, and Kamin themselves "view the links between values and knowledge as an integral part of doing science in this society at all, whereas determinists tend to deny that such links exists" (p. 9). In short, these biologists defend the idea of ideologically neutral science.

The objection of Rose, Lewontin, and Kamin is thus *not* that scientists *qua* scientists should not participate in policy-making, political discussions, or religious and moral debates. Their point is that scientists can and should evaluate (that is, be ideologically partisan scientists), but they *must* explicitly state when they as scientists make evaluative judgments. They must be explicit about their partisanship. Neglecting to do so is the mistake which biologists such as Dawkins and Wilson make. They conflate scientific theories and political or ideological viewpoints. Thus, when scientists do not clearly distinguish between scientific theories and value judgments in their scientific research, in their role as scientific experts, or in their role as popularizers of science, they use science in an ideologically illegitimate way. Making this distinction is required because value statements do not automatically follow from factual statements. As they say in the quotation above, "there is no logical necessity connecting the truth of determinism to its political role." Scientists cannot therefore derive in any straightforward way how society *ought to be* from scientific theories about how things *are*. To be able to do that, scientists must add something extra-scientific, namely, values, to the scientific information they have. Scientists are allowed to do this, but their duty is to be explicit about their linking of "value and knowledge." They should not appear to be "politically disinterested parties" when that is not the case.

The second thing that worries Rose, Lewontin, and Kamin is that these biologists' scientific work serves the ideological interests of the dominant groups in society and not their own ideological interests. According to them, "'Science' is the ultimate legitimator of bourgeois ideology" and it is in this context that claims of biological determinism ought to be understood (p. 31). Biological determinism seems to be related to ideology in at least three different ways, however. First, they write,

> biological determinism *(biologism)* has been a powerful mode of explaining the observed inequalities of status, wealth, and power in contemporary industrial capitalist societies, and of defining human "universals" of behavior as natural characteristics of these societies. As such, it has been gratefully seized upon as a political legitimator by the New Right, which finds its social nostrums so neatly mirrored in nature; for if these inequalities are biologically determined, they are therefore inevitable and immutable. (p. 7)

The idea here is that we have a political movement, the New Right, which has a particular ideological agenda. They discover the scientific theories developed by biological determinists and realize determinism's political value and thus try to legitimate their political ideology and policies by referring to this set of biological theories. This is the first way in which these biologists' scientific work serves the ideological interests of the dominant groups in society.

The second is that, whether or not any political party realizes this, biological determinism — if true — has certain consequences for ideological beliefs and values. In my terminology, this kind of scientific theory is *ideologically relevant,* that is, its content could either support or undermine ideologies, religions, or worldviews. Rose, Lewontin, and Kamin write,

> But [biological determinism] is more than mere explanation: It is politics. For if human social organization, including the inequalities of status, wealth, and power, [is] a direct consequence of our biologies, then, except for some gigantic program of genetic engineering, no practice can make a significant alteration of social structure or of the position of individuals or groups within it. What we are is natural and therefore fixed. We may struggle, pass laws, even make revolutions, but we do so in vain. The natural differences between individuals and among groups played out against the background of biological universals of human behavior will, in the end, defeat our uninformed efforts to reconstitute society. (pp. 18-19)

If these theories are true, then it follows that a particular set of ideologies or ideological ideas is undermined or perhaps even refuted.

It is pointed out that biological determinism is ideological in yet a third way, that is, these theories of human nature and behavior are uncritically accepted by these biologists for ideological reasons. Rose, Lewontin, and Kamin maintain that "what cannot be understood without reference to political events . . . is how these errors [of the biological determinist's explanation of the world] arise, why they come to characterize both the popular and scientific consciousness in a particular era, and why we should care about them in the first place" (p. 28). These scientific ideas would not have been developed and certainly would not have been accepted as true were it not for the influence of right-wing values and beliefs. Thus the best explanation for the development, popularity, and acceptance of biological determinism is not that it is well supported by scientific evidence but that it serves a particular purpose; it benefits the ideological interests of the dominant groups in society.

Hence, Rose, Lewontin, and Kamin do not clearly distinguish between three different ways in which they write about "science as ideology": It is appropriate to talk about "science as ideology"

- if a political party uses scientific theories or results to support some of their ideological ideas or social policies/projects (such as birth control, maternity and paternity leave, etc.),
- if scientific theories or results undermine or support ideological ideas or social policies/projects, or
- if scientific theories or results are developed and accepted because they fit preconceived ideological ideas.

The difference between these senses of "science as ideology" is important and is something we have to come back to in our critical evaluation of ideological expansionism in the next chapter. It is clear, however, that since Rose, Lewontin, and Kamin believe that "science is not and cannot be above 'mere' human politics," they reject the idea of ideologically neutral science and maintain that science must be an ideologically partisan science (p. 8). It is less clear whether this means that they want to replace this right-wing version of "science as ideology" found among the biologists they criticize with yet another ideology, thus claiming that science should be the ultimate legitimator of a socialist ideology (in other words, we should replace right-wing science with a left-wing science), or whether they would allow a plurality of ideologies within science, thus accepting the legitimacy of not just their own ideologically partisan science but also of right-wing science, feminist science, Islamic science, and so forth.

Feminist Science

Some feminists argue that science is inherently oppressive against women because it is guided, or perhaps even determined, by androcentric values. Sandra Harding writes,

> The androcentric ideology of contemporary science posits as neces-sary, and/or as facts, a set of dualisms — culture vs. nature; rational mind vs. prerational body and irrational emotions and values; objec-tivity vs. subjectivity; public vs. private — and then links men and masculinity to the former and women and femininity to the latter in each dichotomy. Feminist critics have argued that such dichotomizing constitutes an ideology in the strong sense of the term. . . . (Harding 1986: 136)

Feminists like Harding thus maintain that mainstream science is disguised androcentric ideology, that is, roughly, a system of ideas that suits men's experiences and minds more than women's and that neglects and misrepresents the latter set of experiences. Helen Longino characterizes androcentrism as a "perception of social life from a male point of view with a consequent failure to accurately perceive or describe the activity of women" (Longino 1990: 129). But it must be more than that, however, since these feminists claim that not only the social sciences but also the natural sciences are androcentric. The perception in question is not only of social life but also of nature. (I shall call science shaped by androcentric ideology simply "androcentric science.")

Further, mainstream science is often also ideological in the sense that it is a "sexist science." Longino claims, for instance, that the man-the-hunter theory in anthropology is dependent upon sexist assumptions (p. 111). According to her, "sexism" is used to refer to attitudes expressing or ideas stating "the inferiority of women, the legitimacy of their subordination, or the legitimacy of sex-based prescriptions of social roles and behaviors" (p. 129). Thus, *male-sexist science* can be understood, roughly, as the practices (choice of research areas, theory constructions, grant applications, tenure track evaluations, and so forth) male scientists *qua* scientists are engaged in which involve or express discrimination against women and are geared (consciously or unconsciously) toward dominating them. A paradigm example of a male-sexist scientific practice would be one that excludes women from becoming scientists merely because of their sex. Notice that I have in my rough definition tried to avoid including Longino's statement that ideas stating "the inferiority of women" are examples of sexism. The reason is simply that although a claim such as "men are in general physically stronger than women" states the (physical) inferiority of women, we would nevertheless hesitate to classify it as a male-sexist idea. This claim would be male-sexist only if it was both false and geared toward dominating women.

The key objections these feminists raise against science are essentially the same as those we have seen Rose, Lewontin, and Kamin raise against a particular kind of research program in biology, although the ideology the feminists criticize is a different one. One objection is that mainstream science serves the ideological interests of men and not of women. More exactly, the claim must be that science serves merely the ideological interests of men *whenever* men's and women's interests diverge, because they could of course also converge. A second objection is that male scientists have falsely appeared to be sex- and gender-neutral parties, when in fact they have been developing an implicit ideologically partisan science.

Feminists maintain that androcentric biases can enter the research process at every stage. They can enter in the concepts and hypotheses selected, in the design of research, and in the collection and interpretation of data. For example, scientists who believed that women should not play a prominent role in public life often gathered data to support the claim that women are not suited for such a role by nature. From Aristotle's pronouncements on women as cold and wet to Darwin's notion of woman as a man whose evolution has been arrested, the ideological character of such research has sometimes passed virtually unnoticed until feminists started pointing it out. The same holds true for many theories of reproduction and anatomy developed over time, which were also plagued by ideological assumptions about female inferiority.[12]

Moreover, feminists have, as Londa Schiebinger documents, criticized several large and influential studies that omitted women as both objects and subjects of recent medical research. For instance, the 1982 Physicians' Health Study of Aspirin and Cardiovascular Disease conducted in the United States was performed on 22,071 male physicians and 0 women. No woman was among the 12,866 persons participating in the Multiple Risk Factor Intervention Trail either; this research studied the correlation between blood pressure, smoking, cholesterol, and coronary heart disease (Schiebinger 1999: 113). Other omissions pointed out are that only in the 1960s did primatologists begin looking seriously at what females do. But since the work of Jeanne Altmann, Linda Ferdigan, and Sarah Hrdy, females have been recognized as having their unique place in primate societies, undermining among other things the stereotype of the passive, dependent female (pp. 126-36).

Another example frequently used to illustrate how male-bias has produced inaccurate science is taken from anthropology. In the 1960s Sherwood Washburn and others developed a hypothesis to explain how quadrupedal apes evolved into bipedal toolmakers with significantly larger brains. According to the man-the-hunter hypothesis, the development of

---

12. For a discussion of this see, for instance, Lloyd (1983: 86-111) and Mosedale (1978).

tool-making among intelligent apes was due to "man-the-hunter," who needed lethal weapons to slay the savage beasts of the African savannah. This hypothesis was not surprising since the evolutionary theory was sharply focused on males. It gave the impression that men evolved by hunting while sedentary women tagged along gathering and giving birth; men actively and aggressively drove evolution forward. The woman-the-gatherer hypothesis, developed in the 1970s by Sally Slocum, Nancy Tanner, and others, claims instead that tool-making developed among intelligent apes because of "woman-the-gatherer," who needed tools to scrounge and forage for scarce vegetarian food. This new hypothesis undermined the notion that early human societies were characterized by strictly observed monogamy and rigid sexual division of labor with females subordinated to males.[13] The lesson to be learned is that the man-the-hunter hypothesis was the accepted hypothesis for so long because it was developed and sustained by a scientific discipline dominated by male scientists with masculine values and experiences.

These together with a number of other examples are taken by feminist critics to show that science is not ideologically neutral or gender-unbiased, but rather is driven by male interests and androcentric ideology. The most significant claim is that the very content of accepted theories in many areas of science reveals the male-bias of the scientists who developed them.

What is then the alternative to mainstream, androcentric science? Among feminists there seem to be basically two answers given. Some feminists, like Susan Haack, maintain that what we need to develop is a better science in which the effect of personal, social, or ideological elements is reduced, and which lives up to the ideal of what science should be (Haack 1992: 9-10). Hence feminists like Haack argue for a non-androcentric science or, in my terminology, an ideologically neutral science, despite the male-bias which has been found in scientific research. Harding calls the view that these feminists take "feminist empiricism" and defines it as the "attempts to bring feminist criticism of scientific claims into the existing theories of scientific knowledge by arguing that sexist and androcentric results of research are simply the consequences of 'bad science'" (Harding 1991: 48). It is worth noticing that although "feminist empiricism" has be-

---

13. For a discussion of this see, for instance, Longino (1990: 106f.) and Schiebinger (1999: 136f.).

come a term frequently used to characterize this kind of feminism, Haack herself rejects it as an inadequate term to describe her and similar views. She writes,

> No position deserves the name "feminist empiricism" unless, like Longino's and unlike mine, it makes some serious conceptual connection between the feminism and the epistemology. The point isn't that I do not think sexism in scientific theorizing is often bad science; I do. It isn't that I don't care about justice for women; I do. It isn't that I don't think there are legitimate feminist questions about science — ethical and political questions — about access to scientific careers, about funding priorities, about applications of scientific discoveries; I do. It is, rather, that I see the aspiration to a feminist epistemology of science — to an epistemology which embodies some specifically feminist insight, that is, rather than simply having the label stuck on adventitiously — as encouraging the politicization of inquiry; which, by my lights, whether in the interests of good political values or bad, is always epistemologically unsound. (Haack 1998: 118-19)

My interest, however, is not primarily in this group of feminists but in the group of feminists who like Harding and Longino argue for a science also on the theoretical level shaped by feminist beliefs and values. Their alternative to androcentric, mainstream science is "feminist science." According to Harding, feminist science is the "scientific knowledge-seeking that is directed by existing feminist theories and agendas" (Harding 1991: 305). She maintains that the feminist sciences "consist of the feminist metatheories of science and the research programs in the natural and social sciences that these metatheories already direct" (p. 307). Feminist science is "politicized research" which is "directed by feminist rather than androcentric goals" (Harding 1986: 24; 1991: 310).

Harding and Longino are positive toward politicized research and a legitimization of ideological commitments in the name of science. Hence they question the idea that ideologically partisan science is always bad science. Longino thinks we must be more realistic: "the ideal of value neutrality places unrealistic constraints on science as we know it" (Longino 1990: 13). She suggests instead that "a feminist scientific practice admits political considerations as relevant constraints on reasoning, which through their influence on reasoning and interpretation shape content" (p. 193). "In order to practice science as a feminist . . one must deliberately adopt a framework expressive of that political commitment" (p. 197). This means, among other things, that feminists "allow [their] political commitments to guide the choice" of what scientific theories to accept (p. 191).

These feminists, then, maintain that *ideologically partisan science* — that is, a science which is used to support or serve the interests of a particular group of people, groups such as feminists, socialists, libertarians, Christians, or naturalists — exists and also ought to exist. If we are realistic, they maintain, we realize that ideologically partisan science is the only kind of science available to us. What is crucial, however, is that we are explicit about our background beliefs or ideological commitments. This is one of their central objections against mainstream science. What these feminists are against, then, is scientists who try to hide their political agenda in doing science or who, falsely, think that their scientific practice is ideologically neutral or, more specifically, gender-neutral. Science is in fact always disguised politics of one or the other kind.

Let me end this section by focusing on a conceptual problem that arises and that could confuse the debate about feminism and science. We have seen that according to Harding, feminist science is "politicized research" which is "directed by feminist rather than androcentric goals" (Harding 1986: 24; 1991: 310). To contrast feminist science with androcentric science, however, as Harding does in this sentence, would be problematic given these feminists' own understanding of androcentrism, because we would then by "feminist science" mean a system of ideas scientists develop that suits women's experiences and minds more than men's and which neglects and misrepresents the latter set of experiences. But I take it that feminists would deny that feminism is, to paraphrase Longino, "a perception of social life from a female point of view with a consequent failure to accurately perceive or describe the activity of men." Let us, therefore, call the kind of science that is the complement (or the symmetrical opposite) to androcentric science, "gynecentric science" to avoid any confusion on this point.

Feminist science would then, roughly, be the practices scientists are engaged in which suit women's experiences and minds more than men's and which serve women's interests in society. A feminist science starts from or at least reflects the experiences and interests of women, but without thereby misrepresenting the experiences and interests of men or trying to dominate them. Thus the proper contrast to feminist science would be what we can call "masculinist science." *Masculinist science* could then be defined as, roughly, the practices scientists are engaged in which suit men's experiences and minds more than women's and which serve men's interests in society. A masculinist science reflects the experiences and interests of men, but without thereby misrepresenting the experiences and interests of women or trying to dominate them.[14]

Thus, androcentric science should, given my definitions, be contrasted with gynecentric science, feminist science with masculinist science, and male-sexist science with female-sexist science. Consequently, a *gender-neutral science* is a nonfeminist and nonmasculinist science. It consists of those practices scientists *qua* scientists are engaged in which do not suit men's experiences and minds more than women's or women's experiences and minds more than men's, and which do not serve any particular gender's social interests at the expense of the other. Given the definitions I suggested in the beginning of this chapter (see p. 175), we could say that any science (or part of science) that is aligned with or supports feminist values or beliefs over masculinist values and beliefs is ideologically partisan, whereas any science (or part of science) that does not do so is ideologically neutral.

IN THIS CHAPTER we have, in addition to introducing some key concepts and distinctions, surveyed some of the claims made by some advocates of religious or ideological expansionism. The basic idea behind worldview expansionism (which is the umbrella term) is that actual scientific practice is not worldview-neutral but filled with ideological and religious partisanship and bias. The proper response to this state of affairs is to allow an expansion of the boundaries of religion or ideology in such a way that it becomes an integrated part of science; the idea of a worldview-neutral science should be abandoned. Worldview expansionists, therefore, think that the most appropriate and honest strategy to adopt is to be explicit about what ideology-plus-science one defends, hence the talk about Augustinian science, Islamic science, left-wing science, and feminist science. Here we have an instance of interaction running in the opposite direction

---

14. Notice, however, that sometimes feminists make no distinction between androcentric science and masculinist science. Keller and Longino write in the introduction to the anthology *Feminism and Science* that "those [papers] in the second part [of the book] demonstrate the inadequacy of the view that masculinist research on sex and gender can be simply dismissed as 'bad science'" (Keller and Longino 1996: 8; cf. p. 39).

from what we considered in the previous chapter and from what has been the main focus of the literature in the science-religion dialogue. In that chapter we saw the level of interaction between science and religion in terms of the relevance of the content of particular scientific theories for religious belief; here we have looked at accounts that seek to show the relevance of religion or ideology for scientific theory construction and method development. It is now time to assess these claims, and that shall be our preoccupation in the following chapter.

Chapter 9

Should Religion Shape Science?

How should we think about worldview expansionism or, in a different terminology, the issue of religiously or ideologically neutral science? To what extent should religion or ideology shape science? In what way (if any) is it appropriate that worldview values and beliefs such as those endorsed by feminists, Marxists, Christians, Muslims, or naturalists enter into the fabric of science? These are the issues that we shall discuss in this chapter. The answer to these questions depends in part, I believe, on what exactly we mean by "science." In the first part of the chapter I therefore distinguish between different aspects of science before in the remainder of the chapter critically evaluating the case for a worldview-partisan science.

Worldview expansionists are right, I think, that it is unrealistic to think that no faith or ideological commitments enter into the fabric of science. As a Christian, I am as worried as, for instance, Plantinga and Golshani about the naturalism that often seems to be presupposed in what many contemporary scientists write and say. The theologian John F. Haught even thinks that this kind of naturalism or materialism "has become so intimately intertwined with modern science that today many scientists hardly even notice the entanglement" (Haught 1995: 33). In my discussion so far I have critically evaluated this form of naturalism (as a version of scientific expansionism) by making the entanglement that some evolutionary biologists are involved with explicit and by pointing out that their ideas typically presuppose the truth of certain philosophical or extra-scientific claims. In terms of the four options I presented in the beginning of the previous chapter it seems as if I have opted for this view:

(1) Scientific naturalism is not proper science because it is shaped by religious or ideological elements.

But if we follow Plantinga's and these other worldview expansionists' advice we cannot really argue in that way, given, of course, that scientific naturalism satisfies the other requirements that scientists typically demand that scientific theories have to satisfy. This is so because if, for instance, Christians maintain that they should be entitled to let their religion shape science to such an extent that they find it appropriate to talk about a theistic or an Augustinian science, then of course people who hold a different worldview such as naturalism must be allowed to let their worldview shape science to a similar degree. Hence, it seems as if Plantinga, Golshani, and other religious expansionists must accept that

(2) Scientific naturalism is proper science.

The importance of this point can be illustrated by Plantinga's attempt to criticize Fredric Crew for "failing to distinguish empirical evolutionary science from a philosophical or religious patina added by those who embrace metaphysical naturalism," in Crew's review essay "Saving Us from Darwin" (Crew 2001). Crew responds by saying that what Plantinga really wants is to replace Darwinism with "Augustinian science" and explains that "this 'science' takes as its starting point what Plantinga calls 'our knowledge of God'" (Plantinga et al. 2001). The issue that Crew probably had in mind but forgot to state explicitly (in a reply that leaves much to be asked for) is "How could Plantinga consistently criticize him for not distinguishing between empirical science and naturalist beliefs, if Plantinga thinks it is proper science to take as a scientist one's starting point in Christian beliefs?"

What Plantinga could, of course, consistently complain about and what goes beyond (2) is that Crew, Dawkins, Simpson, and others tend to hide their metaphysical naturalism and try to sell it as a proper part of public science (that is, as a science that is supposed to be free from religious or ideological commitments), when it is in fact not. Thus, his position might be our third option:

(3) Scientific naturalism is not proper science because the religious or ideological elements which shape it are not made explicit.

The advocates of left-wing science that we have studied hold, as we have seen, a similar position with regard to biological determinism. Recall that Rose, Lewontin, and Kamin write,

> To legitimize their [these biologists'] theories they deny any connection to political events, giving the impression that the theories are the outcome of internal developments within a science that is insulated from social relations. They then become political actors, writing for newspapers and popular magazines, testifying before legislatures, appearing as celebrities on television to explicate the political and social consequences that must flow from their objective science. (Rose et al. 1990: 28)

This is not to deny that Rose, Lewontin, and Kamin think that much evidence is lacking when it comes to these biological theories, but a main complaint (and this is what we are interested in within this context) is directed against the false appearance of these biologists as politically disinterested parties. They use a dishonest strategy when they hide their ideological commitments. Since science is not and cannot be above "mere" politics, the only thing we could ask for in this regard is that it is an explicitly ideologically partisan science.

As soon as Dawkins, Simpson, and these other scientists have made it explicit, however, that they are starting from and taking for granted what they know or at any rate think that they know *as* naturalists (that God does not exist, that the only reliable path to knowledge is science, that matter is all that ultimately exists, and so on) or *as* political agitators, and that they are employing this together with everything else they know in dealing with a scientific problem or project, then it seems that neither Plantinga nor Rose, Lewontin, and Kamin can demur.

But perhaps this is not quite right either. The reason why is that there is actually one other way in which Plantinga or Rose, Lewontin, and Kamin could maintain that scientific naturalism or biological determinism is not really science, namely, if this were their complaint:

(4) Scientific naturalism (or biological determinism) is not proper science because it is shaped by the wrong kind of religious or ideological elements.

211

Scientific naturalism, for instance, is not proper science because it does not assume the pronouncements of Christian faith and only this kind of science is what we really should call "science." I do not think that this is the position Plantinga tries to persuade us to take, nor is it the one that Rose, Lewontin, and Kamin argue for in their criticism of biological determinism. Some feminists seem close to embracing (4) or something very like it, however. Harding, for instance, believes that "feminist natural sciences," when developed, would provide us with "ways to obtain less partial and distorted knowledge of the empirical world" than that provided by the conventional natural sciences (Harding 1991: 56). She writes, "the feminist standpoint [epistemologist] . . . argues that men's dominating position in social life results in partial and perverse understandings, whereas women's subjugated position provides the possibility of more complete and less perverse understandings" (Harding 1986: 26; italics omitted).

So which one of these four positions should we endorse?

What Is Science?

To be able to make up our minds about options (1) to (4) we need to be a bit more specific about what we mean by science. What is it, more exactly, that perhaps should be shaped by religion or ideology?

In the last chapter we distinguished between *actual science* and *good science,* between the issues of whether science as it is done today (or in the past) is (or was) free from worldview considerations, and whether science should be or should strive to be free from worldview considerations. Either we can mean by "science" the activities that scientists are actually engaged in when developing theories and explanations, or we can mean the activities that scientists ought to be engaged in when doing science at its best. To see the relevance of this distinction, consider one of the examples of bias in science which feminists have brought to our attention. In the last chapter we saw that in several large and influential studies women have been omitted as both objects and subjects of recent medical research. For instance, the 1982 Physicians' Health Study of Aspirin and Cardiovascular Disease conducted in the United States was performed on 22,071 male physicians and 0 women. Neither were any women among the 12,866 persons participating in the Multiple Risk Factor Intervention Trial, studying the correlation between blood pressure, smoking, cholesterol, and coronary heart disease (Schiebinger 1999: 113). Here we seem to have a good example of male bias in science (although some scientists have defended their choice of men as research subjects on the ground that men are cheaper and easier to study). Many would argue that we here simply have a case of bad science. The evidence gathered about male physiology and behavior is not sufficient to render conclusions that apply to both males and females. This is not good science.

From the fact that actual science is not always good science, it does not necessarily follow that good science should be identical with actual science. It is therefore not enough to display cases where we can see that faith or ideology commitments have shaped scientific practice, to refute the idea of a worldview-neutral science. It must also be shown that it is unrealistic or perhaps undesirable to accept that idea as a regulative ideal for actual scientific practice. This could be done by arguing that there is no way to institutionalize scientific practice so that it can ensure that theories are accepted by the scientific community independently of ideological or religious concerns; or if it is realistic, to argue that it is still better to let science be shaped by religions or ideologies. Moreover, we have to distinguish between, on the one hand, those who claim that science in general is or should be influenced by ideologies or religions and, on the other hand, those who maintain that merely parts of science are or should be shaped in such a way. Reflecting the former position, Sandra Harding writes, "When we [the feminists] began theorizing our experience . . . we knew our task would be a difficult though exciting one. But I doubt that in our wildest dreams we ever imagined we would have to reinvent both science and theorizing itself to make sense of women's social experience" (Harding 1986: 251). A statement like this seems to indicate that Harding thinks the whole scientific enterprise — at least up until the recent development of feminist science — is not merely ideologically partisan but also biased. The view is then not that merely certain scientific programs or theories are expressions of male bias, but that science as a whole is disguised androcentric ideology. On the other hand, Plantinga writes, as we have seen, that it would be "excessively naive to think that contemporary science is religiously and theologically neutral, standing serenely above this battle and wholly irrelevant to it." Nevertheless, he continues in the next sentence, "Perhaps *parts* of science are like that: mathematics, for example, and perhaps physics, or parts of physics. . . . Other parts are obviously and deeply involved in this battle: and the closer the science in question is to what is distinctively human, the deeper the involvement" (Plantinga 1991: 16). Thus, according to his view, while not every scientific discipline is religiously partisan, this critique does hold true for some of them or some part of them.

If we take into account these two distinctions, we end up with the following list of alternatives:

	Worldview-Neutral Science	Partial Worldview-Neutral/Partisan Science	Worldview-Partisan Science
Actual Science	1	2	3
Good Science	4	5	6

Whether actual science should be understood as characterized by position (1), (2), or (3) is a question that is open to empirical investigation. But I think that the examples these worldview expansionists have given are sufficient to show that position (1) is no longer tenable. My point, however, is that even if we reject position (1), that actual science is worldview-neutral, we are not forced thereby to accept that science should be worldview-partisan (position 6) or even partially worldview-partisan (position 5). We can still argue that science ought to be free from ideological or religious considerations. We can, of course, also make it a matter of degree, by maintaining that the fewer religious or ideological elements that science contains the better.

But the cake can also be cut in different ways. One way to distinguish parts of science from each other is to focus, as Plantinga does, on different disciplines or subject matters. But another is to focus on the ensemble of activities that scientists, whether they are physicists, biologists, or sociologists, are engaged in when doing science. Scientists *qua* scientists choose a research area and problems to solve, develop hypotheses, collect and interpret data; they try to convince their peers to accept their methods and theories; they publish their results in books and journals; they function as peer reviewers both when it comes to what articles to publish and what research projects should be funded; they are involved in the storage and destruction of material used and in its application; they popularize research and explain the scientific results to the public; they function as expert advisers for private firms or governments; they teach and grade student papers and they decide what courses to offer and not to offer; they encourage/discourage students becoming scientists; they hire and fire people at their departments and they promote or do not promote a certain social structure at their institutions; they are engaged in fund-raising and in accepting (and possibly also in rejecting) funds from government agencies, private companies, and foundations. In all these scientific activities ideological or religious considerations could play a larger or smaller role, and are something we could encourage or discourage, accept or reject.

We immediately realize that the ways in which worldviews could enter into the fabric of science are too extensive to be adequately addressed in the last part of this book. To see the extent to which I think we should go along with worldview expansionists and on which point we should be reluctant to do so, however, it is sufficient that we add to the distinctions we already have one between four different aspects of the scientific enterprise:

1. Problem-Stating Phase   Science$_1$
2. Development Phase   Science$_2$
3. Justification Phase   Science$_3$
4. Application Phase   Science$_4$

The first aspect of the scientific practice consists of choosing a topic or problem for research. Call it the *problem-stating phase* or *science$_1$*. Scientists must first decide what is worth studying, what they want to spend their time, energy, and their own or other people's money on. In the second aspect, the *development phase* or *science$_2$*, scientists try to find methods suitable for solving the problem, try to develop hypotheses that would provide adequate explanations of phenomena under investigation and test them against what they consider to be the evidence. If scientists do not have enough or good enough evidence, they try to find more or better evidence. Moreover, they invent concepts to be able to express their hypotheses and evidence and classify the evidence in different categories. Scientists then try to convince the rest of the scientific community of the adequacy of these explanations in order to have their theories accepted as a part of the body of scientifically justified theories. In doing so they enter or take part in the *justification phase* or *science$_3$*. Sometimes the result of scientific inquiries can be used for achieving some practical human purpose. Such scientific theories have a practical utility for society. Thus, in the *application phase* or *science$_4$*, scientific results are used to increase food production, to cure diseases, to manipulate human or animal genes, to produce weapons, to create efficient ways of controlling behavior, and so forth.

Each of these phases could be cut into smaller parts and there are no clear boundaries between them, and moreover there is no one-way traffic between them. For instance, in their attempt to justify a theory, a group of scientists might receive a critical response from other scientists which makes them go back and restate the problem or collect new evidence or interpret the evidence at hand in a different way or modify the theory. I suggest, however, that the distinction between these four phases of scientific research would take us a long way toward identifying some of the key issues in the debate about worldview-neutral science.

This distinction makes it possible to distinguish between four different ways in which one could claim (or deny) that there is a legitimate place for religion or ideology in science:

(a) Worldviews could and should shape the problem-stating phase of science.
(b) Worldviews could and should shape the development phase of science.
(c) Worldviews could and should shape the justification phase of science.
(d) Worldviews could and should shape the application phase of science.

But now we are able to see that although I have maintained that scientific naturalism is not proper science because it is shaped by ideological considerations, the way position (1) expresses the matter may be somewhat misleading. Basically my analysis here and in *Scientism* (2001b) has shown that scientific expansionism typically is a combination of certain scientific theories and a particular ideology or worldview, namely, naturalism or materialism. That is to say, the theories about human nature, morality, and religion its advocates maintain do not merely derive their justification from scientific evidence but presuppose the truth of certain philosophical or extra-scientific claims (such as that the only kind of knowledge we can have is scientific knowledge or that only matter is real) and should therefore not be understood as science proper. Thus all my criticism seems to assume is that we accept the idea of a worldview-neutral science in the sense that worldviews ought not to shape the justification phase of science — that is, a version of (c) above. In other words, my argument so far does not rule out the possibility of a worldview-partisan science in senses (a), (b), and (d) above. Consequently, the key issue concerns the justification phase of science. I shall therefore in my evaluation of worldview expansionism briefly discuss whether religion or ideology should shape the problem-stating phase, the development phase, and the application phase, before focusing my attention to the issue of the acceptance and rejection of scientific hypotheses or theories and the place of worldviews in such an activity.

Worldviews and Science₁, Science₂, and Science₄

Let us then start our inquiry by focusing on the problem-stating, development, and application phases of science and on the place, if any, there should be for religion or ideology in those contexts.

The Problem-Stating Phase of Science

Scientists must first decide what is worth studying, what they want to spend their time, energy, and their own or other people's money on; when scientists do this they do science₁. One way of understanding the idea of a worldview-neutral science is to maintain that it applies to this aspect of the scientific enterprise. Imre Lakatos writes, as we have seen, that in his view "society . . . has a responsibility . . of maintaining the apolitical, detached scientific tradition and allowing science to search for truth in the way determined purely by its inner life" (Lakatos 1978: 258). The idea is that science ought to be *autonomous* in the sense that the direction of research should proceed undisturbed and not be determined by any ideological or religious interests. He argues against the view that it is society which should determine the scientist's choice of problem and research areas.

Lakatos's concern was that science₁ is threatened by political interference. Today this seems to be a matter of fact. In contemporary science more and more research projects require large funding, and consequently governments and large corporations have become increasingly involved. Hence people in power often decide the kind of research that should be undertaken and the kind that should be ignored. Scientists may even have to make a difficult choice between doing their research under these conditions or not doing it at all. Science₁ has become heavily politicized and commercialized. But we do not even have to turn to "Big science" to understand this because it is clearly the case, I take it, that there are certain things that rich but not poor people, white but not colored people, men but not women, Christians but not naturalists, liberals but not socialists, or vice versa, are interested in and which will sometimes determine what they as scientists decide to work on or, just as important, what they choose not to investigate or try to explain. It is quite possible, if you allow me to speculate, that, for instance, Dawkins's interest in evolution and his choice of research area in that field derives from his wish to be an "intellectually fulfilled atheist" (which he thinks Darwin made possible), and his intention is to use his own research for this purpose (Dawkins 1986: 6). Hence, science in the problem-stating phase is often religiously or ideologically partisan.

This also shows that the issue of the autonomy of science merely partially overlaps with the issue of whether ideology or religion should shape science$_1$, because even if scientists were completely free to ask whatever questions they wanted to ask and freely could choose research areas and problems, science$_1$ could still be religiously and ideologically partisan because most scientists adhere (whether or not they are aware of it) to one ideology or another.

Plantinga wants to draw our attention to the fact that many scientific projects start from and are motivated by naturalism. Science$_1$ is not religiously neutral. But the Christian community should not only point this out but do science in its own way and from its own perspective, which includes "deciding what needs explanation" seen from that point of view (Plantinga 1996a: 212). He maintains in his advice to Christian philosophers that "the Christian community has its own questions, its own concerns, its own topics for investigation, its own agenda and its own research program" (Plantinga 1984: 255). So Christians because they are Christians have certain interests and find certain things, but not others, puzzling and thus in need of explanation. Plantinga claims that this is something we should accept in scientific practice. Therefore, we should reject the idea that science$_1$ ought to be religiously neutral. It is entirely appropriate that Christians let their religious convictions influence what they decide to do research on and what questions to ask. Marsden agrees and points out that parity ought to apply in this regard. If there is place within science for feminism, Marxism, or naturalism, then there should be place for explicit Christian points of view as well (Marsden 1997: 52, cf. pp. 6-7).

Some left-wing scientists, on the other hand, believe that many scientific projects are motivated by capitalism. For instance, the Marxist anthropologist Marshall Sahlins criticizes, as do Rose, Lewontin, and Kamin, sociobiology for reflecting the values and ideas of a capitalist society. The sociobiological view of human nature is merely an ideological superstructure to a capitalist social order, an order which he rejects (Sahlins 1977). Hence there are or could be ideological reasons for asking the kind of questions that sociobiologists (and today evolutionary psychologists) ask and for offering the answer that they do. Feminists like Longino and Harding think instead that male interests and androcentric ideology drive the direction of research. In its place (or as a complement) they want a scientific knowledge-seeking that is directed by feminist interests and values (Harding 1991: 305). They argue for a feminist science$_1$. Moreover, Golshani maintains that the Islamic worldview has implications for the practical aspects of science, so, for instance, "Scientists should seriously refrain from conducting any kind of research which could be harmful to the human life, other creatures and our environment" (Golshani 2002: 9). In fact, Islamic science means that scientists see the totality of the things science deals with within an Islamic framework (Golshani 2000: 13). Thus the direction of scientific research also ought to be guided by Islamic convictions.

Should we try to prevent this kind of worldview influence on science$_1$? Not necessarily. The development of science might sometimes even benefit from it because some topics, some things in need of explanation, scientists might simply fail to notice if they shared too many interests or had similar ideological background beliefs. To take one recent example, consider women who have experienced that the society they are a part of denies them certain things, like an equal opportunity irrespective of gender to be hired for doing a job they are qualified to do or an equal salary irrespective of gender when doing the same job as men do. If these experiences together with the ideological interest to have the same opportunities as men determine that a group of female scientists decide to study the question of what causes the oppression of women, who has a right to complain? Hence, it seems quite reasonable to allow ideological or religious motives to guide what kind of research scientists get involved in. But it is, of course, extremely important that we realize that such a rejection of the autonomy of science means that ideological interests are in such a situation allowed to strongly influence the kinds of scientific inquiries which get done and the kinds which do not. Thus, we should perhaps actively try to promote a direction of scientific research that takes into account the interests of a broad variety of groups in our society.

Moreover, the success of science has drawn it into highly contested areas. Not only has the success led to radical modifications of social behavior (such as in reproductive technology), but it now seems possible to compromise the integrity and uniqueness of human life (as in, for instance, gene sequencing and cloning). To argue that science on this issue ought to be shaped by, for instance, Christian or Islamic values so that either this kind of research is not conducted or it is conducted with extreme caution must, it seems, be permitted, since we cannot avoid letting values guide the choice of research areas and problems (see Golshani 2002: 5).

But if one particular ideology or worldview is allowed to determine too heavily the problem-stating phase of science, then this might lead to a situation where some questions cannot be asked for ideological reasons. There might be some issue about the biological nature of humans that feminists such as Harding and Longino might be reluctant to encourage given their political agenda, and the same applies to the Christians, Muslims, and Marxists we have considered. Recall for instance the following criticism made by Rose, Lewontin, and Kamin against sociobiologists:

> For if human social organization, including the inequalities of status, wealth, and power, [is] a direct consequence of our biologies, then, except for some gigantic program of genetic engineering, no practice can make a significant alteration of social structure or of the position of individuals or groups within it. What we are is natural and therefore fixed. We may struggle, pass laws, even make revolutions, but we do so in vain. The natural differences between individuals and among groups played out against the background of biological universals of human behavior will, in the end, defeat our uninformed efforts to reconstitute society. (Rose et al. 1990: 18-19)

Suppose now that there exists a society in which their left-wing science totally dominates the scene. In such a society it might be very difficult to get any research money or approval to do research that might lead to the discovery of evidence supporting the idea that human social organization, including the inequalities of status, wealth, and power, is a direct consequence of our biologies. Hence, if we let (and actually I cannot see how we could avoid this) religious or ideological considerations influence the problem-stating phase of science, we should at least try to ensure that the scientific community consists of people with different ideological or religious backgrounds so that the research topics undertaken and the questions asked reflect the interests of different groups of people. Ironically, this might perhaps be (partially, at least) what lies behind the idea of the autonomy of science, namely, that scientists should be free to ask any kind of question without censorship or political correctness. With these qualifications, I think that on this issue about worldviews and science$_1$ we should go along with worldview expansionists, although the question is more complex than what we have been able to take into account in this context.

The Development Phase of Science

The second issue concerns whether ideology should influence the development phase of science, science$_2$. After scientists have picked their area of research and problems to solve, they try to find methods suitable for solving these problems, try to develop hypotheses that would provide adequate explanations of phenomena under investigation and test them against what they consider to be the evidence. If scientists do not have sufficient or good enough evidence, they try to find more or better evidence. Moreover, they invent concepts to be able to express their hypotheses and the evidence, and to classify the evidence in different categories. They present papers of their findings at symposia, workshops, and conferences, and try to take into account (one hopes) the criticism their ideas encounter on these occasions. At other times, they decide not to present their ideas at symposia, workshops, and conferences because they want to be the first to have published a solution to these problems within the scientific community.

Could religious or ideological considerations play a part, even a legitimate part, in this process? Longino maintains, as we have seen, that the development of the man-the-hunter hypothesis in anthropology was "dependent upon culturally embedded sexist assumptions . . ." (Longino 1990: 111, cf. p. 130). In other words, the tendency of the scientists who developed this hypothesis to think only in terms of male activity and their reluctance to ascribe to early human predecessors any behavior other than hunting have constituted ideological constraints on their capacity to develop and evaluate hypotheses which explain the evolution of the human species and in particular of tool-making. The most reasonable explanation, according to Longino, for the development of this particular hypothesis within paleoanthropology is that its developers were influenced by gender stereotypes that were projected into the past. In the 1970s, as we have already noted, paleoanthropologists such as Adrienne Zihlman, Sally Linton, and Nancy Tanner started to question the man-the-hunter hypothesis and developed instead the hypothesis that tool-making developed among intelligent apes because of "woman-the-gatherer," who needed tools to scrounge and forage for scarce vegetarian food. Instead of seeing prehistoric women as invisible handmaidens to men, they become the active partner who drove evolution forward.

The best explanation for the development of the woman-the-gatherer hypothesis might, on the other hand, be the rise of the 1970s women's movement with its insistence on making women "visible" (see Schiebinger 1999: 137). In such a context it became obvious that one had to start asking questions concerning women's role in evolution. Following Longino's line of reasoning, the most reasonable explanation for the development of the woman-the-gatherer hypothesis might then be that it fitted well with the feminist movement; the movement's "progressive" political values and ideals were projected into the past. Or is that really how we should see things?

The first point I want to make is that research might be motivated by ideological considerations and yet produce reliable knowledge or justified theories. Partisanship, as I have previously pointed out, does not entail bias (unfair or unjustified representation of the way things are or seems to be) (p. 178). This is the fallacy of guilt by association: if you can show that person A is a member of z (for instance, the group of people defending feminist values or masculinist values) then that somehow undermines this person's claims, given the assumption, of course, that it is a bad thing to be a member of z; if it is a good thing then you are supposed to draw the opposite conclusion. Therefore, it is not enough that Longino is able to show that certain masculinist values and ideas influenced the development of the man-the-hunter hypothesis to establish that we are confronted with a case of gender bias, far less that the hypothesis is false. (Recall that the charge of bias merely gives us a *prima facie* reason to think that what is claimed is false [p. 177].) What we need to know is this: did the advocates of this hypothesis accept it for purely nonscientific, ideological reasons, without a shred of scientific evidence that could be cited in its favor? Or was there actually some evidence that supports the man-the-hunter hypothesis, but because of ideological reasons (masculinist values and ideas) these scientists presented as established truth something which in fact should have been regarded as sophisticated but not completely unwarranted speculation? Or did the evidence available at the time actually point in this direction, but new data were soon to be discovered that would undermine the hypothesis?

What seems clear if we are to believe Zihlman is that the women's movement in the 1970s provided, as she says, "the basis for asking questions, but it did NOT provide data."[1] The women's movement *inspired* Zihlman, Linton, and Tanner to develop a new hypothesis that helped organize newly emerging data. These data included Richard Lee's finding from the study of the !Kung (a group of chimpanzee) that females provided two or three times as much food by weight as males. The important point is that the man-the-hunter hypothesis — whether the result of male bias, ideology, or religion — provides resources and constraints on the kinds of questions scientists ask and therefore on the kind of hypotheses they develop and on where they look for evidence.

It seems, therefore, unnecessary (and perhaps impossible) to restrict the ways scientists arrive at their hypotheses. If scientists arrive at their hypotheses by reading the Bible, or the *Qur'an*, or Marx's *Das Kapital*, or by being inspired by contemporary gender stereotypes or by the women's movement and not by a pure curiosity about how nature works, it perhaps does not matter all that much as long as they produce good hypotheses which are well-supported by evidence and which explain the phenomena in illuminating ways. Religions or ideologies could then be allowed to have a *heuristic role* in construing hypotheses within the sciences.

But worldview-partisan science$_2$ is problematic at least in one sense: if science is dominated by a particular group of people (men, women, Christians, naturalists, socialists, or liberals) and their religious or ideological commitments make it difficult, if not almost impossible, to develop certain hypotheses that would better explain the data than the ones actually developed, this would have a detrimental effect on scientific progress. Without the rise of the women's movement perhaps the woman-the-gatherer hypothesis would not have entered any scientist's mind! A good way to avoid this would probably be to make sure that within the scientific community we have people with very different ideologies. A pluralistic scientific community ought to be the ideal to strive toward.

These points apply equally well, I think, to the writings of the other

---

1. Zihlman quoted in Schiebinger (1999: 137).

worldview expansionists we have considered. Golshani, for instance, maintains that the popularity of the steady state theory or the oscillatory model of the universe among physicists can be explained at least partially by the fact that this theory or model provides ground for an atheistic interpretation of the universe (Golshani 2000: 8). The idea that the universe has no beginning appeals to physicists who are atheists or naturalists because it avoids any need to think that a god might lie behind the existence of the universe. Hence, it is not unlikely that the reason or a reason why scientists have developed steady state theory is that it fits nicely with their naturalist beliefs. This provides an example of worldview-partisan physics$_2$. Many Christian and Muslim physicists are, on the other hand, for religious reasons much more inclined to accept the big bang theory because it seems to leave room for a creator, perhaps even demand it. But again, it does not seem to matter much what it is that inspires scientists to develop a particular hypothesis, as long as they produce good hypotheses which are well-supported by evidence and explain the phenomena in illuminating ways.

Many other things besides developing hypotheses are, of course, going on in the development phase of science. For instance, novel concepts are developed to provide a conceptual clarification of the core elements of a theory or to create a useful metaphor that illuminates certain aspects and filters out others. These concepts could be developed and used either mainly or partially for religious or ideological reasons. One might, for example, wonder why an atheist like Dawkins would take a heavily value-loaded cultural term such as "selfishness" and apply it to nature, thus suggesting that the "selfish gene" is a vivid and adequate metaphor to express the idea that genes are the key unit of natural selection in nature (Dawkins 1989). Much more could therefore be said about science$_2$, but I hope that this is sufficient to show not only that religious or ideological considerations may shape the development phase of science, but that we should also accept that this is the case when a plurality of ideological and religious points of views are allowed to flourish within the scientific community.

The Application Phase of Science

Yet another issue about the relevance of worldviews to science concerns the application phase of science, that is, science$_4$. It is about whether it is appropriate that the results of science are used to promote the interests of a certain race, social class, sex, ideology, or religion. Today we face a new kind of situation in which the demarcation between traditional knowledge institutions such as universities and research institutions has eroded. Scientific knowledge production or theory construction is now generated to a large extent in the context of application. In the new research field of the life sciences, especially in biotechnology, the separation of university and industrial research has broken down almost completely.

In light of these changes it seems difficult to uphold the ideal of a worldview-neutral science$_4$, that is, that religion or ideology should not shape the application phase of science. Jonathon Porritt, for instance, maintains in contrast that

> Modern science and technology are themselves major elements in the ideology of industrialism. There are those who would have us believe that science itself is neutral, yet more and more it is being put to ideological uses to support particular interests, especially by those who already wield the power in our society. (Porritt 1984: 50)

Science is therefore not ideologically neutral because it is developed and used to support the ideological interests of certain groups in society.

Golshani maintains that the main difference between Islamic science and secular science is not merely that within the former the metaphysical presuppositions of science are rooted in a religious worldview (the theoretical level), but that religious considerations direct the proper orientation of the applications of science (the practical level). He says, "the Islamic world view should give orientation to the applications of science and technology" (Golshani 2002: 8); religion should shape science$_4$. Here he identifies one of the basic problems associated with modern — that is to say, secular — science. Instead of seeing the goal of science as the discovery of the secrets of God's handiwork in nature, modern science looks upon itself as neutral with respect to ideology and religion, thereby neglecting the responsibility that scientists have for the direction and application of their research as God's vicegerents on the earth. Golshani writes, as we have seen, that

> In the past, ethical considerations were a concern of all faithful scientists, both in the Islamic world and in the Western world. This perspective has been dramatically changed in our era. The development of sci-

ence and technology under the secularist-materialist world view has led to grave consequences for humankind. In this world view, the ethical, philosophical and religious dimensions of science and technology are neglected and humankind's physical comfort is confused with real happiness, though even this one is not achieved. (p. 8)

Once science and values were united in an organic whole. Today we need once more to return to a united view. Thus scientists' training should be accompanied by ethical education in order to stimulate moral concern and responsibility. Such training could "most effectively be done in a religious context" (p. 9). Islam should direct the proper orientation to be adopted with regard to the applications of science.

These ideas of a worldview-partisan science$_4$ go against the received view of the neutrality of science in respect to the practical use of its findings. Lakatos maintains, as we have seen, that

> *In my view, science, as such, has no social responsibility.* In my view it is society that has a responsibility — that of maintaining the apolitical, detached scientific tradition and allowing science to search for truth in the way determined purely by its inner life. Of course, scientists, as citizens, have responsibility, like all other citizens, to see that science is *applied* to the right social and political ends. This is a different, independent question. . . . (Lakatos 1978: 258, italics original)

Edward Teller believes that

> The scientist's responsibility is to find out what he can about nature. It is his responsibility to use new knowledge to extend man's power over nature. . . . When the scientist has learned what he can learn and when he has built what he is able to build his work is not yet done. He must also explain in clear, simple, and understandable terms what he has found and what he has constructed. And there his responsibility ends. The decision on how to use the results of science is not his. The right and the duty to make decisions belong to the people. (Teller 1960: 21-22)

Accordingly, Teller and Lakatos argue that the ends to which scientific results are to be applied should be determined by the people in a democratic society. Within the framework of democracy, people are equally allowed to use the teachings and the findings of science for whatever vision of a good human life they endorse, be it a feminist, a Christian, or a Buddhist vision. Scientists *qua* scientists should themselves remain neutral with regard to such visions. It is not a part of the scientist's task to take a stand in questions about the utility of science. The only thing scientists should care about is finding out the truth or discovering how nature works. Since it is up to society to decide the applications of the results of science, proper science may therefore be described as religiously or ideologically neutral.

Which of these views is the most reasonable one to defend today? This problem has many dimensions, and in this context we can only touch on a few. The first issue is, of course, whether the applications of science ought to be understood as a part of what we call "science," because if applications are never a proper part of science then it is inappropriate to talk about worldview-partisan science in this context. Hence, one kind of response to Porritt is that even if he might be right in maintaining that science more and more is being put to ideological uses to support particular interests in society, science could still be neutral because the application of science is for society to decide. So if science benefits the rich and the powerful rather than the poor, women, and religious minorities, then this says something about the social environment science inhabits rather than about science itself. In other words, it depends on the ideological structure of the society of which science is a part whether the results of science are used to create nuclear weapons and effective propaganda machines or to increase food production, to cure diseases, to restore wilderness areas, or to save endangered species. According to this reasoning, science as such can hardly be blamed for the ideological misuses of its results because the application phase is no proper part of science. So feminists and Muslims, for instance, are free to argue that scientific results should be used to promote their political ideals rather than others, but it is merely confusing to talk about feminist science$_4$ or Islamic science$_4$.

The problem with this line of argument, as I have already indicated, is that funds for scientific research are more and more given with an eye to possible applications, for instance, of a military, industrial, or medical kind. Science has increasingly become what used to be called "applied science." Scientific knowledge production is now generated to a large extent in the context of application. Therefore it has become very difficult to exclude the applications of science from science proper. As Leslie Stevenson and Henry Byerly point out,

By accepting funds from certain sources — and agreeing to make their
result available to those funding them — scientists are participating in
social processes by which knowledge, and hence power, is given to certain social groups rather than others, for example, to industrial corporations, defense departments, or national institutes of health. . . . If
they participate in the process as actually institutionalized, they display tacit acceptance of those institutions' values. (Stevenson and
Byerly 1995: 218)

Thus, much (but of course not all) scientific research done today is done in
the context of application. There has been an explosion of expectations
about science's ability to provide "useful answers" to an ever-increasing
range of problems in society. What is understood to be "useful answers"
depends, of course, on the ideology of the funding institution, be it a religious community, a company, an institution, or a government. But if this is
the situation then it is often appropriate to talk about science$_4$ and about
the possibility that religion or ideology could shape science in the application phase. Should we try to prevent this kind of worldview influence on
science$_4$?

It seems reasonable to assume that good scientists should not begin to
carry out a research project without first trying to consider, to the best of
their knowledge, certain basic questions about the expected results of the
project. How can these results be used? Who will use them? And what is
their purpose? Should it be obvious that these applications violate widely
accepted ethical principles, then scientists should refuse to carry out the research without adequate modifications. Thus, good science$_4$ should be
guided by ethical considerations, but these are of course not free-floating
principles but are often closely linked to a particular religion or ideology. A
reason why scientists might have a responsibility as scientists is that they are
often in a better position than other people to predict the consequences of
scientific research programs. For instance, the physicist Leo Szilard realized
as early as 1933 that the enormous energy resulting from a nuclear chain
reaction could eventually become a powerful weapon, thus suggesting to
other physicists that they should stop publishing their results (see
Stevenson and Byerly 1995: 177). Another example would be the self-
imposed moratorium on recombinant DNA research, decided upon by
prominent molecular biologists at the Asilomar conference in 1975.

This suggests that Golshani is right to propose that scientists' training should be accompanied by ethical education in order to stimulate moral concern and responsibility. Whether such training could most effectively be done in a religious context is a question on which, of course, advocates for different worldviews would disagree. But that Islam should direct or at least influence the proper orientation to be adopted toward the applications of science in countries where the majority of citizens are Muslims seems to be something which must be permitted, and the same holds true for any other religion or ideology. Thus, it is appropriate to talk about an Islamic science$_4$.

Worldviews and the Justification Phase of Science

We have so far considered the idea of a worldview-partisan science with respect to the choice of topics or problems for research (the problem-stating phase of science), the development of hypotheses, methods, and concepts used to solve those problems (the development phase of science), and the application of science to serve the needs of society or of groups within society such as the government, religious communities, industry, poor people, or rich people (the application phase of science). Now it is time to focus our attention upon the justification phase of science or upon what I have called science$_3$, that is, the phase in which scientists try to convince the rest of the scientific community to accept the explanations, theories, concepts, or methods they have developed. Could and should worldviews shape the justification phase of science? It is not possible to discuss all things that scientists test in the justification phase. Let us therefore focus on what I take to be the key element, namely, theories.

Worldview-Partisan Science$_3$

That science$_3$ could be worldview-partisan is something that advocates of worldview expansionism have given us good reasons to believe to be true. Let us again consider Plantinga's discussion of Simon's theory about human docility and limited rationality. It is developed, as Simon tells us, within the framework of neo-Darwinism to explain the spreading of altruistic behavior. By "docility" he means the tendency we can find among humans to accept social influence. He writes, "Docile persons tend to learn and believe what they perceive others in the society want them to learn and believe" (Simon 1990: 1666). His idea is that "because of the limits of human rationality, fitness can be enhanced by docility that induces individuals often to adopt culturally transmitted behaviors without independent evaluation of their contribution to personal fitness" (p. 1665). "Because of bounded rationality, the docile individual will often be unable to distinguish socially prescribed behavior that contributes to fitness from altruistic behavior" (p. 1667). For these and some other reasons Simon concludes that docile persons will necessarily also behave altruistically. But does this not mean that the really rational way to behave is to try to increase one's personal fitness? Is not the assumption underlining Simon's reasoning that if people were smarter (and perhaps a little less docile) they would be able to screen this culturally transmitted altruistic behavior and instead behave in a (nonbounded) truly rational way? But why think that altruistic behavior is a manifestation of limited rationality? Why not instead think, as Plantinga suggests, that it is a manifestation of genuine rationality? Altruistic behavior is, at least from a Christian perspective, very rational because it reflects the character of God. So what is going on here?

I suggest, in accordance with my previous discussion, that the reason why Simon assumes that the rational way to behave is to try to increase one's fitness is that he (consciously or unconsciously) interprets evolutionary theory *scientistically*. Simon assumes that neo-Darwinism is the whole story of human behavior. Maybe he shares with Michael Ruse and Edward O. Wilson the idea that "morality . . . is merely an adaptation put in place to further our reproductive ends" and that "in an important sense, ethics . . . is an illusion fobbed off on us by our genes to get us to cooperate" (Ruse and Wilson 1993: 310; cf. 1986: 186). Given this kind of perspective it is also not particularly surprising that Richard Dawkins writes, "much as we might wish to believe otherwise, universal love and the welfare of the species as a whole are concepts that simply do not make evolutionary sense" (Dawkins 1989: 2). If morality is merely an adaptation put in place to further our reproductive ends and if one *also* believes that evolutionary theory provides us with an all-sufficient explanation, what can practical rationality be other than maximizing personal and genetic fitness?

If Simon shares these ideas with Dawkins, Ruse, and Wilson, then the problem for Christians who maintain that science$_3$ should be religiously neutral is not really, as Plantinga suggests, that his theory of bounded rationality is inconsistent with their religious convictions. This follows if, as I have previously argued, worldview-relevance does not imply worldview-partisanship (see p. 180). The difficulty is rather that his and other biologists' account presupposes the prior acceptance of a rival worldview or ideology, namely, scientific naturalism. But a Christian can rightly point out that claims like "only science provides us with a reliable path to knowledge" and "the only things that exist are the ones science can discover, i.e., matter is what ultimately exists" are not scientific claims or entailed by such claims, and that it is possible to construct scientific theories without any problems whatsoever without making these kinds of epistemological and metaphysical assumptions.

This means that the ideal of science$_3$ as religiously neutral is probably best understood as a claim about what scientific investigation ought not to presuppose. The argument for a nonpartisan science would thus be as follows: *Science should be religiously neutral in the sense that it ought not to presuppose the truth of any particular worldview, religion, or ideology such as Christianity, Marxism, feminism, or naturalism in the justification phase.* This means that ideologies or religions ought not to be among the grounds for accepting and rejecting theories in science. Theories should be accepted by the scientific community only in the light of considerations that involve empirical data, other accepted theories, and cognitive values such as consistency, simplicity, and explanatory power. Ideological or religious considerations are therefore illegitimate ways of deciding between scientific theories. They threaten the integrity of science. The basic idea is that you do not have to agree on what constitutes a good human life or society, what a just social order is, what the appropriate differences (if any) between the sexes are, or whether God exists and who God is if God exists, to be able to evaluate scientific theories properly. The justification of scientific theory should not be determined by moral, personal, ideological, or religious ideas, but by interscientific norms.

Is not this also the real problem with Simpson's claim — which Plantinga brings to our attention — that all attempts to answer that question "What is man?" before Darwin published *The Origin of Species* in 1859 are worthless and that we will be better off if we ignore them completely? It is reasonable to assume that Simpson in telling us these things (and Dawkins in quoting him approvingly) simply presupposes the truth of scientific naturalism. It is only by taking for granted that genuine knowledge can be obtained solely by employing the methods of science that it seems reasonable to state in this *a priori* fashion that all human inquiries of human nature before the development of Darwinism are simply worthless. Only by assuming not merely that "Biology after 1859 gives us knowledge of human nature" but that "Nothing but biology (or the sciences) after 1859 gives us knowledge of human nature" or something along those lines can Simpson and Dawkins *as scientists* maintain by implication that what Christians take to be crucial information, namely, that we are created in God's image and that we are sinners who need God's love and redemption, is really worthless and that we would be better off if we ignore these ideas altogether. But "Nothing but biology (or the sciences) after 1859 gives us knowledge of human nature" and similar pronouncements are of course not something that science has the means to confirm. On this point Simpson and Dawkins violate the regulative ideal of science as religiously and ideologically neutral by assuming the truth of a particular ideology in their scientific reasoning.

The same analysis can, as we have seen, be made about the claim — which Plantinga thinks a Christian cannot take seriously for a moment[2] — made by Dawkins, Futuyma, Gould, and Simpson that evolutionary theory has shown or given us reason to believe that our species is merely accidental, that there was neither plan nor mind nor foresight involved in its coming into existence. If all individual species that come into existence through the process of evolution are random (i.e., have a low probability) with respect to what evolutionary theory (or more broadly, the sciences) can predict or retrospectively explain and if *the only source of knowledge we have is science (or more specifically evolutionary biology, in this case)*, then perhaps it follows that we ought to believe that our existence is the result of pure chance or, in other words, that it is not a part of anyone's plan and serves no one's end. But this is a scientistic and not a scientific argument because its second premise assumes the truth of scientism or scientific naturalism. Merely the first premise, the scientific one, is, however, compatible with the assumption that God knew before the creation of the world that human beings or at any rate intelligent life would be the inevitable product of the evolutionary process and that therefore we (or intelligent life) exist for a reason.

It is therefore somewhat misleading to write that worldview-neutral science, or what Plantinga calls "Duhemian science," "would be maximally inclusive and wholly neutral with respect to the world-view differences

2. But on which I have suggested it is possible to disagree (see p. 163).

that separate us" (Plantinga 1996b: 382). On the contrary, worldview-neutral science might totally undermine a particular ideology or religion if it contains many empirical claims that science can show to be false. The idea is rather that *science₃ ought not to grant a privileged status to any particular worldview, ideology, or religion in the sense of presupposing its truth* in the way, for instance, that Marxism was assumed to be true in "Lysenkoian" biology in the Soviet Union or Nazism in "Aryan" physics in Germany. It is in this way, I suggest, that we should understand the idea that Duhemian science (in contrast to Plantinga's Augustinian science) ought not to be ideologically or religiously partisan but neutral.

But Plantinga rejects, as we have seen, the ideal of science as ideologically or religiously neutral also in the justification phase. He maintains that Christians as scientists should start from what they think that they know as Christians. They should in doing science appeal, where appropriate, to what they know about God or God's activity or to what they know by the testimony of the Bible (p. 380). These beliefs ought to be part of the background evidence with respect to which the plausibility and probability of scientific theories are to be evaluated. Hence, science₃ should not be ideologically or religiously neutral in the sense that it should not presuppose the truth of any particular worldview, religion, or ideology such as Christianity, Marxism, feminism, or naturalism.

Plantinga is not alone among the worldview expansionists we have considered in arguing for a worldview-partisan science₃. Golshani maintains, as we have seen, that "it is on this basis [revealed knowledge and its effect on scientific knowledge] that we want to elaborate on the relevance of religious science, and in particular Islamic science" (Golshani 2000: 4). Moreover, Longino writes,

> The idea of a value-free science presupposes that the object of inquiry is given in and by nature, whereas the contextual analysis [that is, her own] shows that such objects are constituted in part by social needs and interests that become encoded in the assumptions of research programs. Instead of remaining passive with respect to the data and what the data suggest, we can, therefore, acknowledge our ability to affect the course of knowledge and fashion or favor research programs that are consistent with the values and commitments we express in the rest of our lives. From this perspective the idea of a value-free science is not just empty but pernicious. (Longino 1990: 191)

With this last statement Longino claims that the very idea of a value-free science and, I assume, also a worldview-neutral science is dangerous and therefore ought not to serve even as an ideal. On the contrary, scientists should not merely make their ideological commitments explicit when participating in policy-making, religious or moral debates, and so forth, but they should also interpret the data in such a way that those theories which guarantee the reinforcement of their own social ideals will be validated. However, "in order to survive and attract participants" this must be done in such a way that "some of the standards/values characterizing the scientific community within which it is proposed" are satisfied (Longino 1990: 193). Longino points out that on this issue neo-Marxists (like Rose, Lewontin, and Kamin) and radical feminists have a similar view: "the neo-Marxists are understood as advocating an alternative vision of nature and natural processes largely on *moral* and *sociopolitical grounds*. . . . In this regard the neo-Marxists stand on the same ground as the feminist scientist. In order to practice science as a feminist, as a radical, or as a Marxist one must deliberately adopt a framework expressive of that political commitment (Longino 1990: 197, italics added). Thus, according to this way of looking at things, ideological considerations are to be regarded as legitimate constraints on scientific reasoning also in the justification phase.

Why Accept Worldview-Partisan Science₃?

Why Accept Worldview-Partisan Science$_3$?

But *why* should we accept a worldview-partisan science$_3$, that is, that religious or ideological considerations should be allowed to play a legitimate role in determining which theories scientists ought to accept or reject? Does Plantinga or Longino (or any other of these worldview expansionists) give us any good reason why we should develop a worldview-partisan science$_3$?

What is evident is that Plantinga and Golshani have given us convincing examples of naturalist bias within contemporary science. But, as we have seen, this is not in itself sufficient to support the idea of an Augustinian science$_3$ or an Islamic science$_3$. It is not sufficient because one can still maintain that the appropriate way to respond is to reject these scientists' ideas once we discover that they are not based merely on accessible empirical evidence, but depend for their justification on the prior acceptance of certain ideological convictions. More precisely, as soon as we discover that scientists accept scientific hypotheses because they fit their ideological beliefs or values, one could argue that these hypotheses ought not to be considered a part of the body of justified scientific theories. Science ought to be structured so as to discourage scientists from advocating scientific hypotheses because they fit their ideological or religious convictions. In good science, scientists should be encouraged to expose — and receive recognition for exposing — ideological assumptions functioning as control beliefs for what theories are accepted or rejected by the scientific community. This is, in fact, also what has happened many times in the history of science. For instance, the psychologist Cyril Burt (1883-1971) developed a theory that intelligence is innate or genetically determined, which received such an acceptance within both the scientific community and the establishment in Great Britain that it provided the theoretical basis for the English educational practice of selecting pupils for different types of secondary school on the basis of an examination at age eleven. Leon Kamin and others showed how biased Burt's research really was. It seems that Burt's ideological convictions about selective schooling (and his personal ambitions) must have influenced his scientific theory construction to such an extent that he even adjusted evidence to fit his theory. Kamin and others received recognition for their criticism because it was assumed that ideological assumptions should not function as control beliefs for what theories are accepted or rejected by the scientific community (see Stevenson and Byerly 1995: 101f.).

Perhaps Harding and Longino are right that many scientists have failed to see the extent to which male-bias functions as a control belief in scientific reasoning and perhaps Plantinga and Golshani are right that the same is true about naturalist bias in contemporary science. But as long as the scientific community can be constituted in such a way that it contains scientists who adhere to a great variety of religions or ideologies and these people's voices are not silenced, we can still, when it comes to the validation of scientific theories, continue to hold on to the non-Augustinian conception of science as a regulative ideal for $scientific_3$ practice.

Plantinga seems to anticipate this objection because he admits that a possible response to Dawkins, Simon, and other scientists is to maintain that when they say these things about rationality, purpose, pre-Darwinian ideas about human nature, and so on, they are not (strictly speaking) doing science because their conclusions require the acceptance of certain extra-scientific premises. But his comment is that this "is not really the important question for my present purpose" (Plantinga 1996a: 187). This is puzzling because he says that his objective is not merely to give examples of naturalist bias in current science but to "argue that a Christian academic and scientific community ought to pursue science in its own way, *starting from* and taking for granted what we know as Christians" (p. 178). But if one can criticize Dawkins, Simon, and these other scientists on scientific grounds by pointing out that they presuppose naturalism in their scientific reasoning, then one crucial reason why Christians should develop their own kind of science fails. Why develop a theistic science$_3$ if one can show that naturalist science$_3$ is not good science? The same applies to feminism: why promote a feminist science$_3$ if one can argue that masculinist science$_3$ is not good science?

Another reason for developing a worldview-partisan science$_3$ that Plantinga gives is that since we know many important things as Christians, it would be unwise or unnatural if we accepted a constraint that did not allow us to use that information in doing science (p. 192). Why should we not use everything we know in doing science? Notice first — given the distinctions I have made — what the question is about. I am not saying that Christians should not let their knowledge or at any rate their presumed knowledge influence the kind of research topics they undertake or the hypotheses they propose. What I am saying is merely that *they should not claim that their Christian convictions ought to be considered a proper part of scientific theory validation.* They ought not to maintain that worldview-partisan science$_3$ is good science.

Why? Because if they do, then people of other faiths and ideologies who also believe firmly that they know particular things as a result of *their* adherence to these faiths and ideologies can claim that their "knowledge" also ought to be considered a proper part of scientific theory validation. But since it seems as if we cannot come to an agreement about which worldview we should accept, we face a choice. (The situation is that one religion's or ideology's truth is another's bias!) We can either choose to accept a pluralism of worldviews in scientific theory validation or try to limit their influence as much as we can, and whenever a theory is accepted because of worldview considerations point this out and thereby disqualify it as a proper part of the body of scientifically justified theories.

Moreover, the history of science should make even the most convinced Christians hesitate before maintaining that their convictions ought to be a proper part of scientific theory validation. For instance, many

Christians have really thought they *knew* that the Bible taught that the earth was flat, that the earth was at the center of the universe, and that God created the different species on earth in a fixed form roughly six thousand years ago, and for a long time — as we all know — these beliefs hindered the progress of scientific inquiry. None of Plantinga's reasons why Christians ought to develop an Augustinian science is therefore convincing.

Let us now consider a feminist case for a science shaped by ideology in the justification phase because some of the reasons Longino gives are of a different sort than those Plantinga gives. Notice first that Longino is a bit more ambiguous in her writing than what I have indicated so far. In her discussion of the man-the-hunter theory and its rival the woman-the-gatherer theory in anthropology, she is anxious to emphasize that the evidence is indecisive since the data do not conclusively support any of these theories (Longino 1990: 106-11, 129-30).[3] Thus, Longino assumes that under these circumstances scientists with feminist values and beliefs are justified in maintaining that the woman-the-gatherer theory is to be preferred. This indicates that the influence of ideology in the justification phase ought to be accepted *only* in a situation in which the theories scientists have to decide among are fairly equally supported by the evidence. In such a situation we ought to let the scientific theories' ideological or political virtues be the determining factor.

Such an interpretation, however, allows that there also are *other* kinds of theory justification situations, situations in which ideological considerations will not be the determining factor because the evidence for a theory — no matter its ideological virtues — is strong or even overwhelming in comparison to that for any rival theory. But if this is Longino's position she could not really claim that ideologically neutral or value-free science is not just empty but pernicious, since these other kinds of situations are good examples of ideologically *non*determined theory choices.

Let us examine this weaker interpretation of Longino's position first. According to this interpretation she claims the following:

---

3. Recall that according to the man-the-hunter theory the development of tool-making among intelligent apes was due to "man-the-hunter," who needed lethal weapons to slay the savage beasts of the African savannah. The woman-the-gatherer theory claims instead that tool-making developed among intelligent apes because of "woman-the-gatherer," who needed tools to scrounge and forage for scarce vegetarian food.

(a) Scientists should favor a scientific theory which is consistent with the ideological beliefs and values they express in the rest of their lives in situations in which this theory and its rivals are roughly equally supported by the evidence (call this the *inclusive ideology thesis*).

This thesis has one important implication for the present discussion, namely, that neither Longino nor anybody else who accepts this view can on scientific grounds criticize scientists such as Wilson and Washburn for letting their purported masculinist values and beliefs determine why they accept the man-the-hunter theory. Therefore, the acceptance of a scientific theory that expresses a male bias (and not a female bias) is not in itself a valid objection against the theory, provided either that it is the only available theory or that the evidence does not equally support the rival theories. Ideology or religion per se is not intrinsically something bad in scientific theory choice situations if it is made explicit.

A number of feminists would not be happy with the inclusive ideology thesis, however. Longino acknowledges such a result in pointing out that according to these feminists, not only is it the case that "[k]nowledge in a male dominant society reflects the experience and interests of men ... [but a] more objective and transformative knowledge is ... to be found in the perspective of women" (Longino 1990: 12). Sandra Harding, for instance, maintains that feminist natural sciences, when developed, would provide us with "ways to obtain less partial and distorted knowledge of the empirical world" than that provided by the conventional natural sciences (Harding 1991: 56). Hence the ideology thesis should instead be interpreted as saying this:

(b) Scientists should favor a theory that is consistent with feminist beliefs and values in situations in which this theory and its rivals are roughly equally supported by the evidence. (We can refer to this as the *exclusive ideology thesis*.)

On the basis of this thesis scientists such as Wilson and Washburn could be criticized on valid scientific grounds for accepting the man-the-hunter theory, because good scientists should endorse feminism and thus accept the woman-the-gatherer theory (or similar theories).

We can see the obvious problem with the exclusive version of the ideology thesis if we universalize it:

(c) Scientists should favor a theory that is consistent with the correct or best-justified ideological or religious beliefs and values in situations in which this theory and its rivals are roughly equally supported by the evidence.

With the less specific statement we leave it open whether it is, for instance, the feminist, masculinist, Christian, Islamic, naturalist, left-wing, or right-wing ideology which is the correct one. In other words, the exclusive ideology thesis seems to imply that in order to do the best kind of science, scientists should first agree on a *political* agenda, that is to say, they ought to accept the same ideology. But the prospect that scientists should be able to agree on one correct ideology if they thought through things carefully enough and listened to philosophers like Dennett, Harding, Nozick, Plantinga, and Rawls seems wishful thinking. To start with, scientists would probably have to take a number of years off, thoroughly studying the ideological options available. But even if scientists did this, there is no reason to think that they would have more success than philosophers and politicians have had in reaching a consensus on these issues. A feminist would, therefore, be better off rejecting the exclusive ideology thesis and arguing instead for a plurality of ideologies in science since we do not know or at least cannot come to a consensus about which set of ideological values and beliefs is the best or the correct one.

So perhaps (a), the first interpretation of Longino's position, is more plausible than (b), understanding it along Harding's lines. But the inclusive ideology thesis also faces serious difficulties. Even though ideological correctness or the acceptance of feminist values and beliefs is not a necessary condition for proper theory validation in science, it is problematic to bring society's plurality of ideologies or worldviews into science$_3$. Think of scientific education, for instance. What theories should be taught in college or at the university? There seem to be two options available for Longino. Either Longino could say that the universities should teach those theories that fit her own ideological profile or she could argue that the universities should use textbooks in which — whenever the evidence is indecisive between rival theories — it is stated that some scientists because of worldview$_1$ take theory$_1$ to be the best warranted while other scientists take theory$_2$ to be best warranted because of worldview$_2$, and so forth.

But why not leave out the ideological or religious considerations altogether, and simply *withhold* judgment? Is not that what good scientists should do? Thus, it should be written in the textbooks that at the present time theory₁ and theory₂ are equally supported by the evidence, and perhaps noted in the text that future research may or may not settle the issue. Hence, good scientists must maintain that in contemporary science there are two theories that explain the phenomena and they are equally justified. Moreover, scientists can add that they themselves are currently engaged in a research program that is intended to identify new evidence that they hope will show that one of the theories is better justified than the other, and that it is their ideological or religious commitments that make them think this and motivate their research. That is, ideological or religious considerations are legitimate in the development of scientific hypotheses (i.e., in science₂) but not in the justification of them (i.e., in science₃). But if Longino accepts this she could not at the same time claim that

> that *theory* which is the product of the most inclusive scientific community is better, other things being equal, than that which is the product of the most exclusive. It is better not as measured against some independently accessible reality but better as measured against the cognitive needs of a genuinely democratic community. This suggests that the problem of developing a new science is the problem of creating a new social and political reality. (Longino 1990: 214, italics added)

A more radical interpretation of Longino which makes it impossible to withhold judgment is, however, possible, given that we think science a worthwhile activity. Such a reading is conceivable because expressions such as "we should not be passive with respect to data," "value-free science is pernicious," and a theory is "better as measured against the cognitive needs of a genuinely democratic community" seem to indicate a stronger standpoint than the one we just examined.[4] Perhaps the situation is such that in *all* theory justification situations in science, the evidence is not sufficient to make one theory more likely than its rivals. Evidence never obliges scientists to accept one theory rather than another. Thus, any number of theories can be logically consistent with the same data, and it is only when scientists add certain background assumptions that they are justified in picking out a particular theory (Longino 1990: 38-48). It is in fact in this way, Longino thinks, that ideology enters into even the justification phase

---

4. Cf. Longino (1990: 191) and the above discussion.

of science: "Background assumptions are the means by which contextual values and ideology are incorporated into scientific inquiry" (p. 216). Since the evidence always underdetermines theories, the acceptance of theories is and should always be affected by something besides the evidence, namely, the scientists' worldview commitments functioning as background assumptions. The argument from underdetermination shows the impossibility of an ideologically or a religiously neutral process of theory validation in science. Ideology or religion is always relevant in science$_3$ because it fills the slack between evidence and theory.

Notice also that the radical interpretation of Longino's position can be given two different readings:

(d) Scientists should favor a scientific theory which is consistent with the ideological beliefs and values they express in the rest of their lives since scientific theories are always underdetermined by the evidence (call this the *inclusive radical ideology thesis*).

(e) Scientists should favor a scientific theory which is consistent with feminist beliefs and values since scientific theories are always underdetermined by the evidence (call this the *exclusive radical ideology thesis*).

According to these theses, it does not matter if the evidence for a particular scientific theory is stronger or even overwhelming in comparison to any of its rivals, because it is always legitimate to claim that one of its rivals is the one theory that scientists should prefer in that it is more in tune with one's own ideology or with feminism.

The above radical ideology theses also face some major difficulties, however. Recall, for example, the question of what theories should be taught in schools and at the university. If we do not settle for the option of letting the universities teach those theories that fit their own ideological profile, we are in a rather awkward situation. Should good scientific textbooks list the theories that purport to explain the data and say explicitly that since we, the authors, accept worldview$_1$, we maintain that theory$_1$ is the best warranted? Or perhaps the best solution would be to let the textbooks provide the students with the data and then let the students pick the theory which best fits their own worldview? Perhaps people in society should decide what theories should be taught by participating in general elections (thus, a kind of democratic scientific epistemology). People could vote once a year if the man-the-hunter theory or the woman-the-gatherer theory should be taught in school, and the same goes for the evolution theory, quantum mechanics, the big bang theory, and their rivals.

But notice that the difficulty with the radical ideology theses goes deeper than this. Scientists and people in general not only lack knowledge about what scientific theories to accept: they do not even know what ideology or worldview to accept because these too are underdetermined. There is also a slack between evidence and ideologies or worldviews.

Even more problematic is the fact that most people would not know whether the feminist critique of science is true or justified. Nor would they know whether feminist science is better than masculinist science because these claims are also underdetermined by the evidence. Consider the following summary of some of the feminist criticism against modern science:

(1) In all the theory choice situations which feminists have empirically studied, the evidence shows that male-bias has either determined or at least heavily influenced which theories scientists have accepted.

(2) It is likely that the same result would be obtained if any of the other instances of theory choice in the history of science were critically examined.

(3) Therefore, science is male-biased and not ideologically neutral.

One can wonder, however, why anybody other than a feminist should accept this argument as sound, if an appeal to underdetermination is legitimate in the making of theory choices. If it is always legitimate to choose between rival claims or theories on the basis of ideological considerations, even in situations where there is more evidence supporting one claim in comparison with the other, then somebody who is not a feminist can always be warranted in maintaining for ideological reasons that the first premise of the argument is false — that is, in claiming that scientific theory choices are always male-unbiased and ideologically neutral, no matter what feminists say and no matter how good their evidence is. A feminist critique of science that is based on this understanding of the underdetermination thesis is, therefore, in the end self-defeating.

In fact, I do not think the radical ideology thesis is the position Longino really wants to defend, even if the rhetoric sometimes seems to lead her in that direction. She writes, for instance, that her contextual analysis does not imply that "the sciences are completely determined by contextual values [i.e., values about what ought to be the case in society]. Constitutive values [i.e., the norms which are generated from the goals of scientific inquiry] provide a check on the role of contextual values and cultural assumptions" (Longino 1990: 223). She further thinks that ideological commitments can and should be reduced, but not eliminated, through shared procedures in the scientific community (pp. 76-83). But if Longino merely wants to maintain the weaker ideology thesis, she cannot consistently claim that gender-free science is "anathema" or that the idea of a value-free science is not just empty but "pernicious" (p. 191).

So far my argument has been primarily a negative one against the idea that science should be ideologically or religiously partisan in the sense that scientists should let religious or ideological considerations determine what theories to accept or reject. I have maintained that some of the main objections raised against this idea fail. In what follows we will consider whether or not any positive evidence can be provided which supports the idea that science$_3$ should be worldview-neutral. It seems as if we can give examples from the history of science that would indicate that the slack between theory and evidence is not always present, at least not in the sense that ideology or religion always fills the gap. The realist in Larry Laudan's dialogue on science and relativism points out,

> If you're right [that is, the relativist] that a number of very specific facts about Einstein's social and political background explain why *he* adopted the theories he did — and maybe you're right about that — I cannot see how those same causes could possibly be invoked to explain why a huge number of theoretical physicists, with backgrounds and interests vastly different from Einstein's, have also come to accept most of his theories. Englishmen and Americans, Christians and atheists, capitalists and libertarians, scientists from working-class and aristocratic families, young and old . . . the backgrounds of current-day advocates of, say, relativity theory cut directly across all the usual ways of categorizing noncognitive concerns. (Laudan 1990: 152)

In a similar way the acceptance of the relativity theory cuts across all usual ways of categorizing ideological concerns. Thus, at least sometimes science has shown itself to have an *ideology-transcending capacity*; it can overcome the various ideological barriers that divide people of different sex, gender, culture, religion, and economic status. If we can find examples of ideologically or religiously nondetermined scientific theory acceptance in actual science, why should we hesitate to claim that good science, that is, science at its best, ought to be worldview-neutral in the process of evaluation and justification? The scientific community is structured (or, at least, should be structured) so that in the process of justifying scientific theories, the advocating of scientists' ideological or religious convictions is discouraged. Science is set up so that it is in the professional interest of scientists to make sure that their acceptance of a theory is based on the best empirical evidence available. Otherwise, they may have their reputations severely damaged by other scientists who are keen to expose the weaknesses of the proposed evidence or the inferences from data to theory. This does not, of course, make contemporary science infallible — as Longino, Plantinga, and those other worldview expansionists we have discussed have correctly pointed out — far from it; but it indicates that contemporary scientific practice already tacitly accepts worldview-neutral science$_3$ as an ideal. As Ronald N. Giere points out,

> Historical studies have revealed many cases in which a scientific consensus on a particular hypothesis was in fact due as much to shared [ideological] values as to empirical evidence. What the history of science (since the Scientific Revolution) does not reveal is many cases in which participants *explicitly* argued for a hypothesis because of its ideological desirability. And those who have, as following publication of Darwin's *Origin,* tended to be outside the scientific community. Evaluation of scientific hypotheses is *supposed* to be strongly based on empirical data, even if in practice this is not always the case. If the data fail to agree more with one hypothesis than another, one is *supposed* simply to withhold judgment, even though there is often in fact a rush to judgment that goes beyond the data. Moreover, discovery of ideological bias in the evaluation of scientific hypotheses is usually taken as a basis for criticism within the scientific community. (Giere 2003: 20)

What I think Longino, Plantinga, and those other worldview expansionists we have discussed have shown, however, which is important enough, is that a proper scientific education ought always to contain a study of examples of ideological or religious influences on past and present scientific research projects, so scientists can develop a better and less naive understanding of how their own and other people's worldview commitments interact with scientific practice also in the justification phase.

We can state the position defended here more exactly if we use two of the distinctions developed in earlier chapters, the one between justification and rationality and the one between individual practice and collective practice (see pp. 23-24, 102). The *individual practice* consists of the commitments, beliefs, and goals that individual scientists accept, whereas the ones that are shared by the scientific community constitute the *collective practice*. One of the central goals of the collective scientific practice is to produce knowledge or at least justified theories about the natural world. This collective epistemic goal is a goal all the sciences should share, although the methods and the data appealed to might be of different sorts. Once one accepts the professional role of a scientist, it follows that one thereby consents to this goal. Scientists therefore have an obligation not only to make their theories accessible to other scientists (to avoid duplication of work), but to try to justify them, that is, to try to convince other scientists that their own theory better fits the evidence than rival theories in the field do, and that therefore this theory ought to be a part of the collective scientific practice. Scientists have an obligation to get involved in the process of justification (which includes peer evaluation), and this is typically done by presenting one's research in scientific journals and at scientific conferences. This is a part of what I have called the justification phase of science or science$_3$. It is in *this* context, I have argued, that ideological or religious reasons for scientific theory acceptance should not be permitted and in fact should be discouraged.

This does not mean, however, that we could not accept that individual scientists always have their own epistemic and practical goals besides the ones maintained by the scientific community. A scientist could (and should) accept the *collective epistemic goal* of contributing to the long-term scientific community project of understanding some aspect of the world, for example, human nature. But she could at the same time also have the *personal epistemic goal* of showing that a particular theory about gender which is not accepted at the present time by the scientific community is actually the best theory. This personal ambition may in part be motivated by the *personal practical goal* of promoting a society shaped by feminist values — a goal that the scientific community perhaps either rejects as its *collective practical goal* or tries to be neutral toward. (Notice that we by allowing the development of a worldview-partisan science$_1$ and science$_4$ have also accepted that science's collective practical goals could be shaped by ideologies and religions.)

If we now add the distinction between rationality and justification, we can see that such a symbiosis of personal and collective goals need not be problematic for a worldview-neutral science₃. This is so because on my account scientists need not convince their colleagues that they are wrong, to be rationally entitled to accept their own theories. At most they need to convince other scientists that they themselves are rationally entitled to them. Whether other scientists are equally rational in accepting them is another question, which brings us to the issue of scientific justification. Scientists' exercise of informed judgment is necessary for satisfying the demands of scientific rationality, whereas in addition the social requirement (peer evaluation) is necessary for obtaining scientific justification. The question of *scientific rationality* concerns whether scientists are rationally entitled to believe that their own theory is true or that it is better or more promising than the others in the field. The question of *scientific justification* concerns whether scientists have succeeded in giving an account that should convince their colleagues that they also ought to accept the theories they propose so that these theories can become part of the collective scientific practice.

Hence it is compatible with the idea of a worldview-neutral science₃ that individual scientists can be rationally entitled to accept theories (as a part of the individual practice) that are not accepted by the scientific community (or as a part of the collective practice) and do this for ideological or religious reasons. The point is merely that this kind of reason (or evidence) should not be allowed in scientific justification and thus in the justification phase of science.

In conclusion, the central insight of the worldview expansionists we have considered is that scientific research does not take place in a vacuum. Science is also a social institution and as such is integrated into all our other social institutions. At the personal level, people get involved in science for a number of reasons: out of pure curiosity about how nature works, a desire for reputation or power, a need to earn a living, or a desire to serve humanity or influence public policy. As Lewontin writes, at a social level "science is molded by society because it is a human production that takes time and money, and so is guided by and directed by those forces in the world that have control over money and time" (Lewontin 1993: 3). If this is so, it is unrealistic, as Longino points out, to think that no ideological commitments enter into the fabric of science, that "science is free of personal, social, and cultural values, that is, independent of group or individual subjective preferences regarding what ought to be" (Longino 1990: 4). It is, as Plantinga says, naive to "think that contemporary science is religiously and theologically neutral, standing serenely above this battle [between theism and naturalism] and wholly irrelevant to it" (Plantinga 1991: 16).

On all these issues we could agree, but *should* it be like this? Should we accept and endorse without reservation a worldview-partisan science and develop different kinds of sciences depending on what ideology or religion we adhere to? I have suggested that the answer depends on what aspects of the scientific enterprise we have in mind. In the problem-stating phase of science (or science$_1$), it seems almost unavoidable that religious and ideological interests influence the direction of research. I have argued that we should accept this, although it might be crucial for scientific progress that no one particular ideology or religion be allowed to determine the problem-stating phase of science too heavily because this might lead to a situation where some questions cannot be asked for ideological or religious reasons. Thus, we should try to promote a direction of scientific research that takes into account the interests of a broad variety of groups in society.

In respect to the development phase of science (or science$_2$), we have reached a similar conclusion. It does not much matter, to put it simply, what inspires scientists to develop hypotheses as long as they produce hypotheses that are well supported by evidence and explain the phenomena in illuminating ways. But again, a pluralistic scientific community is desirable because otherwise the dominance of a particular ideology or religion might block the creativity so essential for scientific$_2$ development.

If it is acceptable that worldviews influence the direction of research (or science$_1$) then it seems strange to not allow worldviews to also give orientation to the application phase of science (or science$_4$). This is so because often it is the possible application that determines the direction of research. Moreover, a decision about applications cannot be reached unless values enter into the picture, and values often are a subset of worldviews. A worldview-partisan science$_4$ might therefore be not only possible but also desirable because it gives a foundation to the values that guide applications of science and technology.

The key issue concerns, however, the justification phase of science (or science$_3$). I have argued that irrespective of whether it is appropriate with a worldview-partisan science$_1$, science$_2$, and science$_4$, we should be much more reluctant to accept a worldview-partisan science$_3$. Science should instead be religiously neutral in the sense that it ought not to presuppose the truth of any particular worldview, religion, or ideology such as Christianity, Islam, feminism, Marxism, or naturalism in the justification phase. Theories should be accepted by the scientific community only in the light of considerations that involve empirical data, other accepted theories, and intra-scientific norms such as consistency, simplicity, and explanatory power. The basic idea is that you do not have to agree on what constitutes a good human life or society, what a just social order is, what the appropriate differences (if any) between the sexes are, or whether God exists and who God is if God exists, to be able to evaluate scientific theories properly. This holds true even if worldview expansionists are right that violations of this ideal in the actual life of scientific inquiry happen more frequently than we have previously thought.

In sum, the traditional view of a religiously or ideologically neutral science could be expressed in terms of the following matrix:

	Worldview-Neutral Science	Worldview-Partisan Science
Problem-Stating Phase	X	
Development Phase	X	
Justification Phase	X	
[Application Phase		X]

The application phase is bracketed because some of the advocates of the traditional view of a worldview-neutral science maintain that applications are not a proper part of science but something distinct from it. The alternative proposed by the worldview expansionists we have considered is as follows:

	Worldview-Neutral Science	Worldview-Partisan Science
Problem-Stating Phase		X
Development Phase		X
Justification Phase		X
Application Phase		X

Whereas I have suggested that we instead should accept this matrix:

	Worldview-Neutral Science	Worldview-Partisan Science
Problem-Stating Phase		X
Development Phase		X
Justification Phase	X	
Application Phase		X

Note that these matrixes fail to do justice to the fact that the extent to which religion should (or should not) shape science is not merely to be understood in terms of these four phases but also as a matter of degree within each phase. In our discussion of, for instance, Longino's view, we have seen that it is possible to argue for a worldview-partisan science$_3$ in the sense that ideological or religious reasons ought to be accepted *only* in a situation in which the theories scientists have to decide among are equally supported by the empirical evidence. In such a situation we ought to let the scientific theories' religious or ideological virtues be the determining factor. A much stronger view of worldview-partisan science$_3$ is the one which entails that ideological or religious reasons ought always to determine which theories the scientific community should accept or reject.

What our discussion entails, however, is that contemporary science (that is, the natural sciences) needs to be transformed. Few scientists today seem to feel any need to be aware of the effects of various ideological or religious influences on the questions that are asked, on the gathering of data, and on the formulation and assessment of theories. But if scientists frequently are (mis)led by dominant ideologies or religions, to the extent that the worldview expansionists argue, then what we need is a change of scientific education and not merely a change in the constitution of the scientific community (so that a plurality of ideologies and religions is encouraged among scientists). We need a scientific education which contains a study of examples of worldview influences on past and present scientific research, so that scientists can develop a better and less naive understanding of how their own and other people's ideological or religious commitments interact with scientific practice at different levels.

Chapter 10

How To Relate Science and Religion

I n this last chapter of the book I shall discuss how my ideas should be related to Ian Barbour's well-known typology of science and religion, and
in the process I shall give an answer to the key question of this book,
namely, how should we relate science and religion?

As a result of the influence of Barbour's important work in the
science-religion field, the standard way to present the relationship between
science and religion is in terms of four views or models (Barbour 1997: 77f.;
2000: 2f.). These four views — conflict, independence, dialogue, and integration — are taken to give a systematic but simplified overview of the
main options today. Advocates of the *conflict view* maintain that science
and religion are rivals. They compete on the same turf and in the end one
will emerge as the winner. Barbour takes two paradigm examples of advocates of the conflict view, scientific materialists (or proponents of scientific
naturalism or scientism) and religious literalists: "They both claim that
science and theology make rival literal statements about the same domain,
the history of nature, so that one must choose between them" (Barbour
1997: 78). Defenders of the *independence view,* on the other hand, maintain
with regard to science and religion that each "has its own distinctive domain and its characteristic methods that can be justified on its own terms.
Proponents of this view say there are two jurisdictions and each party
must keep off the other's turf" (p. 84). Barbour also identifies two mediat-
ing positions between these extremes. The advocates of the *integration
view* hold that "some sort of integration is possible between the content of

theology and the content of science" (p. 98). Thus, for example, proponents of this view could maintain that changes in scientific theories may affect the reformulation of certain religious beliefs (such as ideas about creation, original sin, and divine omnipotence). Barbour maintains that in the fourth model, the *dialogue view,* a less direct relationship between science and religion is defended than in the integration view. An exchange between the two practices may take place about the metaphysical presuppositions, the methods, or the conceptual tools of science and religion, but, in contrast to the integration view, reformulation of the content of science or religion will seldom be called for (p. 92). What consequences does our discussion have for Barbour's four basic ways of relating science and religion?

Five Science-Religion Views

I suggested in chapter 1 that we think about the relationship of science and religion in terms of three models or views: the independence view, the contact view, and the monist view (p. 9). There is or should be either (a) no overlap between science and religion, (b) overlap (or intersection) between science and religion, or (c) a union of the domains of science and religion. This threefold typology applies whether or not science and religion change over time, whether or not we have a particular religion or a particular science in mind, and independent of which aspect or dimension of these two practices we focus on.

Picturing the relationship between science and religion simply in terms of no overlap, overlap, and union does not tell us *how large* a possible overlap between science and religion could be. It also does not specify precisely *where* exactly a proponent of the contact view finds the overlap; it could be in the methods or rationalities of science and religion (as with van Huyssteen) or in the theoretical content (as with Kaufman) or somewhere else.

How is Barbour's fourfold typology related to this threefold typology? I suggest that Barbour's dialogue view and integration view should be interpreted as two different versions of (b). The advocates of the integration view would on such an account maintain a larger overlap between science and religion than the proponents of the dialogue view. Barbour claims that those who argue for the integration view "seek a closer integration of the two disciplines," implying that those who advocate the dialogue view seek a less close integration (Barbour 2000: 3). But it then creates some confusion merely to call one of these two views "the integration view" and the other "the dialogue view." It would be better to talk about two perhaps important versions of the integration view, which each in its turn could, at the next level, be divided into subviews such as natural theology, theology of nature, and process theology. Alternatively, there is my approach, which is to follow Haught and talk about two versions of the contact view (Haught 1995: 9).

Moreover, there are, as I also pointed out in the first chapter, actually two versions of the monist view. There I wrote that if one believes that science and religion offer rival answers to the same kinds of problems, then one is a proponent of the *conflict* version of the monist view. But if one holds that science and religion could or at least eventually will offer the same answers to the same kinds of problems, then one is a proponent of the *harmony* version of the monist view. The conflict version seems to be the most widely accepted of the two today, however.

If we take these considerations into account, Barbour typology could be expressed and related to mine in the following way:

Level 1	(the monist view)[1]	(the contact view)	the independence view
Level 2	the conflict view (the harmony view)	the integration view the dialogue view	
Level 3	religious literalists scientific materialists	natural theology theology of nature process theology presuppositions methodological parallels	neo-orthodoxy existentialism

Level 1 is more fundamental than level 2, and level 2 is more fundamental than level 3. On level 3 we can find the people or schools and the like that Barbour identifies as exemplifying the views we can find at levels 1 and 2. (The first three examples in level 3 of the second column illustrate the inte-

---

1. I have put in parentheses those science-religion views that are omitted in Barbour's typology.

gration view and the last two the dialogue view). A difficulty with Barbour's typology, then, is that he identifies four core science-religion views, but they are not located at the same logical level.

There are also some other problems with Barbour's typology that we need to address. The first one is simply a terminological difficulty but one of great importance. Irrespective of which of these science-religion views we hold, we could argue that its advocates ought to get engaged in a *dialogue* with each other and thus drop the polemics or stop ignoring each other. Dialogue is thus a way in which people who hold different views can relate to each other. It is therefore infelicitous to call one science-religion view the "dialogue view" because it is desirable that people — regardless of whether they accept the conflict view, the contact view, or the independence view — should at least sometimes try to become involved in a dialogue with each other and listen carefully to what people with differing views think about these issues. Those who are reluctant to participate in a dialogue are probably those who are most certain that their view is the correct one and therefore see no need to listen to anyone holding a different view. I really hope that I can convince you on this point, so that we all immediately stop talking about a dialogue view.[2]

Second, as soon as one allows an intersection between science and religion, one opens the door for potential conflict or harmony between science and religion. Drawing on the recent work of astronomers, Nancey Murphy and others have argued that the physical constants in the early universe appear to be fine-tuned as if by design, thus providing additional confirmation for a belief in God as the designer and creator of the universe (Murphy 1993: 407f.). Religious practitioners could by religious ways of belief formation obtain this knowledge, but now it seems as if information obtained by scientific ways of belief formation can also confirm this religious belief. But not only does intersection between science and religion allow the possibility of harmony; it also allows the possibility of conflict. Gordon Kaufman, as we have seen, argues that changes in scientific theory make it necessary to reconstruct the conception of God that has traditionally been endorsed by Christians, Muslims, and Jews. There is a conflict between a personal con-

---

2. Not surprisingly this is one of the models or views which Barbour himself endorses. But who could really be against dialogue? Only the dogmatic people! But neither defenders of the conflict view nor defenders of the contact view nor defenders of the independent view need be dogmatic *merely as a result of holding their view*. (By which I am not denying that dogmatic people probably could be found in all three camps.)

ception of God and scientific theories about cosmic and biological evolution. But nevertheless, Kaufman does not (in terms of Barbour's typology) accept a conflict view: he holds an integration view. Here we have a conceptual problem. In other words, we must keep in mind that even if a scholar engaged in the religion-science dialogue maintains that there is a conflict between science and religion this does not automatically make him or her a proponent of the conflict view. *Conflict* between science and religion is compatible with both the conflict view and the contact view. *No conflict* between science and religion is compatible with not merely the monist view (in both of its versions) and the contact view but also the independence view. Of course, the larger the intersection between science and religion is, the larger the area of *potential* conflict between science and religion is.

But who is to be classified as a proponent of the conflict view? Phrased differently, why would Barbour classify a religious literalist like Philip E. Johnson (or any other religious literalist) as an advocate of the conflict view, but not someone like Kaufman (Barbour 1997: 84)? Johnson, like Kaufman, believes that the theory of evolution conflicts with religious faith (Johnson 1995). But to maintain, as we have just seen, that there is a conflict between science and religion on a particular topic cannot be sufficient for being classified as a proponent of the conflict view. What else is required? What constitutes the difference between the conflict view and the integration or contact view?

One obvious difference between them is of course that Johnson, in contrast to Kaufman, thinks that there is something wrong with actual scientific theory formation and not with religious belief. So one possibility would be to say that a person who believes that there is a conflict between science and religion and who gives priority in such a conflict to religious belief at the expense of scientific theory is a proponent of the conflict view, whereas someone who in such a conflict gives priority to scientific theory at the expense of religious belief is a proponent of the contact view. But what about scientific materialists such as Dawkins and Wilson; they would then fail to qualify as proponents of the conflict view, which hardly makes sense.

Another idea would be to focus on Barbour's statement about scientific materialists and religious literalists: "They both claim that science and theology make rival literal statements about the same domain, the history of nature, so that one must choose between them" (Barbour 1997: 78). So if you claim that science and religion make rival statements about the same domain or object then you are a proponent of the conflict view. This is, of course, a possible way of defining the conflict view, but then this position would most likely be a version of the contact view. It would certainly be so if its advocates at the same time maintained that the methods of obtaining these rival statements are different; for instance, one could maintain that scientists obtain them by inferring a hypothesis from empirical data and that religious people obtain them by reading and interpreting what they consider to be God's revelation, the Bible or the *Qur'an*. If that is the case, then there is a theoretical but no methodological overlap between science and religion.

This way of defining the conflict view would (based on the quotation above) also conflict with Barbour's own writing because he writes in response to Haught's typology that Haught's "first two categories, Conflict and Contrast, are identical with those in my scheme. His third category, Contact, combines most of the themes in what I have called Dialogue and Integration" (Barbour 2000: 4). Recall that to qualify as a proponent of the conflict version of the monist view, one must claim that science and religion offer rival answers to the same kinds of problems. This characterization is, however, somewhat ambiguous. The reason is that the monist view actually holds that science and religion offer rival (the conflict version) or harmonious (the harmony version) answers to the same kinds of problems, and deal with *only* these problems. That is to say, there is nothing in the domain of science that is not in the domain of religion, and vice versa; there is a union of domains. But all religious literalists would hardly claim that. I suppose they would typically maintain that religion also deals with other questions than science deals with, for instance, that religion deals with moral values and their grounds, something completely different from what science is supposed to deal with.

Wilson seems to be the best example of a proponent of a conflict version of the monist view. As a scientific expansionist, he believes that science will (one day if not today) be able to take over the functions of religion; it could actually become our new religion and offer us ethical guidelines. But we have also seen that not all scientific expansionists think that the boundaries of science could be expanded to such an extent. Dawkins is such a person: he thinks that science could offer us some help in solving our existential questions but that science cannot provide us with a new ethics. Since two essential functions of religion are to help us deal with our existential questions and to offer us ethical guidelines, Dawkins does not believe that science alone should replace religion. Rather, we could say that he presupposes a very large intersection between science and religion in his writing. His view would therefore be a version of a greatly expanded contact view, whereas Wilson would perhaps end up endorsing the conflict view in Barbour's typology.

Perhaps the reason why Barbour does not want to count Dawkins as belonging to the middle position between the conflict view and the independence view has to do with the name he gives it, namely, the "integration" view. It seems as though we can talk about integration between two things only if we believe that both are worthwhile but different in some important respect. It does not make real sense to try to integrate science and religion if you think that only religion or only science is worthwhile. Dawkins appears to believe that science wherever possible should replace religion and that what is left should be discarded for other reasons. In addition to the problem with positively value-loading the two middle views by picking the terms "integration" and "dialogue," the difficulty is that this explication of Barbour's position does not help us understand why Kaufman but not Johnson would qualify as a spokesperson for the integration view. Surely both Kaufman and Johnson believe that both science and religion are worthwhile practices to be engaged in.

Perhaps Barbour would defend his classification by maintaining that Johnson and other religious literalists, and Dawkins and other scientific materialists, mostly fall within the scope of the conflict view even if they sometimes endorse the contact view or even the independence view; therefore, religious literalists and scientific materialists are good examples of proponents of the conflict view. This would accord with the way in which Barbour characterizes his own position. He writes, for instance, "I will try to do justice to what is valid in the *Independence* position, though I will be mainly developing the *Dialogue* position concerning methodology and the *Integration* thesis with respect to the doctrines of creation and human nature" (Barbour 1997: 105). Barbour's own position is therefore not the integration view but a combination of the integration view, the dialogue view, and the independence view (but apparently not of the conflict view).

The difficulty with this claim is that it sounds as if these science-religion views (whether we accept a threefold or fourfold typology) are compatible with each other. But they are not! It is true that it is compatible with both the dialogue view and the integration view that something is valid in the independence view, because if one maintains that there is merely an intersection between science and religion then this entails that some part of religion is independent of some part of science. But as soon as there is an overlap in respect to methodology then this is not compatible with the independence view because by definition it contains the claim that there are no overlaps between science and religion. Moreover, if there is an overlap with respect to the doctrines of creation and human nature, then this undermines the dialogue view because it presupposes that the overlap is limited to methodology and boundary questions and the like. (It was on these grounds that in chapter 1 I criticized Gould for being inconsistent in his discussion of the principle of NOMA.) Therefore, I propose that we stick to the characterization of the conflict view that I earlier proposed. The price we pay is that few people involved in the science-religion discussion would fall within the first category, namely, the monist view, and there will be many of them in the second category, the contact view. We therefore need to develop conceptual tools to differentiate versions of the contact view.

Before suggesting how to do this, let me address a different sort of criticism that has been directed against Barbour's typology and see to what extent it affects my typology as well. Brooke, Cantor, van Huyssteen, and others maintain that Barbour's typology is too a-historical, universal, and static to map in any fruitful way the relationship between science and religion that people throughout the ages have advocated (Brooke and Cantor 2000: 275; van Huyssteen 1998: 3; Stahl et al. 2002: 6).[3] This problem can, I think, be avoided if his typology or mine is linked to the ideas of expansion and restriction and to the idea of a multidimensional relationship (to which we soon shall return), indicating that the relationship between science and religion is dynamic and evolving.

What the concepts of scientific expansionism, restrictionism, and religious expansionism indicate is that if we accept that science and religion are social practices which change over time, then it is possible that at time t_1 there is no overlap between science and religion, but due to, say, scientific theory development at time t_2 there is an overlap between these two practices, and perhaps at time t_3 there will be a union (if we are to believe Wilson) between science and religion.[4] It is a development that will come at the

---

3. Barbour has also responded to this kind of criticism in Barbour (2002).

4. But it is also possible that at time t_4 there is merely overlap again and at time t_5 science and religion are completely separate practices, and so on.

expense of traditional religion and not of science (again if we are to believe Wilson). Alternatively the direction could be the opposite, as Plantinga and Golshani maintain, with religious beliefs influencing the direction of scientific research and the justification of scientific theories. In other words, we ought to go from a religiously neutral science to a religiously partisan science. I have in contrast argued that we ought to endorse restrictionism in respect to scientific theory justification and disallow an overlap between science and religion on this point. This also shows a problem with my terminology, however, because I would rather characterize my view as an example of "restriction" than of "restrictionism." The "ism" terminology indicates something much stronger or more thorough than the position I am advocating. We therefore need the terms "expansion" and "restriction" as supplements to those of restrictionism and expansionism.

If, as I have suggested, scientific expansionism (in the form of scientific naturalism) should be seen as an expansion of the domain of science into the territory of religion, and religious expansionism (in the form of Augustinian science and Islamic science) should be understood as an expansion of the domain of religion into the territory of science, both of them could be classified as either a version of the contact view or a version of the monist view. It depends, so to speak, on how far into the territory of the other practice the first practice is supposed to extend, all or merely a part of the way. But notice if we accept that science and religion are practices that change over time and use the terminology of expansion and restriction as a means to characterize changes in the relationship between science and religion, then we cannot immediately identify scientific/religious restrictionism with the independence view. This is so because restriction or expansion is always related to a previous situation and that situation could be characterized by a particular kind of overlap between science and religion rather than by two autonomous, non-overlapping practices. A restrictionist would in such a situation be someone who argues against expansionists' attempt to further expand the overlap either at the expense of religion or at the expense of science.

But scientific and religious expansionism need not be versions of either the contact view or the monist view. We can see this if we recall that the monist view holds that science and religion offer rival (the conflict version) or harmonious (the harmony version) answers to the same kinds of problems, and deal with only these problems. There is nothing in the domain of science that is not in the domain of religion, and vice versa; there is a union of domains. Scientific and religious expansionism need not be versions of either the contact view or the monist view because its proponents could claim that the domain of one practice, *S*, should be expanded to such an extent that the other practice, *R*, becomes a subset of the first practice, *S*, but still deny that the first practice, *S*, thereby becomes a subset of the second practice, *R*. We could say that *R* is a subset of *S* if *S* fulfills all the functions of *R* but also has other functions than those *R* has. The idea is simply that one could maintain that, for instance, the domain of religion could be expanded to such an extent that science becomes a part of religion, but that there still are functions of religion such as those of providing salvation or ethical guidelines that fall outside the task of science.[5] This would follow if, for instance, we accepted a far-reaching version of theistic science.

I have failed to find any good names for these science-religion views, but let us call them (d) the *complete scientific expansionist view* and (e) the *complete religious expansionist view*. It is thus possible that a scientific materialist like Wilson should not be classified as a proponent of the conflict version of the monist view but as an advocate of the complete scientific expansionist view. This would be the case if he were to claim that science could fulfill all the functions of religion, whereas science also has functions other than those religion has. In a similar fashion a religious practitioner could claim that although science should be a part of religion, and consequently there would be no science apart from religion, religion is more than merely science.

We can conclude that there are actually five basic ways in which science and religion could be related — the monist view, the contact view, the independence view, the complete scientific expansionist view, and the complete religious expansionist view — although we also have seen that it may in reality be hard to find protagonists for some of these views. In what follows I shall, therefore, primarily focus on science-religion views (a), (b), and (c).

---

5. The obvious parallel, well known to many involved in the science-religion dialogue, would be the difference between pantheism and panentheism. According to the pantheist, God and the world are identical, whereas the panentheist believes that there is no world apart from God, but that God is more than the world.

A Multidimensional Typology of Science and Religion

To be able to know whether any person's claims actually presuppose the acceptance of any of these five science-religion views (or for that matter any of the views in Barbour's fourfold typology), it would be very helpful if we could identify those *parameters* which are involved in relating science and religion. It is exactly at this point that I hope the multidimensional matrix developed in this study could be of help. We need to get beyond the one-dimensional picture of science and religion that the monist view, the contact view, and the independence view give us, and apply the multidimensional framework composed of social, teleological, methodological, and theoretical dimensions in our attempt to characterize and identify interesting positions in the religion-science field. We need to know, for instance, where exactly potential overlaps between the two practices can be found and the grounds which allow us to distinguish between different versions of the contact view.

Barbour's distinction between the dialogue view and the integration view seems to be based on such content-related considerations. This is so because he develops the dialogue view in respect to methodology and the integration view in terms of the doctrines of creation and human nature. My suggestion of how we should identify such parameters and develop them in a systematic way is based on the idea of seeing science and religion as social practices. A practice, as I have defined it, is a set of complex and fairly coherent socially established cooperative human activities through which its practitioners (religious believers or scientists) try to obtain certain goals by means of particular strategies. A practice can thus be distinguished by identifying the goals that its practitioners roughly share and by the means that they have developed and used to achieve these goals. Science and religion can, therefore, be related at least in terms of the goals, the methodology (or the means), and the result of applying these methods to achieve these goals, which includes the formation of beliefs, stories, or theories. (Later on we shall come back to the issue of how we could combine these teleological, methodological, and theoretical dimensions with the social dimension of science and religion.)

We could then say that people who claim or assume that the goals (the teleology), the methods (the methodology), and the theoretical output of science and religion are or should be completely different are proponents of the *independence view*. People who claim or assume that there is or should be an overlap between the goals (the teleology), the methods (the methodology), or the theoretical output are proponents of the *contact view*. Lastly, people who claim or assume that the goals (the teleology), the methods (the methodology), and the theoretical output of science and religion are or should be the same are proponents of the *monist view*.

Such definitions would make it possible for us to distinguish between a teleological contact view, a methodological contact view, and a theoretical contact view. A *teleological contact view*, for example, would hold that the goals of science and religion are or should be the same or partially the same, whereas their methods and theoretical output are completely different. A strong version of the teleological contact view would hold that the goals are or should be the same and a weak version would hold that there is or should be merely an overlap of goals. It is frequently argued, for instance, that although both science and religion have epistemic goals, that is to say, they are both intended by their practitioners to say something true, they are nevertheless not intended to say something true about the same thing. (Let us call this "thing" their *area of inquiry and expertise* or *competence*.) Religion (or at least Christianity) could on such an account be taken to say something true about salvation, people's relationship to God, and what is morally right and wrong. This is the area of inquiry and expertise of religion. The area of inquiry and expertise of science, on the other hand, is to discover truths about natural objects and events. For this reason these practices have developed different, non-overlapping methods, and as a consequence fail to have any overlapping theoretical content or outcome. This provides an example of a weak teleological contact view.

By presenting this particular version of the teleological contact view in this way, we can see that there is one more element we could include in our typology, namely, the area of inquiry and expertise or competence. The general idea is this: We typically make a distinction between, for instance, the humanities and the natural sciences on the basis of their different areas of inquiry and expertise. Roughly, the area of inquiry and expertise of the humanities is cultural phenomena, whereas the area of inquiry and expertise of the natural sciences is natural phenomena. This partially explains why they have developed different methods of studying these phenomena. The idea would then be that this kind of reasoning and classification could be applied to religion as well. Thus, a common view based on this kind of differentiation of areas is the view that the area of inquiry of science is composed of empirical questions and the area of inquiry of ethics is composed of moral questions, whereas the area of inquiry of religion is concerned with existential questions. I shall not, however, add this as a fourth element to the typology I propose for two reasons. One is that it increases the complexity of the typology too much, given that the aim of developing a typology is primarily to give a map which sets out the main positions regarding how to relate science and religion. The second reason is that in specifying the goals of a practice, its area of inquiry is typically identified. If one claims that the main goal of science is to discover truth about natural objects and events then its area of inquiry and expertise is also identified.

A *methodological contact view* would say that the methods of science and religion are or should be the same or partially the same, but that the goals are completely different and there is no overlap in theoretical output. A strong version of the methodological contact view holds that the methods of the two practices are or should be the same, while a weak version holds that there is or should be merely an overlap of methods. For instance, the idea could be that both science and religion employ the deliverance of reason (understood perhaps in terms of judgment-based evidentialism), but whereas the goal of science is to obtain true beliefs about the natural world, the goal of religion is to tell us how to become morally virtuous persons or how to live a good human life; and therefore there is no overlap in the theoretical outcome of the two practices.

A *theoretical contact view* would maintain that the content of science is or should be the same or partially the same as the content of religion, but it would assert at the same time that the goals and methods of the two practices are completely different. A strong version of the theoretical contact view holds that the theoretical output of the two practices is or should be the same, while a weak version holds that there is or should be merely an overlap of theoretical output. People of this inclination could, for instance, argue that both religion and science offer us explanations of the origin of the universe and of life, even if they have different goals and use different methods. There is therefore a theoretical intersection between the two practices.

But other combinations than these three are of course possible as well (and the particular versions of these combinations could of course be many, many more). One could also make the classification in matter of degrees, emphasis, or tendency, saying that among those scholars engaged in the science-religion dialogue who endorse a contact view, there is one group that understands the overlap between science and religion primarily in terms of the goals of science and religion, another that does it mainly in terms of the methodologies of science and religion, and one last group that does it for the most part in terms of the theoretical output of science and religion.

If we define the science-religion views as I have suggested, the difference between Barbour's dialogue view and integration view can be understood as the difference between those who maintain that there is merely a methodological overlap between science and religion and those who claim that there is also a theoretical overlap between the two practices. Hence, van Huyssteen would be a proponent of at least a weak methodological contact view, whereas Kaufman would be a proponent of at least a weak theoretical contact view. Van Huyssteen believes that judgment-based evidentialism constitutes one such epistemological overlap (or transversality, in his terminology) between the two practices. Kaufman argues that scientific theories about cosmic and biological evolution directly imply changes in the conception of God; there is therefore a theoretical overlap between science and religion.

Barbour appears to think, as we have seen, that proponents of a methodological contact view seek a closer integration than those who argue for a theoretical contact view. This may perhaps be the case if we survey the current science-religion literature, but it is important that we notice that this is not automatically so. If a spokesperson for a strong methodological contact view maintains, for instance, that the only kind of evidence that ought to be allowed in both science and religion is observational evidence of the kind that is used in the natural sciences, this might entail far more radical changes in religion than if we accept the claim of an advocate for a theoretical contact view that the Christian doctrine of original sin must be modified due to changes in scientific theory. Hence, to be able to draw such conclusions we have to become even more specific in our account and specify on what issues within the teleological, epistemological, or theoretical dimension of science and religion there is or should be an overlap. Is the issue about epistemic and practical goals, existential and soteriological goals (the teleological dimension), evidence, standards of rationality (the methodological dimension), the creation, human nature, God, ethics, or the meaning of life (the theoretical dimension)? And so on.

If we take these considerations into account it would give us three levels of analysis:

Level 1   the monist view
           the contact view
           the independence view
           the complete scientific expansionist view
           the complete religious expansionist view

Level 2   the teleological contact view
           the methodological contact view
           the theoretical contact view and so on

Level 3   epistemic and practical goals
           existential and soteriological goals
           kinds of evidence
           standards of rationality
           creation
           human nature
           conceptions of God (or divine reality)
           ethics
           the meaning of life and so on

Notice that whereas there are only five possibilities on level 1, the views on level 2 and the examples of topics on level 3 are merely illustrations. To this scheme we can add two more levels:

Level 4   conflict
           tension
           no conflict
           harmony

Level 5   conformism
           nonconformism
           dogmatism

Someone who claims, for instance, that a personal conception of God is incompatible with a particular scientific theory holds that there is a *conflict* between religion (or a particular religious tradition) and science. The occurrence of a conflict is compatible with the conflict version of the monist view and the contact view, but incompatible with the independence view. Someone who on this or any other topic maintains that there *seems* to be a conflict between science and religion holds that there is a *tension* between the two practices. Such a stance is compatible with not merely the monist view (in both of its versions) and the contact view but also with the independence view; an advocate of the independence view must simply be convinced that the solution of the tension will not fall within the category of conflict but within the category of no conflict. Someone who claims that on a particular topic religion and science are compatible holds that there is *no conflict* between the two practices. This is a claim which proponents of all science-religion views could make. A fourth possibility is that on a particular topic, say the order of the universe, something more than merely the absence of conflict can be found between science and religion. Perhaps in this particular case there is actually a fit or an integrated combination of elements of religion and elements of science; the relationship is characterized by *harmony*. Harmony on any particular religion-science topic is compatible with both the harmony version of the monist view and the contact view, but it is questionable whether proponents of an independence view can consistently endorse it. If two things, *S* and *R*, are totally independent from each other then there seems to be no basis for talking about harmony between *S* and *R* because harmony connotes a fit between *S* and *R* or an integrative element which relates *S* to *R*. The possibility for this kind of fit is lacking in a consistently elaborated independence view.

In fact, religious practitioners often believe that there is no genuine conflict between science and religion. Although conflict between science and religion may appear at times, it is only apparent; in the end no conflict will be revealed, and perhaps harmony will even be revealed. Notice, however, that in saying this, "science" and "religion" in these sentences do not necessarily mean "actual science" and "actual religion," but rather mean something akin to "perfect science" and "perfect religion" (that is, what science and religion should really be like if ideally performed and developed). The reason for this belief that there is no genuine conflict between science and religion is thus that either actual religious beliefs have been misunderstood or are based on the wrong grounds and thus mistaken, or that actual scientific theories have been misunderstood or are based on the wrong grounds and thus mistaken. It is these mistakes that make it look as though there is a conflict between science and religion. This does not mean, however, that those who hold such a view must deny that there is a conflict between contemporary science and contemporary religion or between any other instantiation of science and religion in the past.

Suppose that there really is a conflict between, for instance, a personal conception of God and contemporary scientific theories about cosmic and biological evolution, or between the selfish gene theory developed by Dawkins and others and a religious belief in human beings as free and responsible agents, capable of genuinely altruistic action; what should we do? By asking this kind of question we have reached level 5 in my analysis scheme and here I suggest that we can give three different kinds of answers:

(1) religious beliefs should take precedence;
(2) scientific theories should take precedence;
(3) neither religious beliefs nor scientific theories should automatically take precedence; this must be decided on a case-by-case basis.

I have failed to find any value-neutral name for these views and their advocates and I therefore hope somebody else will find a better terminology, but until this happens let us call the first position *dogmatism*, the second *conformism*, and the third *nonconformism*. I have elsewhere argued for position (3) (Stenmark 1999). I shall not repeat my arguments here but merely highlight that in my view religious practitioners face a dilemma. The problem is that the religion that is married to science today will be a widow tomorrow because scientific methods and theories come and go. But the religion that is divorced from science today will leave no offspring tomorrow. Hence, as Rolston points out, "religion that has too thoroughly accommodated to any science will soon be obsolete. It needs to keep its autonomous integrity and resilience. Yet religion cannot live without fitting into the intellectual world that is its environment. Here too the fittest survive" (Rolston 1987: vii). What I want to suggest is that not only can different versions of the contact view be distinguished on the basis of how they view the teleological, methodological, and theoretical relationship between science and religion, but they are also distinguishable on the basis of their assumptions about how to handle conflict situations that arise or could arise because of the intersection between science and religion.

Notice also one crucial limitation of my (but also of Barbour's)

266

typology of science and religion, structured on the basis of how people understand the relationship between the *goals*, the *methods* (or means), and the *theoretical output* of science and religion. If one accepts and to some extent even advocates, as I did in chapter 9, that religious beliefs and values should influence the direction of science (science$_1$), the development of science (science$_2$), and the application of science (science$_4$), then one must reasonably be understood to presuppose the contact view. But this kind of intersection or interaction between science and religion is hard to capture within the framework of an explication of the goals, the methods, and the theoretical output that these methods developed to achieve the goals generated in either science or religion. Perhaps it could be squeezed into the methodological dimension and thus be understood as an issue about what extra-scientific criteria (if any) should be used in certain scientific processes. Or perhaps it indicates that somehow we need to develop a typology of science and religion which includes not merely teleological, methodological, and theoretical parameters, but also a social parameter or structuring category. After all, what I have called the "problem-stating phase," the "development phase," the "justification phase," and the "application phase" of science refer to social processes taking place within the scientific practice. The idea is that religion could and should play a role in some of these social processes of a scientific inquiry. This would give some support for the idea that an adequate typology of science and religion ought to be developed in such a way that it includes besides a teleological, a methodological, and a theoretical parameter also a social parameter. I do not know at the present time how to do this in an elegant and illuminating way, and on this issue we certainly need help from the historians and sociologists who are engaged in the science-religion dialogue.

THE KEY QUESTION of the book, "How should we relate science and religion?" has been answered in dialogue with scientific expansionists (those who claim that the boundaries of science can be expanded in such a way that religion becomes a part of science), restrictionists (those who believe in a strict separation of science and religion), and religious expansionists (those who maintain that the boundaries of religion can be expanded in such a way that religion influences science).

I have developed the critical reflections on these three views into a multilevel or multidimensional model of science and religion. The thesis defended has been that we need to take into account at least four different levels or dimensions of science and religion in order to understand how to relate them:

(1) the *social* dimension (science and religion as social practices performed by people in cooperation within a particular historical and cultural setting);
(2) the *teleological* dimension (the goals of scientific and religious practice);
(3) the *epistemological* or *methodological* dimension (the means developed and used to achieve the goals of science and religion); and
(4) the *theoretical* dimension (the beliefs, stories, theories, and the like that the practice of science and religion generates).

I have argued that we should begin by thinking about science and religion in terms of social practices (the social dimension). A social practice such as science or religion can be distinguished in terms of what its practitioners claim or assume the goals of their activity are (the teleological dimension), in terms of the means developed to obtain these goals (the methodological dimension), and in terms of the outcome, including the formation of beliefs, stories, and theories, that those means generate (the theoretical dimension).

If science and religion are understood to be *multidimensional, social practices* then we must take into account that they change over time and look differently in different places. But if both science and religion are evolving and changing practices then no *a priori* or once-and-for-all answer can be given about how science and religion should be related (in respect to any one of these dimensions). Nevertheless, it is true that the logical possibilities are limited to union, overlap, or complete separation of the practices, or that one of the two practices is understood to be a subset of the other. Because of changes in either science or religion or both, however, the actualization of any of these five science-religion views (the monist view, the contact view, the independence view, the complete scientific expansionist view, and the complete religious expansionist view) may at time t_1 be justifiably thought to be correct, but at time t_2 turn out to be incorrect. This holds true irrespective of which scientific discipline or religious tradition we are focusing on.

We must therefore take seriously the claims of scientific or religious expansionists who argue that the boundaries of one practice could be expanded to such an extent that it would cover at least parts of the other practice. We cannot, like Gould, simply define these practices as non-overlapping — not, that is, if we take their social and evolving character seriously. In each case those who hold a different view must respond by considering the details of these expansions and by showing exactly why they are inappropriate, unjustified, or misconceived.

Bibliography

Abraham, William J. 1985. *An Introduction to the Philosophy of Religion.* Englewood Cliffs, N.J.: Prentice-Hall.

Alexander, Richard D. 1987. *The Biology of Moral Systems.* New York: Aldine De Gruyter.

Alston, William P. 1991. *Perceiving God.* Ithaca, N.Y.: Cornell University Press.

Andersson, Jan, and Mats Furberg. 1986. *Om världens gåta.* Lund: Doxa.

Atkins, Peter. 1995. "The Limitless Power of Science." In *Nature's Imagination,* ed. John Cornwell. Oxford: Oxford University Press.

Augustine. 1961. *Confessions.* London: Penguin.

Barbour, Ian. 1990. *Religion in an Age of Science.* New York: Harper and Row.

————. 1997. *Religion and Science.* San Francisco: HarperSanFrancisco.

————. 2000. *When Science Meets Religion.* San Francisco: HarperSanFrancisco.

————. 2002. "On Typologies for Relating Science and Religion." *Zygon* 37:345-59.

Basinger, David. 1996. *The Case for Freewill Theism.* Downers Grove, Ill.: InterVarsity.

Batson, C. Daniel, and W. Larry Ventis. 1982. *The Religious Experience.* Oxford: Oxford University Press.

Berger, Peter L. 1998. "Protestantism and the Quest for Certainty." *Christian Century* 115.23 (Aug. 26-Sep. 2).

Black, Max. 1972. "Reasonableness." In *Reason,* ed. R. F. Dearden et al. London: Routledge and Kegan Paul.

Braithwaite, R. B. 1971. "An Empiricist's View of the Nature of Religious Belief." In *The Philosophy of Religion,* ed. Basil Mitchell. Oxford: Oxford University Press.

Brooke, John, and Geoffrey Cantor. 2000. *Reconstructing Nature: The Engagement of Science and Religion*. Oxford: Oxford University Press.

Brown, Harold I. 1988. *Rationality*. London: Routledge.

Brümmer, Vincent. 1981. *Theology and Philosophical Inquiry*. London: Macmillan.

————. 1992. *Speaking of a Personal God*. Cambridge: Cambridge University Press.

————. 1993. "Wittgenstein and the Irrationality of Rational Theology." In *The Christian Understanding of God Today*, ed. James M. Byrne. Dublin: Columba.

————. 1994. "Has the Theism-Atheism Debate a Future?" *Theology* 97.

————. 1999. "How Rational Is Rational Theology? A Reply to Mikael Stenmark." *Religious Studies* 35:89-97.

Cherniak, Christopher. 1986. *Minimal Rationality*. Cambridge, Mass.: MIT Press.

Chopp, Rebecca S. 1989. *The Power to Speak: Feminism, Language, God*. New York: Crossroad.

Clayton, Philip, and Steven Knapp. 1996. "Rationality and Christian Self-Conceptions." In *Religion and Science*, ed. W. Mark Richardson and Wesley J. Wildman. London: Routledge.

Clifford, W. K. [1877] 1947. "The Ethics of Belief." In *The Ethics of Belief and Other Essays*, ed. Leslie Stephen and Frederick Pollock. London: Watts.

Crew, Fredric. 2001. "Saving Us from Darwin." *The New York Review of Books* (October 4).

Crowder, Colin. 1995. "Back to the Future. Vincent Brümmer and the Theism-Atheism Debate." *Theology* 98.

Daly, Mary. 1973. *Beyond God the Father: Toward a Philosophy of Women's Liberation*. Boston: Beacon.

Dawkins, Richard. 1986. *The Blind Watchmaker*. New York: W. W. Norton.

————. 1989. *The Selfish Gene*. Second ed. Oxford: Oxford University Press.

————. 1992. *The Independent* (April 16).

————. 1995a. *River Out of Eden*. New York: Basic.

————. 1995b. "A Reply to Poole." *Science and Christian Belief* 7.

Dennett, Daniel C. 1995. *Darwin's Dangerous Idea*. London: Penguin.

Dupré, Louis. 1989. "Reflections on the Truth of Religion." *Faith and Philosophy* 6:260-74.

Duve, Christian de. 1995. *Vital Dust: Life as a Cosmic Imperative*. New York: Basic Books.

Evans, C. Stephen. 1996. *Why Believe?* Grand Rapids: Eerdmans.

Foley, Richard. 1988. "Some Different Conceptions of Rationality." In *Construction and Constraint*, ed. Ernan McMullin. Notre Dame, Ind.: University of Notre Dame Press.

————. 1991. "Rationality, Belief, and Commitment." *Synthese* 89.

Gellman, Jerome. 2000. "In Defense of a Contented Religious Exclusivism." *Religious Studies* 36:401-17.

Giere, Ronald N. 2003. "A New Program for Philosophy of Science?" *Philosophy of Science* 70:15-21.

Gillispie, Charles C. 1951. *Genesis and Geology*. Cambridge, Mass.: Harvard University Press.

Goldman, Alvin I. 1986. *Epistemology and Cognition*. Cambridge: Harvard University Press.

Golshani, Mehdi. 2000. "How to Make Sense of 'Islamic Science.'" *American Journal of Islamic Social Sciences* 17.

———. 2002. "Values and Ethical Issues in Science and Technology: A Muslim Perspective" (unpublished paper).

Gould, Stephen Jay. 1977. *Ever Since Darwin*. London: Penguin.

———. 1983. "Extemporaneous Comments on Evolutionary Hope and Realities." In *Darwin's Legacy, Nobel Conference XVIII*, ed. Charles L. Hamrum. San Francisco: Harper and Row.

———. 1999. *Rocks of Ages: Science and Religion in the Fullness of Life*. New York: Ballantine.

Graham, Loren R. 1981. *Between Science and Values*. New York: Columbia University Press.

Gross, Paul R., and Norman Levitt. 1994. *Higher Superstition: The Academic Left and Its Quarrels with Science*. Baltimore: John Hopkins University Press.

Gutting, Gary. 1982. *Religious Belief and Religious Skepticism*. Notre Dame, Ind.: University of Notre Dame Press.

Haack, Susan. 1992. "Science 'From a Feminist Perspective.'" *Philosophy* 67:5-18.

———. 1998. *Manifest of a Passionate Moderate*. Chicago: University of Chicago Press.

Harding, Sandra. 1986. *The Science Question in Feminism*. Ithaca, N.Y.: Cornell University Press.

———. 1991. *Whose Science? Whose Knowledge?* Ithaca, N.Y.: Cornell University Press.

Harman, Gilbert. 1986. *Change in View: Principles of Reasoning*. Cambridge, Mass.: MIT Press.

Hasker, William. 1989. *God, Time and Knowledge*. Ithaca, N.Y.: Cornell University Press.

Haught, John F. 1995. *Science and Religion*. New York: Paulist.

———. 2000. *God After Darwin*. Boulder, Colo.: Westview.

Helgesson, Gert. 2002. *Values, Norms and Ideology in Mainstream Economics*. Uppsala: Ekonomikum.

Helm, Paul. 1994. *Belief Policies*. Cambridge: Cambridge University Press.

Hempel, C. G. 1966. *Philosophy of Natural Science.* Englewood Cliffs, N.J.: Prentice-Hall.

Herrmann, Eberhard. 1995. *Scientific Theory and Religious Belief.* Kampen, Holland: Kok Pharos.

Hick, John. 1989. *An Interpretation of Religion.* New Haven: Yale University Press.

Hoodbhoy, Pervez. 1991. *Islam and Science.* London: Zed.

Jaggar, Alison M. 1989. "Love and Knowledge." In *Gender/Body/Knowledge: Feminist Reconstructions of Being and Knowing,* ed. Alison M. Jaggar and Susan R. Bordo. New Brunswick, N.J.: Rutgers University Press.

Jeffner, Anders. 1981. *Vägar till teologi.* Arlöv: Skeab Förlag.

———. 1988. "Religion and Ideology." In *The World's Religions,* ed. S. Sutherland et al. London: Routledge.

Johnson, Phillip. 1995. *Reason in the Balance.* Downers Grove, Ill.: InterVarsity.

Kaufman, Gordon. 1985. *Theology for a Nuclear Age.* Manchester, U.K.: Manchester University Press.

———. 2001. "On Thinking of God As Serendipitous Creativity." *Journal of the American Academy of Religion* 69.

———. 2003. "Rejoinder to Mikael Stenmark." *Journal of the American Academy of Religion* 71:183-86.

Keller, Evelyn Fox, and Helen E. Longino, eds. 1996. *Feminism and Science.* Oxford: Oxford University Press.

Kenny, Anthony. 1969. *The Five Ways.* New York: Schocken.

Kitcher, Philip. 1993. *The Advancement of Science.* New York: Oxford University Press.

Kuhn, Thomas. 1970. *The Structure of Scientific Revolution.* Second ed. Chicago: University of Chicago Press.

Lakatos, Imre. 1978. *Mathematics, Science and Epistemology: Philosophical Papers.* Vol. 2. Ed. John Worrall and Gregory Currie. Cambridge: Cambridge University Press.

Laudan, Larry. 1984. *Science and Values.* Berkeley: University of California Press.

———. 1990. *Science and Relativism.* Chicago: University of Chicago Press.

Lewontin, R. C. [1991] 1993. *The Doctrine of DNA: Biology as Ideology.* London: Penguin.

Lloyd, G. 1983. *Science, Folklore and Ideology.* Cambridge: Cambridge University Press.

Longino, Helen E. 1990. *Science as Social Knowledge.* Princeton, N.J.: Princeton University Press.

MacIntyre, Alasdair. 1987. *After Virtue.* Second ed. London: Duckworth.

Mackie, J. L. 1990. "Evil and Omnipotence." In *The Problem of Evil,* ed. M. M. Adams and R. M. Adams. Oxford: Oxford University Press.

Marsden, George M. 1997. *The Outrageous Idea of Christian Scholarship*. Oxford: Oxford University Press.

Mavrodes, George I. 1970. *Belief in God*. New York: University Press of America.

McFague, Sallie. 1982. *Metaphorical Theology*. Philadelphia: Fortress.

―――. 1987. *Models of God: Theology for an Ecological, Nuclear Age*. Philadelphia: Fortress.

McMullin, Ernan. 1998. "Cosmic Purpose and the Contingency of Human Evolution." *Theology Today* 55.

Midgley, Mary. 1992. *Science as Salvation*. London: Routledge.

Mitchell, Basil. 1973. *The Justification of Religious Belief*. London: Oxford University Press.

Mosedale, S. 1978. "Science Corrupted: Victorian Biologists Consider 'The Woman Question.'" *Journal of the History of Biology* 11:1-55.

Murphy, Nancey. 1993. "Evidence of Design in the Fine-Tuning of the Universe." In *Quantum Cosmology and the Laws of Nature*, ed. Robert John Russell et al. Notre Dame, Ind.: University of Notre Dame Press.

Murphy, Nancey, and George F. R. Ellis. 1996. *On the Moral Nature of the Universe*. Minneapolis: Fortress.

Nasr, Seyyed Hossein. 1976. *Islamic Science*. London: World of Islam Festival Publishing Company.

―――. 1993. *The Need for a Sacred Science*. London: Curzon.

Newton-Smith, W. H. 1981. *The Rationality of Science*. London and New York: Routledge and Kegan Paul.

Numbers, Ronald L. 1985. "Science and Religion." *OSIRIS*, second series, 1:59-80.

Ochs, Peter. 1998. *Peirce, Pragmatism and the Logic of Scripture*. Cambridge: Cambridge University Press.

O'Neill, John. 1993. *Ecology, Policy and Politics*. London: Routledge.

Peacocke, Arthur, ed. 1981. *The Sciences and Theology in the Twentieth Century*. London: Oriel.

―――. 1993. *Theology for a Scientific Age*. Minneapolis: Fortress.

―――. 2001. *Paths from Science towards God*. Oxford: Oneworld.

Peterson, Michael, William Hasker, Bruce Reichenbach, and David Basinger. 1991. *Reason and Religious Belief*. Oxford: Oxford University Press.

Phillips, D. Z. 1976. *Religion without Explanation*. Oxford: Basil Blackwell.

―――. 1988. *Faith After Foundationalism*. London: Routledge.

Plantinga, Alvin. 1983. "Reason and Belief in God." In *Faith and Rationality*, ed. Alvin Plantinga and Nicholas Wolterstorff. Notre Dame, Ind.: University of Notre Dame Press.

―――. 1984. "Advice to Christian Philosophers." *Faith and Philosophy* 1.

―――. 1991. "When Faith and Reason Clash: Evolution and the Bible." *Christian Scholar's Review* 21.

————. 1996a. "Methodological Naturalism?" In *Facets of Faith and Science*, vol. 1, ed. Jitse M. van der Meer. Lanham, Md.: University Press of America.

————. 1996b. "Science: Augustinian or Duhemian?" *Faith and Philosophy* 13.

Plantinga, Alvin, Benjamin Kissing, Roger Shattuck, Charles Gross, and Fredric Crew. 2001. "Saving Us from Darwin: An Exchange." *The New York Review of Books* (November 29).

Poincaré, H. 1958. *The Value of Science.* New York: Dover.

Poole, Michael W. 1994. "A Critique of Aspects of the Philosophy and Theology of Richard Dawkins." *Science and Christian Belief* 6.

Popper, Karl. 1963. *Conjectures and Refutations.* London: Routledge and Kegan Paul.

Porritt, Jonathon. 1984. *Seeing Green.* Oxford: Blackwell.

Proctor, Robert N. 1991. *Value-Free Science?* Cambridge, Mass.: Harvard University Press.

Provine, William. 1988. "Evolution and the Foundation of Ethics." *MBL Science* 3.

Rescher, Nicholas. 1988. *Rationality.* Oxford: Clarendon.

Robbins, J. Wesley. 1988. "Seriously, But Not Literally: Pragmatism and Realism in Religion and Science." *Zygon* 23:229-45.

————. 1993. "A Neopragmatist Perspective on Religion and Science." *Zygon* 28:337-49.

Rolston, Holmes, III. 1987. *Science and Religion.* Philadelphia: Temple University Press.

————. 1999. *Genes, Genesis and God.* Cambridge: Cambridge University Press.

Root, Michael. 1993. *Philosophy of Social Science.* Oxford: Blackwell.

Rose, Steven, R. C. Lewontin, and Leon J. Kamin. [1984] 1990. *Not in Our Genes: Biology, Ideology, and Human Nature.* London: Penguin.

Ross, Andrew, ed. 1996. *Science Wars.* Durham, N.C.: Duke University Press.

Ruether, Rosemary Radford. 1991. "Imago Dei, Christian Tradition, and Feminist Hermeneutics." In *Image of God and Gender Models,* ed. K. E. Børrensen. Oslo: Solum Forlag.

Ruse, Michael. [1986] 1998. *Taking Darwin Seriously.* Second ed. Oxford: Blackwell.

Ruse, Michael, and Edward O. Wilson. 1986. "Moral Philosophy as Applied Science." *Philosophy* 61.

————. 1993. "The Evolution of Ethics." In *Religion and the Natural Sciences,* ed. James E. Huchingson. Fort Worth: Harcourt Brace.

Russell, B. [1946] 1984. *A History of Western Philosophy.* London: Unwin Paperbacks.

Sahlins, Marshall. 1977. *The Use and Abuse of Biology.* London: Tavistock.

Sardar, Ziauddin. 1989. *Explorations in Islamic Science.* London: Mansell.

Schiebinger, Londa. 1999. *Has Feminism Changed Science?* Cambridge, Mass.: Harvard University Press.

Schrag, C. O. 1992. *The Resources of Rationality.* Bloomington: Indiana University Press.

Searle, John R. 1995. *The Construction of Social Reality.* New York: Free Press.

Sennett, James F., ed. 1998. *The Analytic Theist: An Alvin Plantinga Reader.* Grand Rapids: Eerdmans.

Shults, F. LeRon. 1999. *The Postfoundationalist Task of Theology: Wolfhart Pannenberg and the New Theological Rationality.* Grand Rapids: Eerdmans.

Simon, Herbert. 1990. "A Mechanism for Social Selection and Successful Altruism." *Science* 250.

Simpson, George Gaylord. 1967. *The Meaning of Evolution.* Rev. ed. New Haven: Yale University Press.

Smart, J. J. C. 1996. "Atheism and Theism." In *Atheism and Theism,* by J. J. C. Smart and J. Haldane. Oxford: Blackwell.

Stahl, William A., et al. 2002. *Webs of Reality.* New Brunswick, N.J.: Rutgers University Press.

Stenberg, Leif. 1996. *The Islamization of Science.* Lund: Novapress.

Stenmark, Mikael. 1995. *Rationality in Science, Religion, and Everyday Life: A Critical Evaluation of Four Models of Rationality.* Notre Dame, Ind.: University of Notre Dame Press.

———. 1997a. "Behovet av Nya Gudsbilder." *Svensk Teologisk Kvartalskrift* 33.

———. 1997b. "What Is Scientism?" *Religious Studies* 33.

———. 1998. "The End of the Theism-Atheism Debate? A Response to Vincent Brümmer." *Religious Studies* 34:261-80.

———. 1999. "Religion och vetenskap — en olöslig konflikt?" *Signum* 25.

———. 2001a. "Evolution, Purpose and God." *Ars Disputandi: The Online Journal for Philosophy of Religion.*

———. 2001b. *Scientism: Science, Ethics and Religion.* Aldershort: Ashgate.

———. 2003. "Science and a Personal Conception of God: A Critical Response to Gordon D. Kaufman." *Journal of the American Academy of Religion* 71:175-81.

Stevenson, Leslie, and Henry Byerly. 1995. *The Many Faces of Science.* Boulder, Colo.: Westview.

Swinburne, Richard. 1977. *The Coherence of Theism.* Oxford: Oxford University Press.

———. 1979. *The Existence of God.* Oxford: Oxford University Press.

———. 1996. *Is There a God?* Oxford: Oxford University Press.

Teller, Edward. 1960. *The Reluctant Revolutionary.* Columbia: University of Missouri Press.

Tilley, Terrence W. 1995. *The Wisdom of Religious Commitment.* Washington, D.C.: Georgetown University Press.

van der Meer, Jitse M., ed. 1996. *Facets of Faith and Science.* Vols. 1-2. Lanham, Md.: University Press of America.

van Huyssteen, J. Wentzel. 1988. "Experience and Explanation: The Justification of Cognitive Claims in Theology." *Zygon* 23:247-61.

———. 1998. *Duet or Duel? Theology and Science in a Postmodern World*. Harrisburg, Pa.: Trinity Press International.

———. 1999. *The Shaping of Rationality*. Grand Rapids: Eerdmans.

van Inwagen, Peter. 1996. "It Is Wrong, Everywhere, Always, and for Anyone, to Believe Anything upon Insufficient Evidence." In *Faith, Freedom, and Rationality*, ed. Jeff Jordan and Daniel Howard-Snyder. Boston: Rowman and Littlefield.

Ward, Keith. 1996a. *God, Change, and Necessity*. Oxford: Oneworld.

———. 1996b. *Religion and Creation*. Oxford: Clarendon.

Weber, Max. 1969. *The Methodology of the Social Sciences*. Trans. and ed. Edward Shils and Henry Finch. New York: Free Press.

Westphal, Merold. 1984. *God, Guilt, and Death*. Bloomington: Indiana University Press.

Wilson, Edward O. 1978. *On Human Nature*. Cambridge, Mass.: Harvard University Press.

———. 1998. *Consilience: The Unity of Knowledge*. New York: Knopf.

Wolterstorff, Nicholas. 1983. "Can Belief in God Be Rational?" In *Faith and Rationality*, ed. Alvin Plantinga and Nicholas Wolterstorff. Notre Dame, Ind.: University of Notre Dame Press.

Wykstra, Stephen. 1990. "Reasons, Redemption, and Realism." In *Christian Theism and the Problems of Philosophy*, ed. M. D. Beaty. Notre Dame, Ind.: University of Notre Dame Press.

Zackariasson, Ulf. 2002. *Forces by Which We Live*. Uppsala: Almqvist and Wiksell.

Index

278

and worldview-neutral science, 245.
See also Teleological dimensions of
science and religion

Contact view: and expansionism, 258-
59; methodological, 262, 263; and
multidimensional model, 251, 258-59,
261; teleological, 261-62; theoretical,
262, 263; and threefold typology, 9-10

Contemporary Darwinism and religion,
1-15; conflict view, 10-11; contact view,
9-10; epistemological dimension, 12-
13, 14, 268; four dimensions of science and religion, 12-15; independence view, 9-10, 11; monist view, 9-
10; and multidimensional science-
religion relationship, 12-15; and principle of NOMA, 3-5, 10-12; scientific
expansionism, 5-9; scientific
restrictionism, 1-5; social dimension,
12, 14, 268; teleological dimension, 12,
14, 268; theoretical dimension, 13, 14,
268; and threefold typology of science-religion views, 9-15. *See also*
Evolutionary biology and religion;
Multidimensional model of science
and religion

Crew, Frederic, 210

Daly, Mary, 40, 123, 124, 133, 135-36

Dawkins, Richard, x; atheistic bias of,
64, 192; criticism of blind trust, 54-55,
58; and epistemic norms of science
and religion, 54-60, 80-81; integration
view, 255-56; monist view, 9-10; on
morality and rationality, 230; on natural selection, 191, 224; and naturalist
bias, 186, 210, 211; no-purpose arguments, 158; on religious rationality,
111, 112; on science and evidentialism
as norm of rationality, 54; and scientific expansionism, 5-9, 30, 36-37, 73-
74, 120-21, 157, 186; and scope of rationality in religion-science dialogue,
120-21; and selfish gene, 6, 224; and

teleological dimensions of science
and religion, 30, 36-37; worldview
and problem-stating phase of science, 218; and worldview-partisan
science, 230, 232

Dennett, Daniel C., xv, 6, 239

Development phase of science, 215-16,
221-24, 247, 248-49

Dogmatic religious beliefs, 107-10

Dupré, Louis, 37-38

Duve, Christian de, 165

Epistemic goals, 22-23, 28-42; defining,
32. *See also* Teleological dimensions
of science and religion

Epistemological dimensions and rationality, 82-115; and academic disciplines, 101-3, 115; and adequate model
of rationality, 87-89; agent-rationality, 111, 113; and belief revision, 104-7;
comparing religious and everyday-
life rationality, 103-4; comparing religious and scientific rationality, 111-14;
deliberation and rationality, 89, 90-
91, 98; and dogmatic religious beliefs,
107-10; everyday-belief formation
and regulation, 87-89, 92-94, 98-101;
evidentialism and postfoundational
model, 85-86, 88-89; external
evidentialism, 94; and the "ideal"
postfoundationalist, 84; and intelligent use of intelligence, 87-88; internal evidentialism, 91; judgment-
based evidentialism, 86-87, 89-97, 98-
101, 114-15; modernist model of rationality, 83, 85; peer evaluation and scientific rationality, 100; and
postfoundational model of rationality, 83-89, 97-103, 119-20; and
presumptionism, 90, 94-97, 104-7,
114-15, 120; and principle of concern,
106; problems with postfoundational
model of rationality, 86-87, 89-97,
114-15; rational persons/agents, 85; ra-